Blond hair, good look'n',
wants me to marry, get a home, settle down,
        write a book—
                ahhhhhhhhhhhh!
Too much monkey business,
            too much monkey business.
                —CHUCK BERRY

Contents

Preface

This book grew out of my earlier comparative study of Russian Formalism and Prague Structuralism. The juxtaposition of these schools, I was surprised to find, pointed up their fundamental difference much more than their similarity. The Prague School, with its single organizational center, shared frame of reference, and unified epistemological stance, could easily be conceived as a coherent movement. But its Russian counterpart was far more resistant to synthesis. I began to see Formalism, in fact, not as a school in the ordinary sense of the word, but as a peculiar developmental stage in the history of Slavic literary theory.

This fact is reflected in the relative agreement among students of Prague Structuralism about the coherence of their subject matter and the corresponding lack of a consensus among scholars of Formalism. It is this feeling of discord that I wish to convey in my first chapter. Because of the great variety of meanings that the label "Formalism" has attracted in the course of time, it seems legitimate to question its utility and to offer my own understanding of the term as a historical concept.

The middle two chapters treat the Formalists from what I

term a metapoetic stance. That is, their discourse about poetics is analyzed in terms of poetics itself, or more precisely, in terms of the poetic tropes that structure their theorizing. Chapter 2 focuses on the major metaphors of Formalist thought: the three tropological models that describe the literary work as a mechanism, an organism, and a system. The third chapter addresses the synecdochic reduction of the work to its material stratum—language—and the consequent substitution of linguistics for poetics. In particular, I deal here with the two mutually incompatible concepts of poetic language advanced by the Formalists and the basic tenets of their metrics.

I return to the question "what is Formalism?" in the last chapter, where I take up the issue of the movement's unity. As I see it, the intellectual coherence of Formalism lies in its developmental significance within the overall history of Slavic literary theory. This significance consists in the conjunction of two factors: the movement's effectively dividing pre-Formalistic from post-Formalistic scholarship, and its positing of a uniquely literary subject matter to be approached "scientifically," without presuppositions. From this perspective, the baffling heterogeneity of Formalist theorizing can be seen as an "interparadigmatic" stage in the history of literary scholarship.

In writing this book I have relied on the advice and help of a great many people. These were, first of all, René Wellek, Victor Erlich, and Vadim Liapunov at Yale. At later stages, Miroslav Červenka, Sergej Davydov, J. Michael Holquist, Joseph Margolis, and Stephen Rudy provided valuable criticism, insightful suggestions, and much-needed encouragement. My special thanks go to Bernhard Kendler of Cornell University Press for the manner in which he guided my book through its numerous rites of passage. I am grateful for the support of the American Council of Learned Societies, whose grant-in-aid in the summer of 1977 presented a palpable incentive for continuing my work, and to the Research Foundation of the University of Pennsylvania, which furnished funds for the final typing of the manuscript. But most of all, I am indebted to that "good look'n' girl" who wanted me to write a book, and consequently had to put up with all the unpleasantness and deprivation that this process entailed.

PETER STEINER

Philadelphia, Pennsylvania

Russian Formalism

1

Who Is Formalism,
What Is She?

History as a scholarly discipline recognizes only a
single source of its knowledge—*the word.*
  —GUSTAV ŠPET, "History as an Object of Logic"

These words of Špet's encapsulate the historian's dilemma.
Writing about a school of literary theory from the past, I indeed
have nothing but words at my disposal and no Polonius as a
whipping boy. "Words are chameleons," declared the Formalist
Jurij Tynjanov, whose own words I shall soon have occasion to
reclothe in my own language; his phrase in turn is borrowed
from a famous Symbolist poet, with whose generation the Formalists had locked horns in an animated dialogue. Words
change meaning as they pass from one context to another, and
yet they preserve the semantic accretions acquired in the
process.
  "Russian Formalism" is just such a *locus communis* out of which
the history of ideas is made. Such terms are used over and over
again until their repetition lends them the air of solid, univer-
sally accepted concepts whose referential identity is beyond
doubt. A closer scrutiny, however, reveals a different picture.
On sifting through the myriad texts in which "Russian For-

malism" occurs, I discovered a wide diversity of functions the
term was meant to serve: for example, as a stigma with unpleas-
ant consequences for anybody branded with it, a straw man
erected only to be immediately knocked over, and a historical
concept that on different occasions refers to very different literary scholars. Given the wide divergence of these speech acts (the
preceding list can be easily augmented), "Russian Formalism,"
far from serving as a stable basis for scholarly discussion, resembles more an empty sign that might be filled with any content.

Let me illustrate this contention with some concrete examples.
Those we customarily call Formalists always rejected the label as
a grossly misleading characterization of their enterprises. In his
tongue-in-cheek essay, "The Formal Method: In Lieu of a Nec-
rologue," Boris Tomaševskij described the baptism of this
movement:

> Formalism screamed, seethed, and made a noise. It also found its
> own name—"OPOJAZ." In Moscow it was called the Linguistic
> Circle (by the way, the Moscow linguists never called themselves
> Formalists; this is a Petersburg phenomenon).
>
> It is worthwhile to say a few words about the name. Only its
> future biographer will have to decide who christened it the "For-
> mal method." Perhaps in those noisy days it itself courted this ill-
> suited designation. [But] Formalists who rejected the very notion
> of form as something opposed to content do not seem to square
> too well with this formula.[1]

Boris Èjchenbaum voiced similar objections to the label "Formal method" in his gloves-off polemics with contemporary anti-
Formalists:

> First of all, there is obviously no "*Formal method.*" It is difficult to
> recall who coined this name, but it was not a very felicitous coin-
> age. It might have been convenient as a simplified battle cry but it
> failed as an objective term that delimits the activities of the "Soci-

1. "Formal'nyj metod: Vmesto nekrologa," *Sovremennaja literatura: Sbornik
statej* (Leningrad, 1925), pp. 146–47. Unless indicated otherwise, all translations
are my own.

ety for the Study of Poetic Language" ("OPOJAZ") and the Section for Verbal Arts at the Institute for the History of the Arts. . . .

What is at stake are not the methods of literary study but the principles upon which literary science should be constructed—its content, the basic object of study, and the problems that organize it as a specific science. . . .

The word "form" has many meanings which, as always, cause a lot of confusion. It should be clear that we use this word in a particular sense—not as some correlative to the notion of "content" (such a correlation is, by the way, false, for the notion of "content" is, in fact, the correlative of the notion "volume" and not at all of "form") but as something essential for the artistic phenomenon, as its organizing principle. We do not care about the word "form" but only about its one particular nuance. We are not "Formalists" but, if you will, specifiers.[2]

Èjchenbaum was not the only member of the Formal school to suggest a more fitting name. "Morphological school," "expressionist" approach, and "systemo-functional" approach are only some of the labels concocted. This wealth of designations, however, indicates not merely dissatisfaction with the existing nomenclature, but a fundamental disunity in the movement itself. In part this disunity was a function of geography. From its very beginnings, Russian Formalism was split into two different groups: the Moscow Linguistic Circle with such young scholars as Pëtr Bogatyrëv, Roman Jakobson, and Grigorij Vinokur, and the Petersburg OPOJAZ, which included Boris Èjchenbaum, Viktor Šklovskij, and Jurij Tynjanov, among others. Even though their relations were cordial, the two groups approached literature from different perspectives. According to the Muscovites Bogatyrëv and Jakobson, "while the Moscow Linguistic Circle proceeds from the assumption that poetry is language in its aesthetic function, the Petersburgers claim that the poetic motif is not always merely the unfolding of linguistic material. Further, while the former argue that the historical development

2. "Vokrug voprosa o 'formalistach,'" *Pečat' i revoljucija*, no. 5 (1924), 2–3.

of artistic forms has a sociological basis, the latter insist upon the full autonomy of these forms."[3]

The reorganization of scholarly life under the Soviet regime further encouraged these divergences. OPOJAZ was dissolved in the early twenties, to be incorporated into the State Institute for the History of the Arts in Petersburg. The Moscow Circle—transformed by the departures of Jakobson and Bogatyrëv in 1920 for Czechoslovakia—became part of the State Academy for the Study of the Arts in Moscow. In these two research centers, the original Formalists began to collaborate with other students of literature and entered into an exchange of ideas with significance for both sides. Many Formalist notions were accepted by non-Formalists, and in turn, the Formalists modified their views in response to the intellectual trends around them. This dialogue produced a wide spectrum of literary-theoretical ideas labeled "Formalist."

Though this dilution of "pure" Formalism occurred in both branches, it was the Muscovites who were most deeply influenced by the philosophical ideas propounded at the State Academy by Edmund Husserl's pupil, Gustav Špet. This intellectual cross-pollination gave rise to what some commentators have termed the "formal-philosophical school" of the late twenties, within whose orbit belonged such literary scholars as Michail Petrovskij, Grigorij Vinokur, and Michail Stoljarov.[4] Rejecting the iconoclastic tenor of early Formalism, the members of this group rehabilitated many concepts and methods of traditional philology. The introduction to their 1927 anthology, *Artistic Form*, announced what the followers of Špet perceived as their special character: "In contrast to the Formalists of the 'OPOJAZ' type who usually confine their research to the sphere of outer form, we understand artistic form here as 'inner form.' Thus we pose the question [of artistic form] more broadly and seek its

3. "Slavjanskaja filologija v Rossii za gg. 1914–1921," *Slavia* 1 (1922), 458.
4. See N. I. Efimov, "Formalizm v russkom literaturovedenii," *Smolenskij gosudarstvennyj universitet: Naučnye izvestija*, vol. 5, pt. 3 (Smolensk, 1929), p. 56.

solution in the interrelations of various forms—logical, syntactic, melodic, poetic per se, rhetorical, etc."[5]

Given the vicissitudes of geography and history, the identity of Russian Formalism might be sought more profitably outside its organizational structures. One possibility advocated by Tomaševskij in his informative survey, "The New School of Literary History in Russia," was to focus on the protagonists of this movement in order to distinguish the core of genuine Formalists from the peripheral fellow travelers:

> It is people that one should consider now, rather than a school constituting an intellectual unity. Contemporary historians of literature can be classified, according to their relations with the new school, into three groups: the orthodox, the independents, and the influenced.
>
> The orthodox are those faithful to OPOJAZ. They represent the extreme left of Formalism. The best known among them are Šklovskij, Ėjchenbaum, and Tynjanov. The independents took part in the creation of the Formalist school and contributed to its works, but did not accept its discipline and went their separate ways: thus, Žirmunskij and Vinogradov. As for the influenced, it would be futile to pretend to specify their number.[6]

The classification of the Formalists drawn by Tomaševskij has all the authority of an eye-witness account. Yet one wonders what the common denominator between Šklovskij and Tynjanov actually is. This question cannot be dismissed easily, for there are historians of the Formalist movement who see these key figures as quite dissimilar. Ewa Thompson, for example, divides the Russian Formal school into "idealistic" and "positivistic" trends, with Šklovskij gravitating toward idealistic aesthetics and Tynjanov a clear-cut representative of the positivistic orienta-

---

5. "Predislovie," in *Chudožestvennaja forma: Sbornik statej*, ed. A. G. Cires (Moscow, 1927), p. 5.

6. "La nouvelle école d'histoire littéraire en Russie," *Revue des études slaves* 8 (1928), 239–40.

tion.[7] For quite different reasons, Jurij Striedter also maintains that the two leading Formalists are conceptually distant. Šklovskij's notion of the artistic work "as a 'sum of devices' with the function of 'de-familiarization' to make 'perception more difficult'" was, in Striedter's opinion, rendered obsolete by Tynjanov's more comprehensive definition of the artwork "as a 'system' composed of devices whose functions are specified synchronically and diachronically."[8] And although to their contemporaries the difference between the two men might have appeared unimportant, within Striedter's developmental scheme it is of great significance. According to Striedter, Šklovskij stands as the orthodox Formalist, whereas Tynjanov turns out to be the John the Baptist of Structuralism.

There is yet another reason Tomaševskij's categorization should be taken *cum grano salis*. His "state of the movement" is presented from a particular standpoint: that of the insider. This perspective might, of course, be instructive in some respects, for he was privy to information unavailable to strangers. But, at the same time, his point of view is that of the movement he belonged to, and this collective ideology inevitably slanted his presentation. Tomaševskij's contemporary, the psychologically inclined critic Arkadij Gornfel'd, for example, wrote in 1922 that "the Formalists are, of course, very diverse: there are among them simple-minded ones like Kušner and Šengeli clumsily parodying the method, talented thieves like Viktor Šklovskij, and cautious eclectics like Žirmunskij."[9] Boris Arvatov, the father of the "formalist-sociological" approach, cut the pie in the following way: "The researchers of OPOJAZ do not represent anything homogeneous. On the contrary, by now three different groups can be discerned in it: the extreme right which insists on the total separation of poetry and praxis (Èjchenbaum, Žirmunskij), the cen-

---

7. *Russian Formalism and Anglo-American New Criticism: A Comparative Study* (The Hague, 1971), pp. 55–110.

8. "Einleitung," in Felix Vodička, *Die Struktur der literarischen Entwicklung* (Munich, 1976), p. xvii.

9. "Formalisty i ich protivniki," *Literaturnye zapiski*, no. 3 (1922), 5.

ter adhering to a so-called linguo-poetic theory (Jakobson, Šklovskij), and the extreme left—sociological and technological (Brik, Kušner)."[10] Wary of other critics' triads, the Marxist Pavel Medvedev identified four trends in Formalism: "The first tendency is an academic Formalism characterized by its desire to gloss over contradictions and to avoid a formulation of problems according to a single principle" (Žirmunskij); "the second tendency amounts to a partial return to the psychological and philosophical treatment of literary problems" (Èjchenbaum); "a shift toward the sociological method characterizes the third tendency" (Tomaševskij, Jakubinskij); and "finally the fourth tendency is Šklovskij's frozen Formalism."[11]

This sampling of contradictory, incompatible classifications applied to the Formalists illustrates the futility of any attempt to pin down the identity of this movement by sorting out its central and marginal protagonists. Ultimately, it seems, one must come to the same conclusion as Medvedev, that "there are as many Formalisms as there are Formalists."[12] This conclusion, however, should not be interpreted as a sign of hostility toward the Formalist enterprise or of deliberate perversity on the commentator's part. It corresponds to the methodological pluralism of the Formalist approach openly displayed by its practitioners. In his stock-taking article, "The Question of the 'Formal Method,'" Viktor Žirmunskij characterized the Formal school in this way:

> The general and vague name "Formal method" usually brings together the most diverse works dealing with poetic language and style in the broad sense of these terms, historical and theoretical poetics, studies of meter, sound orchestration, and melodics, stylistics, composition, and plot structure, the history of literary genres and styles, etc. From my enumeration, which does not pretend to be exhaustive or systematic, it is obvious that in princi-

10. "Jazyk poètičeskij i jazyk praktičeskij: K metodologii iskusstvoznanija," *Pečat' i revoljucija*, no. 7 (1923), 59.

11. *Formal'nyj metod v literaturovedenii: Kritičeskoe vvedenie v sociologičeskuju poètiku* (Leningrad, 1928), pp. 97–98.

12. Ibid., p. 97.

ple it would be more correct to speak not of a new *method* but rather of the new *tasks* of scholarship, of a new sphere of scholarly problems.[13]

Žirmunskij was not the only Formalist who insisted that this approach should not be identified with any single method. Other more militant proponents such as Èjchenbaum, who blasted Žirmunskij for his "eclecticism," concurred with him on this point.[14] In Èjchenbaum's assessment, "the Formal method, by gradually evolving and extending its field of inquiry, has completely exceeded what was traditionally called methodology and is turning into a special science that treats literature as a specific series of facts. Within the limits of this science the most heterogeneous methods can be developed. . . . The designation of this movement as the 'Formal method,' which by now has become established, thus requires a qualification: it is a historical, not a definitional term. What characterizes us is neither 'Formalism' as an aesthetic theory, nor 'methodology' as a closed scientific system, but only the striving to establish, on the basis of specific properties of the literary material, an independent literary science."[15]

Despite their agreement on the necessity of methodological pluralism, however, there is an important difference between Žirmunskij's "eclecticism" and Èjchenbaum's "principled stance." While Žirmunskij characterizes Formalism somewhat nebulously as a "new sphere of scholarly problems," Èjchenbaum identifies it as something much more concrete—a new "independent literary science." Perhaps by taking advantage of Èjchenbaum's insight, one could look for a more deep-seated identity for Russian Formalism. Beneath all the diversity of method there may have existed a set of shared *epistemological* principles that generated the Formalist science of literature.

13. "K voprosu o 'formal'nom metode,'" *Voprosy teorii literatury: Stat'i 1916–1926* (Leningrad, 1928), p. 154.

14. See, for example, "'Metody i podchody,'" *Knižnyj ugol*, no. 8 (1922), 21–3.

15. "Teorija 'formal'nogo metoda,'" *Literatura: Teorija, kritika, polemika* (Leningrad, 1927), p. 117.

Unfortunately, the Formalists' methodological pluralism is more than matched by its epistemological pluralism. The principle that literature should be treated as a specific series of facts is too general to distinguish either the Formalists from non-Formalists, or genuine Formalists from fellow travelers. A similar concern was voiced by earlier Russian literary scholars, and the autonomy of literary facts vis-à-vis other phenomena was never solved by the Formalists themselves. Neither did they agree on what the specific properties of the literary material are or how the new science should proceed from them.

The epistemological diversity of this new literary science becomes obvious when we compare those who were methodologically similar, for example, the two leading Formalist students of verse, Tomaševskij and Jakobson. The former, rebutting the charge that the Formalists shirk the basic ontological issues of literary studies (that is, what literature is), wrote: "I shall answer by comparison. It is possible to study electricity and yet not know what it is. And what does the question, 'what is electricity,' mean anyway? I would answer: 'it is that which, if one screws in an electric bulb, will light it.' In studying phenomena one does not need an a priori definition of essences. It is important only to discern their manifestations and be aware of their connections. This is how the Formalists study literature. They conceive of poetics precisely as a discipline that studies the phenomena of literature and not its essence."[16]

Jakobson, in contrast, argues that such an ad hoc procedure was the modus operandi of old-fashioned literary scholarship. "Until now, the literary historian has looked like a policeman who, in trying to arrest a person, would, just in case, grab everyone and everything from his apartment, as well as accidental passers-by on the street." To pursue accidental phenomena instead of the literary essence is not the correct way to proceed, Jakobson insisted. "The object of literary science is not literature but literariness, i.e., what makes a given work a literary work."[17]

16. "Formal'nyj metod," p. 148.
17. *Novejšaja russkaja poèzija: Nabrosok pervyj* (Prague, 1921), p. 11.

Seemingly, the epistemological underpinnings of Formalist literary science were fluid enough to accommodate both Tomaševskij's blatant phenomenalism and Jakobson's implied phenomenology.

Perhaps such a conclusion should not surprise us. After all, Boris Èjchenbaum declared that epistemological monism—the reduction of the heterogeneity of art to a single explanatory principle—was the cardinal sin of traditional Russian literary scholarship:

> OPOJAZ is known today under the alias of the "Formal method." This is misleading. What matters is not the method but the principle. Both the Russian intelligentsia and Russian scholarship have been poisoned by the idea of monism. Marx, like a good German, reduced all of life to "economics." And the Russians who did not have their own scholarly *Weltanschauung*, but only a propensity toward it, did like to learn from German scholarship. Thus, the "monistic outlook" became king in our country and the rest followed. A basic principle was discovered and schemes were constructed. Since art did not fit into them it was thrown out. Let it exist as a "reflection"—sometimes it can be useful for education after all.
>
> But no! Enough of monism! We are pluralists. Life is diverse and cannot be reduced to a single principle. Blind men may do so, but even they are beginning to see. Life moves like a river in a continuous flow, but with an infinite number of streams, each of which is particular. And art is not even a stream of this flow, but a bridge over it.[18]

This brief foray into Formalist methodology and epistemology illustrates the difficulty of discerning a common denominator in this new literary science. Its identity appears to be that of a Wittgensteinian family resemblance: a set of overlapping ideas about literature, none of which is shared by every Formalist.

With all hope lost of establishing an intrinsic definition of Formalism, we might at least discover extrinsic criteria of identity for the movement. For instance, there seems to be a distinct

---

18. "5=100," *Knižnyj ugol*, no. 8 (1922), 39–40.

pattern in the way the Formalists characterize their collective enterprise. Again and again they speak of the novelty of their approach, or their deliberate departure from previous modes of literary studies. This, for example, is how Èjchenbaum describes the field of Russian letters in 1922:

> Something characteristic and significant has happened. There used to be "subjective" criticism—impressionistic, philosophical, etc., presenting its "meditations" about this and that. There also used to be "objective" scholarship—academic, internally hostile toward criticism, a lecturing from the cathedra full of certitudes. And suddenly all of this became a laughable anachronism. The scholarly certitudes preached from cathedras turned out to be naive babble and the critics' meditations a mere empty set of words, more or less clever chatter. What was demanded was a business-like criticism—precise and concrete—that would encompass both genuine theoretical ideas and genuine keenness of perception. Both pedantic [*intelligentskij*] criticism and scholarship began to be viewed as dilettantism; both were sentenced to death.[19]

Èjchenbaum's vivid depiction of the shift in Russian intellectual life created by the Formalist revolution suggests a possible source of unity for this school. Whereas a positive identity— some form of methodological or epistemological consensus— seems out of reach, a negative identity—the Formalists' dissent from previous literary scholarship—appears much less problematic. Of course, this path has its difficulties. Even if we manage to establish what Russian Formalism is *not* vis-à-vis its predecessors, our knowledge of what it actually *is* will be quite vague. And without some understanding of Formalism itself, the line we draw between it and pre-Formalism will be accordingly imprecise. Before the advent of Formalism, a great many ideas, concepts, and methods were floating about in Russian criticism that later turned out to be crucial to the movement.

The Formalists' detractors pointed to these very notions in disputing the movement's novelty. They tried to denigrate For-

19. "'Metody i podchody,'" 13–14.

malist literary theory by portraying it as unoriginal and derivative, since in Russian letters the concern with literary form had
preceded the birth of this group by decades. According to A.
Maškin, "as early as 1884, even the famous 'sociologist' idealist
N. Kareev urged his pupils at Warsaw University to study the
formal elements of the literary tradition."[20] The Marxist P. S.
Kogan, president of the Moscow Academy for the Study of the
Arts, found the spiritual father of Formalism in the "impressionistic" literary critic Kornej Čukovskij: "Čukovskij is older
than our learned 'Formalists.' His critical acumen and artistic
taste helped to anticipate many conclusions which the various
linguistic circles and 'OPOJAZ' are reaching only now. In his
critical practice he was applying to poets methods which V. Žirmunskij and his confederates are now trying to put on a scholarly footing."[21] And for those who knew better than to equate
Kareev or Čukovskij with Formalism there were always other
"early" Formalists, for example, the poet-theoreticians of the
Symbolist generation. Žirmunskij acknowledged their importance after his enthusiasm for OPOJAZ had cooled:

> The actual impulse for our own methodological inquires into the
> problems of literary form in fact came from the theoreticians of
> Symbolism, who compelled us to revise traditional academic poet-
> ics. I should mention in the first place Andrej Belyj. He not only
> propelled the theory of verse from a dead issue to a vital topic,
> but was also the first to criticize the traditional eclecticism of the
> pedantic "history of literature" and posed the question of a sci-
> ence devoted to the specifically artistic features of poetic
> works. . . . Next to him Valerij Brjusov discussed the problems of
> form in a number of essays and notes devoted to the technology
> of the poetic craft and Vjačeslav Ivanov offered both a concrete
> treatment of these problems in his analyses of poetry and a gener-
> al, theoretical one in the meetings of the "Poetic Academy." The
> interest in formal problems corresponded to the general literary
> posture of the Symbolists: the defense of the self-contained
> meaning of art and its "autonomy" from extra-artistic goals.[22]

20. "'Formalizm' i ego puti," *Krasnoe slovo*, nos. 2–3 (1927), 164.
21. "*Nekrasov, kak chudožnik.* Peterburg. Izdatel'stvo 'Èpocha.' 1922," *Pečat' i revoljucija*, no. 2 (1922), 351.
22. "Predislovie," *Voprosy teorii literatury*, pp. 8–9.

One need not take these hostile assertions at face value. One should be aware, however, that not all the Formalists shared Èjchenbaum's radical attitude toward history. To be sure, they viewed their common enterprise as a new and original chapter in Russian literary studies, but not necessarily one totally outside of its tradition. As Tomaševskij stressed in his 1928 lecture at the Prague Linguistic Circle, the Formalist negation of the past was selective. They rebelled above all against the main approaches to literature practiced in Russia at that time: (1) the biographical, which interpreted a text in terms of its author's life; (2) the sociohistorical, which reduced the work to a mere mirror of ideas current at the time of its origin; (3) the philosophical, which used literature as an illustration of the interpreter's philosophical system. "But one should not assume," Tomaševskij continued, "that the new school rejected the entire heritage of Russian scholarship. If it sometimes opposed Veselovskij's and Potebnja's ideas, it did so merely to emphasize its own independent stance. It must be stated, however, that the new school is obligated to these two predecessors and that it borrowed many of its basic concepts from them. The Formalists—as the proponents of this new system of literary studies were called—rejected more than anything else the excessive tendency toward inertia."[23]

Bogatyrëv and Jakobson's 1922 survey of current Russian philology also underlined the intellectual affinity between the Formalists and some of the older critics. The Formalist call for an independent literary science emerges from their account as the crystallization of a theoretical tendency that was in the air. "In recent years," the two Muscovites wrote,

> different philologists in a variety of ways arrived at the conclusion that current literary history is antiscientific. . . . The academic Peretc in his *Lessons on the Methodology of Russian Literary History* published in Kiev in 1914, sharply attacks the views of literary

23. "Nová ruská škola v bádání literárně-historickém," tr. J. Mukařovský, *Časopis pro moderní filologii* 15 (1929), 12–13.

history that were prevalent not so long ago and demands the systematic implementation of the formal method as a first step in the study of the evolution of literary forms. A. S. Orlov, in his 1921 lecture . . . "Thoughts about the Study of Literature as an Art," has insisted on the same. N. N. Konov in the pamphlet *Introduction to the History of Russian Literature* (Moscow, 1920) and to some degree Geršenzon in the booklet *A Poet's Vision* (Moscow, 1920) speak about this as well, though not without reservation and with a compromise in view. It is the works of the philologists grouped around the Petersburg Society for the Study of Poetic Language [OPOJAZ] and the Moscow Linguistic Circle that manifest the most radical demand for a fundamental switch in the history of literature and strict formal analysis.[24]

As the foregoing discussion suggests, a clear-cut separation of Formalist critical practice from that of the previous era is impossible without some overall understanding of the new school. A theoretical movement is obviously more than the sum total of ideas that it propounds; without the whole picture we cannot fit together its individual elements.

Demarcating Formalism from its predecessors, however, is only half the problem. The movement's negative identity consists as well in its distinctness from the theories that followed in its footsteps. Indeed, here the confusion seems even greater. Not only did Formalist principles and methods become the common property of literary scholars, but some of the original members of this school managed to continue the Formalist tradition outside its native land. Thus, the label of Formalism is commonly extended to movements whose members considered their own theorizing clearly non-Formalist and referred to themselves by quite different names.

Let me illustrate this point with two examples. The first is the Prague Linguistic Circle established in 1926, which labeled its approach "Structuralism." The close link between the Prague School and Russian Formalism is indisputable. The two not only had common members (Bogatyrëv and Jakobson) but the

24. "Slavjanskaja filologija v Rossii," 457.

Prague group consciously named themselves after the Moscow branch of the Formal school—the Moscow Linguistic Circle. Several leading Formalists (Tomaševskij, Tynjanov, and Vinokur) delivered lectures at the Prague Circle, and thus familiarized Czech scholars with the results of their research. A number of Formalist works, including Šklovskij's *On the Theory of Prose*, were translated into Czech in the late twenties and early thirties.

Given this close relationship, it is not surprising that Victor Erlich's pioneering work, *Russian Formalism,* contains a chapter dealing with the Prague school. To account for the repercussions of Russian Formalism in the neighboring countries, Erlich introduces the umbrella concept of "Slavic Formalism" whose Prague mutation is called "Structuralism." Although he points out the difference between what he terms "pure Formalism" and "Prague Structuralism,"[25] for Erlich the literary theory of the Prague school is ultimately a restatement of the "basic tenets of Russian Formalism in more judicious and rigorous terms."[26] Because of the wide acclaim of Erlich's book in the West, the conflation of Prague Structuralism with Russian Formalism has become commonplace in many subsequent histories of literary theory. Fredric Jameson, for instance, who regards Erlich's work as the "definitive English-language survey of Formalism,"[27] mentions the Prague school in his comparative study of Russian Formalism and Structuralism only in connection with the Russian movement, and refers to its members as "Czech Formalists."[28]

In Czech criticism, a similar view of the Prague school was often advocated by those hostile to Structuralism. Earlier we saw that the Russian foes of Formalism attacked its theories as derivative. Czech anti-Structuralists employed the same strategy.

25. *Russian Formalism: History—Doctrine,* 3d ed. (The Hague, 1969), pp. 154–63.

26. "Russian Formalism," *Princeton Encyclopedia of Poetry and Poetics: Enlarged Edition,* ed. A. Preminger (Princeton, N.J., 1974), p. 727.

27. *The Prison-House of Language: A Critical Account of Structuralism and Russian Formalism* (Princeton, N.J., 1972), p. 85.

28. Ibid., p. 51.

They declared the Prague school approach to be a mere intellectual import from Russia, a continuation of Formalism by emigrés who could no longer practice it in their own land. Concluding his 1934 survey of the Formalist movement, Karel Svoboda wrote: "Russian Formalism *tries to make up* in our country for the losses it has suffered in its homeland. It was brought here by R. Jakobson; on his initiative in 1926 the Prague Linguistic Circle was established, modeled on the Moscow Linguistic Circle and incorporating Formalist principles."[29] Some thirty years later, Ladislav Štoll, the Czech Communist Party's authority on literary matters, faced with the ideologically subversive resurrection of Structuralism in his territory, proclaimed: "At a time when Prague *literary* Structuralists . . . accepted all the basic concepts, procedures, and terminology of the Russian Formal school, the followers of this school in the U.S.S.R., under the influence of Marxist literary theory, were rethinking their previous positions and gradually departing on new paths. In its essence, Prague literary Structuralism is a belated echo of the Russian school."[30] Needless to say, the villain of Štoll's account was the "agent of the worldwide bourgeoisie," Roman Jakobson, whose insidious influence set back the development of Czech literary studies many years, returning it to the cul-de-sac of Formalism.

Predictably, the Prague Structuralists disagreed with these portrayals of their movement. The Circle's leading aesthetician, Jan Mukařovský, retorted by poking fun at Svoboda's account: "The matter is often presented as if Czech scholarship one day discovered Russian Formalism and copied it, almost like a village carpenter who was 'doing Art Nouveau' until he suddenly discovered a pattern book with the plan of a constructivist house." Russian Formalism, in Mukařovský's opinion, was welcomed in Bohemia only because it meshed with a domestic tradition of empirical aesthetics whose foundations were laid in the nineteenth century by the Herbartian Formalists (Josef Durdík,

29. "O tak zvané formální metodě v literární vědě," *Naše věda* 15, no. 2 (1934), 45.
30. *O tvar a strukturu v slovesném umění* (Prague, 1966), p. 86.

Otakar Hostinský). "Under these conditions, it would be wrong to believe that Formalism penetrated Czech scholarship like an alien body. Proceeding from the inevitably international nature of the scholarly enterprise, Czech scholarship consciously and actively absorbed a theory that suited its own developmental tendencies and facilitated its further development. . . . [It] did not collapse under the influence [of Russian Formalism], but overcame in Structuralism the one-sidedness of Formalism."[31]

The conflation of Formalism with Structuralism, whether justified or not, adds yet another twist to the problem of demarcating the Russian movement. Its most obvious effect is to extend the label across temporal and geographical boundaries. Yet at times the conflation has had just the opposite result. In the sixties, when Structuralism was becoming an international movement, historians often divided the Russian precursors into early "pure Formalists" and more advanced "Structuralists." This reshuffling of Formalism was facilitated by the vagueness of the historical label of Structuralism. Coined by Roman Jakobson in his brief account of the First International Congress of Slavicists in 1929, "Structuralism" was used to designate the "leading idea of present-day science in its most various manifestations."[32] As a new holistic and teleological paradigm of scholarship, Structuralism attempted to displace the atomistic and genetic-causal paradigm of positivism, the work of the Prague Linguistic Circle being its clearest exemplification in the fields of linguistics and poetics. By defining Structuralism so broadly, however, Jakobson created an overlap between Formalism and Structuralism. For in its heterogeneity, Russian Formalism certainly contained some of the ideas informing the new paradigm, and some of the Formalists had treated their data in a holistic manner and/or eschewed a genetic-causal mode of explanation.

In this way, what previously was regarded as a single the-

31. "Vztah mezi sovětskou a československou literární vědou," *Země Sovětů* 4 (1935–1936), 14.
32. "Romantické všeslovanství—nová slavistika," *Čin* 1 (1929–1930), 11.

oretical movement suddenly split in two. P. N. Smirnov points out in his encyclopedia entry, "Structuralism in Literary Studies," that some of the Russian Formalists should correctly be called Structuralists.

> In the U.S.S.R. Structuralism began to emerge in the twenties, separating itself from the Formal school (see OPOJAZ). While the Formalists identified the artistic text with the object (artifact) and put forward as their primary theoretical terms the notions "material" and "device," the structuralists juxtaposed to this the difference between the text and structure implicit already in V. Ja. Propp's *Morphology of the Folktale* (1928). . . . Ju. Tynjanov, one of the first to introduce the term "structure" into literary-theoretical discourse, proposed to study the constructive elements of the poetic work in relation to the artistic whole, i.e., from a functional point of view (instead of a technological one).[33]

The limitation of the designation "Formalism" to only the early stage of the Russian movement is not the practice of Soviet historians alone. As I mentioned before, Striedter draws the line between Šklovskij's and Tynjanov's theories in roughly the same way. Another advocate of this view is the Dutch comparatist, Douwe Fokkema. Surveying modern Slavic criticism, he writes, "Within the context of this paper my main point is that the Russian Formalists gradually came to accept the view that the various factors in verbal art are interrelated. The dominant function of one factor subordinates the importance of other factors and deforms them, but seldom completely annihilates their functions. If the Formalists viewed literature as a system characterized by the interdependence of its elements, this position must be called *structuralist* although they rarely used that label before 1927."[34]

The problematic boundaries between Formalism and Struc-

---

33. "Strukturalizm v literaturovedenii," *Kratkaja literaturnaja ènciklopedija*, vol. 7 (Moscow, 1972), p. 231.

34. "Continuity and Change in Russian Formalism, Czech Structuralism, Soviet Semiotics," *PTL: A Journal for Descriptive Poetics and Theory of Literature* 1 (1976), 163. This journal hereafter cited as *PTL*.

turalism are not the only hindrance to an understanding of the Russian movement. With the rise of a new critical star on the current intellectual horizon—post-Structuralism—another Russian literary-theoretical group with ties to Formalism has caught the attention of historians. I speak here of the Bachtin circle, whose most prominent members, aside from Michail Bachtin himself, were the literary scholar Medvedev and the linguist V. N. Vološinov. Since this group produced some of the most penetrating critiques of Formalism from a self-proclaimed Marxist position,[35] the Bachtinians were left out of the picture in older accounts of the Formal school.

Erlich's classic work does not mention Bachtin, although it notes Medvedev's book on Formalism, calling it "the most extended and scholarly critique of *Opojaz* ever undertaken by a Marxist."[36] Striedter's 1969 introduction to a German anthology of Formalist texts fails to mention the Bachtin circle altogether. Well aware of the conceptual heterogeneity and developmental fluidity of the Formal school, Striedter conceives of its unity in a dialectic fashion, as a "dialogic form of theorizing." From this perspective, "the history and theory of Russian Formalism are an uninterrupted dialogue between the Formalists and their opponents, but even more so among the Formalists themselves, who opposed and criticized one another. . . . they were all at one and the same time partners and adversaries in the fascinating dialogue which produced and represented the formal method."[37] Yet Striedter is unwilling to include in this "uninterrupted dialogue" the very scholars who made the notion of dialogue the center of their theory—the Marxist critics of Formalism who gathered around Bachtin. Because of the alleged

35. See, for example V. N. Vološinov, *Marksizm i filosofija jazyka: Osnovnye problemy sociologičeskogo metoda v nauke o jazyke* (Leningrad, 1929); and Medvedev's book mentioned in note 11.

36. *Russian Formalism: History—Doctrine*, p. 114.

37. "Zur formalistischen Theorie der Prosa und der literarischen Evolution," in *Texte der russischen Formalisten*, vol. 1, ed. J. Striedter (Munich, 1969); quoted from English tr. by M. Nicolson, "The Russian Formalist Theory of Prose," *PTL* 2 (1977), 435.

rigidity among the Russian Marxists of the late twenties, Stried-ter claims that "any combination of Formalist and Marxist meth-ods remained, of necessity, a one-sided compromise. Individual Marxist literary scholars did in fact in the course of time take over individual elements of Formalist theory, or at least parts of their analytical technique. . . . But such 'appendages' have no more in common with actual Formalism and its decisive insights than does the Formalists' own contribution to 'literary life' with Marxism."[38]

Erlich's and Striedter's views of Russian Formalism are now being challenged by the youngest generation of Slavicists. In the most comprehensive and meticulous book written on the sub-ject, the Viennese scholar Aage Hansen-Löve divides the history of the Formal school into three successive stages. The last stage in his account includes not only the sociological and historical approaches propounded by such "clear-cut" Formalists as Èjchenbaum and Tynjanov, but also semiotics and communica-tion-theoretical accounts. This is the model advanced, according to Hansen-Löve, by the Bachtinians and the psychologist Lev Vygotskij.[39] From a similar position, Gary Saul Morson re-proaches the historians of Formalism for ignoring the Bachti-nians: "The work of the Bachtin group is, in fact, a logical devel-opment of Formalist thinking. It follows that to leave Bachtin out of an account of Russian Formalism is profoundly to misun-derstand the nature and objectives of the movement: and this is what has largely been done."[40]

One may question Morson's argument for the necessity of including the Bachtinians in the Formal school. As long as he fails to clarify what the nature and objectives of this movement are, his charge of misunderstanding remains a rhetorical device.

38. "Zur formalistischen Theorie der Prosa und der literarischen Evolution," quoted from English tr. by M. Nicolson, "The Russian Formalist Theory of Literary Evolution," *PTL* 3 (1978), 18.

39. *Der russische Formalismus: Methodologische Rekonstruktion seiner Entwicklung aus dem Prinzip der Verfremdung* (Vienna, 1978), pp. 426–62.

40. "The Heresiarch of *Meta*," *PTL* 3 (1978), 408.

Nevertheless, the point raised by the young scholars has been recognized by their seniors as at least deserving attention. "Were I writing this book today," says Erlich in the introduction to the American edition of *Russian Formalism,* "I would undoubtedly pause before the achievements of Mikhail Bakhtin. . . . the essentially structural and metalinguistic thrust of his *Problems of Dostoevsky's Poetics* attests to a strong affinity for the mature phase of Formalist theorizing."[41] Likewise, Striedter mentions Bachtin in a comparative study of Russian Formalism and Prague Structuralism when he searches within the Russian critical tradition for the precursors of the semiotic approach that subsequently flourished in Prague. In this connection, he also speaks of the "Leningrad group centered around M. Bachtin at the end of the twenties, which, in part as a continuation of Formalist theses and in part as a critical opposition to them, proposed to develop a theory of art that can be characterized as communicational and semiotic."[42]

It must be stressed, however, that while aware of the problem the Bachtinians present for the history of Formalism, neither Erlich nor Striedter accepts them as true Formalists. Erlich is particularly strict on this issue. He merely includes Bachtin in what he calls "neo-Formalist developments," and declares categorically that "Bakhtin, who made his debut in the late twenties only to lapse into enforced obscurity until the sixties, could not be labeled a Formalist."[43] Striedter is somewhat more flexible here, willing to consider the semiotic trends within the Russian literary studies of the twenties under the heading of Formalism. But he is also quick to point out that these are merely the fringes of genuine Formalism. "To be sure, it is no accident that [my] examples came mostly from the 'periphery,' whether in the sense of a group affiliation, i.e., the 'margins' rather than from the very 'core' of Formalism, or in the sense of a particular subject matter. . . . In terms of time it is also striking that the

---

41. *Russian Formalism* (New Haven, 1981), p. 10.
42. "Einleitung," p. xlvi.
43. *Russian Formalism* (1981), p. 10.

works quoted appeared mostly toward the end of the twenties just before the end of Formalism as an independent school (and immediately after the founding of the Prague Linguistic Circle)."[44]

The two competing opinions about the status of the Bachtinians, which I have presented as a dialogue between generations, pose an obvious challenge for anyone writing on Russian Formalism. However, it is not my intention to argue one way or the other here. The argument over the Bachtinians is merely another example of the imprecision in the critical usage of the label "Russian Formalism," even as a negative concept.

Having failed to ascertain either a positive or a negative identity for the movement, we might legitimately ask whether it is worthwhile to retain the label at all. Perhaps what we need is a new, more suitable and precise concept—to start over with a clean slate. But as the title of my book reveals, I have refrained from this attractive proposition. The reason for this conservatism lies in my understanding of the role that historical concepts play. To explain this, I shall take a short detour into the field of semiotics.

As I have been showing throughout this chapter, historical labels, such as "Russian Formalism," are vague. To create more precise replacements, it seems logical to turn to less equivocal types of verbal signs. Let us take, for example, proper names. They denote individuals, places, and so forth on a one-to-one basis. If historical concepts could successfully emulate the exact referentiality of proper names, historical discourse might become less impressionistic.

But how do proper names signify? Traditional logic drew a strict line between the proper name of an object and its definite description. Description is always partial, for it provides knowledge about only some of an object's properties. The name, on the other hand, does not impart any knowledge about the object but rather points to the identity of the object in its entirety. The

44. "Einleitung," p. xlviii.

proper name thus conceived is a senseless mark, an index whose meaning is merely the object to which it points, or, in John Stuart Mill's terminology, a sign with denotation but without connotation. From the standpoint of this theory it is immediately obvious why concepts like "Formalism" are so ambiguous. They do not simply name stages or trends in literary theory but describe them by referring to them through some of their randomly selected features. Because formal concerns are far from limited to Russian Formalism, these concepts are easily transferable to other literary theoretical schools.

The theory of proper names thus provides me with a criterion for replacing ambiguous historical concepts with less ambiguous substitutes. The names selected should be devoid of connotations which could motivate their homonymic extension. To separate the metalanguage of historical discourse completely from the object-language of literary-theoretical discourse, I might designate Russian Formalism as "79." It is doubtful, however, whether such a radical change of nomenclature would produce any actual gain. The problem is not that the procedure would not work, but that it would work only too well. A number-name is such a senseless mark that no one would understand what it designated. And yet, in the very moment that the name is explained through a synonym, in this case, "79 is Russian Formalism," it is automatically subject to the same slippage and ambiguity as the previous concepts.

According to some logicians, this attempt at replacing traditional historical concepts with new ones is doomed from the start, for it proceeds from a mistaken assumption about proper names. The theory propounded by Gottlob Frege, for instance, holds that proper names are not at all senseless marks, but rather shorthand descriptions. Their sense stems from the fact that the naming always presents an object in a particular mode, as a part of a particular context. "The morning star" and "the evening star," for example, are two names for the same object captured in different phases. This account of proper names fits quite well the conceptual muddle of historical discourse. Terms such as "the morphological school," "OPOJAZ," or "Structuralism" can indeed be seen as partial descriptions of "Russian Formalism," since they present this movement from different perspectives. Although Frege's theory legitimizes this interchanging of historical concepts, it provides no criteria for selecting among them. There is no reason that I could not call the Russian Formalists "neo-Aristotelians" (referring in this way to some principles of Aristotle's poetics incorporated into Formalist poetics) or any other name, provided that it grasps at least one feature of the movement.[45] Given the extreme heterogeneity of Russian Formalism, the acceptance of Frege's theory would lead to the direct opposite of what I intended to achieve: a proliferation of historical concepts rather than their limitation and clarification.

These two theories of proper names lead nowhere because they represent two extreme views of the act of naming: in the traditional theory, naming is prior to description, whereas in Frege's countertheory, description precedes naming. The traditional view conceives of names as static tags attached on a one-to-one basis to equally static objects; Frege conceives of names as an unlimited set of signs whose significations are a function of the contexts of the entity designated. The proper name in fact falls somewhere between these two poles. The traditionalists correctly point out that its signification is much more specific than that of other nouns, but Frege's argument also has weight; as long as the proper name is a linguistic sign it remains inadequate in some way to the object named. The two theories appear mutually exclusive because of their either/or presentation. For those who believe that the name is a senseless mark, only a word that identifies a single object in its entirety is a name proper; for

45. For analogies between Aristotle and the Formalists, see, for example, K. Svoboda, "O tak zvané formální metodě," 39, or A. A. Hansen-Löve, *Der russische Formalismus*, pp. 24–30. However, the Formalists themselves resented any parallelism drawn between their poetics and Aristotle's, and they certainly would have rejected the label "neo-Aristotelian." See, for example, B. Tomaševskij's letter to Šklovskij of April 12, 1925 (*Slavica Hierosolymitana*, no. 3 [1978], 385–86).

their opponents, no name can achieve this absolute goal and therefore there are no proper names but merely definite descriptions.

One can, however, assume a more moderate position allowing the name some degree of imprecision. Taking for granted the essential inadequacy of the relationship between a name and its object, one can argue that this inadequacy is not strong enough to prevent the proper name from referring to a particular object. This position, adopted by some modern logicians, is well illustrated in John Searle's discussion of the use of the name "Aristotle."

> To ask for the criteria for applying the name "Aristotle" is to ask in the formal mode what Aristotle is: it is to ask for a set of identity criteria for the object Aristotle. "What is Aristotle?" and "What are the criteria for applying the name 'Aristotle'?" ask the same question, the former in the material mode, and the latter in the formal mode of speech. So if, prior to using the name, we came to an agreement on the precise characteristics which constituted the identity of Aristotle, our rules for using the name would be precise. But this precision would be achieved only at the cost of entailing some *specific* descriptions by any use of the name. Indeed, the name itself would become logically equivalent to this set of descriptions. But if this were the case we would be in the position of being able to refer to an object solely by, in effect, describing it. Whereas in fact this is just what distinguishes proper names from definite descriptions . . . the uniqueness and immense pragmatic convenience of proper names in our language lies precisely in the fact that they enable us to refer publicly to objects without being forced to raise issues and come to an agreement as to which descriptive characteristics exactly constitute the identity of the object. They function not as descriptions, but as pegs on which to hang descriptions.[46]

Searle's "pragmatic" view of proper names opens up a new perspective on the function of historical concepts. These concepts do not simply denote segments of the historical continuum

46. *Speech Acts: An Essay in the Philosophy of Language* (Cambridge, 1969), p. 172.

but refer to them in such a way that the issue of the identity of these segments is avoided. This view of historical concepts provides the most convincing argument against the wholesale rejection of vague terms like "Russian Formalism." It is concepts like these rather than their more precise replacements that *refer* in the manner outlined by Searle. "Nonconnotative" concepts, as long as they remain truly senseless, cannot refer at all, while shorthand descriptions identify objects through some of their characteristics and become too easily embroiled in disputes over the identity of their referents.

Strange as it might seem, what makes established labels best suited to the act of referring is their vagueness. They become established not because they are more adequate to their objects than other signs but because of their semantic "elasticity"—their capacity to accommodate different, often contradictory usages. In this respect, established concepts are multiperspectival, transtemporal representations of their respective historical segments. They contain many points of view and many layers of semantic accretion, thus presenting their objects synthetically in their manifold heterogeneity. It is precisely this institutionalized slippage of established concepts that makes them indispensable for historical discourse. Only through them is it possible for historians to refer to roughly the same temporal segments, intellectual schools, and trends, while at the same time providing different accounts of them. In other words, though historians of literary theory disagree widely in their descriptions of Russian Formalism, their disagreement is meaningful only if an intuitive agreement that they are speaking of the "same" thing underlies their discussion.

What remains to be explained is my own method of dealing with Russian Formalism. From the very beginning I have faced a dilemma. On the one hand, I am only too aware of the pitfalls of a piecemeal approach toward Formalist critical practice. As long as we focus merely on the individual ideas, concepts, or principles that constitute it, the unity of the movement (if it exists) will always elude us. On the other hand, I have at my disposal no methodological or epistemological denominator common to all of Formalist theorizing.

Pondering plausible holistic approaches to the Formal school, I began to wonder whether the theoretical program the Formalists advanced for the study of literature might not, *mutatis mutandis*, be applied to their own writings. Just as they, in searching for the differential quality of literature, had shied away from *what* the writer said to focus on *how* he said it, I began to study not what the Formalists had to say about literature but how they conceptualized it. But even after turning the Formal method upon itself, I learned that there is no single "how" to Russian Formalism. The propounders of this "pure science of literature" indiscriminately borrowed frames of reference from other realms of knowledge. As I realized that the unity of the movement must be sought elsewhere, I began to have some inklings about where it might be found.

At the same time, I found this transference of conceptual frameworks from one realm of knowledge to another quite intriguing. It reminded me of the poetic tropes I often discussed as a teacher of literature. I soon discovered that some modern philosophers of science also call attention to the figurative nature of scientific knowledge. Max Black, perhaps the best-known proponent of this view, observed that "a memorable metaphor has the power to bring two separate domains into cognitive and emotional relation by using language directly appropriate to the one as a lens for seeing the other; the implications, suggestions, and supporting values entwined with the literal use of the metaphorical expression enable us to see a new subject matter in a new light."[47] Because of its simplicity and ad hoc character, however, the explanatory power of a metaphor is low. Therefore Black introduced a second notion, the complex metaphor, which he terms a model. "You need only proverbial knowledge, as it were, to have your metaphor understood; but the maker of a scientific model must have prior control of a well-

47. *Models and Metaphors* (Ithaca, N.Y., 1962), pp. 236–37.

knit scientific theory if he is to do more than hang an attractive picture on an algebraic formula. Systematic complexity of the source of the model and capacity for analogical development are the essence."[48] With this in mind, I have happily applied Black's insights to my own material. But in doing so I have found that the limitation of his theory to transferences based on similarity or analogy—that is, metaphors—is too narrow for my purposes. Obviously, not only metaphors but other complex tropes can provide conceptual frameworks. The biographical approach, common in literary studies, is metonymic in that it is based on an association of contiguity: the life of the author is studied not necessarily because it is analogous to his or her work but because it supposedly provides the cause for the organization of meaning in it. I decided therefore to employ the term "model" somewhat more broadly than Black, as an umbrella term for any complex language transference used as an explanatory tool, regardless of the type of associations that underlie it—metaphoric or metonymic.

This way of dealing with Russian Formalism, of course, is not entirely new. A similar strategy was employed by Fredric Jameson in his *Prison-House of Language*. Explicitly stating in his preface that "the history of thought is the history of its models," Jameson proceeded to discuss *the* model which in his opinion molded the literary theory of the Formal school.[49] Here we part company, for obviously I do not believe that any one model is capable of accounting for Russian Formalism in all its diversity. Jameson identifies the "absolute presuppositions" of this school with the "linguistic model." The source of this reductivism may very well lie in Jameson's Marxist stance, since such a treatment of Formalism fits rather well what Viktor Šklovskij had to say of Maksim Gor'kij's "ironic bolshevism." According to Šklovskij, "The Bolsheviks believed that what counts is not material but its

48. Ibid., p. 239.
49. *The Prison-House of Language*, p. 3.

formation. . . . They could not understand the anarchy of life, its subconscious, the fact that the tree knows best how to grow."[50] Though one need not be a neo-Hegelian to agree with Jameson's claim that the linguistic model is more progressive than the organic one he consigns to the dustbin of the nineteenth century, this judgment did not stop some of the Formalists from regressing into organicism. Had they read *The Prison-House of Language* perhaps things would have been different. But they were such an unruly bunch!

My task, then, is to separate the tangled threads in the confusing and often contradictory frameworks utilized by the Formalists, and to outline a typology for the theoretical models that they applied to the study of literature. I call my work a "metapoetics" because it attempts to examine a poetics in terms of poetics itself, or more precisely, in terms of the poetic tropes that molded the Formalist discourse on poetics. This exercise might appear frivolous to those who prefer other ways of writing intellectual history. But I have taken this path nevertheless, convinced that it not only might shed new light on a movement whose significance for modern literary study is undeniable, but also might enable me, finally, to formulate what the distinctive quality of Formalist theorizing is.

50. *Sentimental'noe putešestvie: Vospominanija 1917–1922* (Berlin, 1923), p. 266.

2

The Three Metaphors

The Machine

> To make two bald statements: There's nothing sen-
> timental about a machine, and: A poem is a small
> (or large) machine made of words. When I say
> there's nothing sentimental about a poem I mean
> that there can be no part, as in any other machine,
> that is redundant. [. . .]
> There is no poetry of distinction without formal
> invention, for it is in the intimate form that works
> of art achieve their exact meaning, in which they
> most resemble the machine, to give language its
> highest dignity, its illumination in the environment
> to which it is native.
>
> —WILLIAM CARLOS WILLIAMS, *Collected Later Poems*

Probably the best known Formalist model was advanced by
Viktor Šklovskij, the self-proclaimed "founder of the Russian
school of Formal method."[1] His answer to the question "what is
Formalism?" was very clear: "In its essence the Formal method is

1. *Sentimental'noe putešestvie: Vospominanija 1917–1922* (Berlin, 1923), p. 317.

simple—a return to craftsmanship."[2] Technology, that branch of knowledge pertaining to the art of human production, was the predominant metaphor applied by this model to the description and elucidation of artistic phenomena.[3]

Šklovskij's obsession with the machine analogy was well known to his contemporaries. In a commemorative article about Jurij Tynjanov, Lidija Ginzburg recalls a random chat of 1925 in which Tynjanov had tried to differentiate his own approach to literature from Šklovskij's. "Viktor is a fitter, a mechanic.—And a chauffeur, someone prompted.—Yes and a chauffeur too. He believes in construction. He thinks that he knows how the car is made. . . ."[4] Tynjanov did not have to explain his phrase because the hint was transparent to everyone. He was alluding to Šklovskij's bon mot in a 1922 letter to Roman Jakobson: "We know how life is made and how *Don Quixote* and the car are made too."[5]

Šklovskij did not reserve his car/literature analogy for the inner Formalist circle. Quite the contrary: it recurs again and again as the central image in his scholarly, pedagogical, and creative texts as well. For example, in his booklet *The Technique of the Writer's Trade* (1928), Šklovskij advises aspiring prose writers about how to read literature:

> If you wish to become a writer you must examine a book as attentively as a watchmaker a clock or a chauffeur a car.

2. Ibid., p. 327. See also Osip Brik's succinct account of the program of OPOJAZ: "OPOJAZ studies the laws of poetic production" ("T. n. 'formal'nyj metod,'" *Lef*, no. 1 [1923], 214).

3. The Formalist S. Baluchatyj characterized his method as a "technological literary discipline" (*Problemy dramaturgičeskogo analiza Čechova* [Leningrad, 1927], p. 7). G. Vinokur described stylistics as "a kind of 'linguistic technology'" (*Kul'tura jazyka*, 2d ed. [Moscow, 1929], p. 9). B. Èjchenbaum summed up the early phase of Formalism as follows: "In recent years, students of literature and critics have paid attention above all to questions of literary 'technology'" ("Literaturnyj byt," *Moj vremennik: Slovesnost', nauka, kritika, smes'* [Leningrad, 1929], p. 50).

4. *Jurij Tynjanov: Pisatel' i učënnyj*, ed. V. Kaverin et al. (Moscow, 1966), p. 90.

5. *Knižnyj ugol*, no. 8 (1922), 24. For another reference to this quip of Šklovskij's, see Boris Larin, "O raznovidnostjach chudožestvennoj reči," *Russkaja reč': Sborniki statej*, vol. 1, ed. L. Ščerba (Petersburg, 1923), p. 89.

Cars are examined in the following ways: The most idiotic people come to the automobile and press the balloon of its horn. This is the first degree of stupidity. People who know a little more about cars but overestimate their knowledge come to the car and fiddle with its stick-shift. This is also stupid and even bad, because one should not touch a thing for which another worker is responsible.

The understanding man scrutinizes the car serenely and comprehends "what is for what": why it has so many cylinders and why it has big wheels, where its transmission is situated, and why its rear is cut in an acute angle and its radiator unpolished.

This is the way one should read.[6]

What this technological metaphor meant for the study of literature is apparent in the introduction to *On the Theory of Prose*—the most scholarly of Šklovskij's books: "In the theory of literature I am concerned with the study of the internal laws of literature. To draw a parallel with industry, I am interested neither in the situation in the world cotton market, nor in the policy of trusts, but only in the kinds of yarn and the methods of weaving."[7] Because of the repeated use of the machine analogy, I shall term this trend in Formalism "mechanistic."

The source of Šklovskij's technological metaphor is rather complex. It betrays first the influence of Italian Futurism, with its cult of the machine as the most crucial factor in the birth of the modernist artistic sensibility. But in Russia it also indicated a certain political stance. It was related to the leftist intelligentsia's yearning for a radical transformation of Russian society. The mastery of technology was often seen as the ultimate means to this end. Lenin's famous equation—"socialism = the Soviet government + electrification"—was an expression of this belief, as were the unrealizable Constructivist projects of scientifically designed socialist cities, or Vladimir Majakovskij's statement that a single Ford tractor is better than a collection of poems.

Šklovskij's interest in literary know-how was conditioned by

6. *Technika pisatel'skogo remesla* (Moscow, 1928), pp. 7–8.
7. "Predislovie," *O teorii prozy* (Moscow, 1925), p. 5.

pragmatic concerns too. The Formalist leader did not enter the field of Russian letters as an academic observer or an armchair theoretician, but as an active participant—a creative writer. From this perspective, the problems of literary production were of paramount significance. Yet it was precisely in this area that previous Russian criticism exhibited a curious lacuna. Whereas for all the other arts technical knowledge was considered vital to both historical and practical study, in literature technique was relegated to schoolbooks on poetics that were mere catalogues of tropes, figures, and meters derived from Greek and Latin models. It was this gap that mechanistic Formalism, concerned with the literary *techné*, set out to close.

The selection of the machine as the controlling metaphor of his theoretical model served Šklovskij in yet another way. It furnished a frame of reference that enabled him to treat literature in a manner radically different from that of pre-Formalist critics. At the risk of oversimplification, one might claim that traditional literary scholars were concerned above all with *what* the work conveyed. To understand this "what," students of Russian literature looked beyond the work: into its author's life, the philosophy supposedly embodied in it, or the sociopolitical events that gave rise to it. This "what," customarily called the content of the literary creation, was opposed to its *how*, its form. And even though the meaning of these two notions varied from critic to critic, the "what," the message of the literary work, always seemed the decisive member of the pair. Form was relegated to a mere auxiliary mechanism necessary for expressing content, but completely dependent upon it.

By focusing on the nuts and bolts of poetic texts, the internal laws of literary production, mechanistic Formalism radically reversed the value of content. Mocking traditional critics, Šklovskij wrote: "The present-day theoretician, in studying a literary work and considering its so-called form as a shroud that must be penetrated, is mounting a horse while jumping over it."[8] The

---

8. "Literatura vne 'sjužeta,'" *O teorii prozy*, p. 162.

"how" of literature gained decisive prominence in the mechanistic model, and the machine analogy furnished the conceptual viewpoint that enabled Šklovskij to redirect attention from the external conditions of the literary process to the internal organization of the work.

Disjunction was the key logical principle by which mechanistic Formalism organized its basic concepts. This principle split art decisively from nonart, and expressed their mutual exclusivity in the following set of polar oppositions:

art	byt (everyday life)[9]
de-familiarization	automatization
teleology	causality
device	material
plot (sjužet)	story (fabula)

The first concept in the table, de-familiarization (ostranenie), has today gained wide currency. The word was coined by Viktor Šklovskij to account for the special nature of artistic perception. In his 1914 manifesto, *The Resurrection of the Word*, Šklovskij presented the dialectics of de-familiarization and automatization in this way: "By now the old art has already died, but the new has not yet been born. Things have died too: we have lost the

---

9. My translation of *byt* as "everyday life" is a rather inadequate rendition of a highly evocative Russian term. According to Roman Jakobson, *byt* is "the tendency toward stabilizing the immutable present and the gradual accretion of the stagnant slime to it, the stifling of life by tight and petrified molds," the antithesis of "the creative impulse toward the transformed future. . . . It is curious," Jakobson continues, "that while in the Russian language and literature this word and its derivatives play quite a significant role . . . European languages lack any corresponding nomenclature" ("O pokolenii rastrativšem svoich poètov," *Smert' Vladimira Majakovskogo* [Berlin, 1931], p. 13). For this reason, I have retained the Russian *byt* in all quotations from Formalist texts. In my own prose I alternate *byt* with "life." If, however, the word "life" appears in quotation marks it is a translation of the Russian *žizn'*. The adjective *bytovoj* is rendered as "extra-artistic" or "extraliterary" depending on the context.

sensation of the world. We are like a violinist who has stopped feeling his bow and strings. We have ceased to be artists in our quotidian life; we do not like our houses and clothes and easily part with a life that we do not perceive. Only the creation of new forms of art can bring back to man his experience of the world, resurrect things and kill pessimism."[10]

In this early formulation, the principle of de-familiarization is closely linked to the poetics of Russian Futurism, a movement that sentenced past art to death and set out to create artistic forms more attuned to the iconoclastic tastes of radical youth. As his mechanistic model developed, Šklovskij began to replace the existential frame of reference with terminology that would better fit his machine metaphor. It was economy, or more precisely, energy-efficiency, that eventually became the criterion for differentiating between automatized and de-familiarizing modes of perception.

Šklovskij's concept of artistic perception has its roots in the positivistic belief in art's economizing of mental energy, in particular the principle of least effort that Herbert Spencer (1820–1903) had declared the universal law of style. In the Russian context, Spencer's theory had found an echo in the writings of Aleksandr Veselovskij (1838–1906), one of the few critics of the past whom the Formalists did not completely disregard. In the third chapter of his unfinished *Historical Poetics*, Veselovskij had used Spencer's principle of the economization of mental energy to support his differentiation of poetic from prose style. Poetry achieves its results with a paucity of means impossible in prose, as witnessed in its unfinished periods, elisions, and omissions. Veselovskij especially stressed the role of rhythm and rhyme, the predictability of which purportedly saves us from wasting energy in frustrated expectations.[11] It was this assertion that Šklovskij challenged. "The idea of the economy of energy as the

---

10. *Voskrešenie slova*, repr. in *Texte der russischen Formalisten*, vol. 2, ed. W.-D. Stempel (Munich, 1972), p. 12.

11. "Tri glavy iz istoričeskoj poètiki," *Istoričeskaja poètika*, ed. V. Žirmunskij, (Leningrad, 1940), p. 356.

law and goal of creativity might be correct when applied to a particular case of language, 'practical' language"; but "the language of poetry is a difficult language, language which is made difficult and hampered."[12] According to Šklovskij, the perception of art manifests not the law of least effort but the law of maximal effort.

The explanation of this claim offered by the mechanistic Formalists is elegant in its simplicity: artistic form is difficult because it is made so. The teleology used in this argument is in perfect harmony with the technological metaphor. The work of art as a product of an intentional human activity is a functional object whose purpose is to change the mode of our perception from practical to artistic. This change can be effected in several ways, most simply by displacing an object from its customary context. "In order to render an object an artistic fact it must be extracted from among the facts of life . . . it must be torn out of its usual associations."[13]

The Formalists were not so much interested in ready-made objects or found art as in the artistic work as a complex artifact. For this reason the concept of "displacement" was always secondary to that of the "device," which pertains specifically to the production of the work. "Every art," argued Šklovskij, "has its own organization—that which transforms its material into something artistically experienced. This organization is expressed in various compositional devices, in rhythm, phonetics, syntax, the plot of the work. It is the device that transforms extra-aesthetic material into the work of art by providing it with form."[14] The device changes extra-artistic material into art, forming it anew and in this way de-familiarizing it. The cardinal position of the concept of the device is apparent in Jakobson's programmatic statement: "If literary history wishes to become a scholarly discipline it must recognize the artistic device as its sole hero."[15]

---

12. "Iskusstvo, kak priëm," *O teorii prozy*, pp. 10 and 18.
13. Šklovskij, "Zakon neravenstva," *Chod konja* (Moscow, 1923), p. 115.
14. "Iskusstvo cirka," ibid., p. 138.
15. *Novejšaja russkaja poèzija: Nabrosok pervyj* (Prague, 1921), p. 11.

It must be stressed, however, that despite their obvious similarity there is an important difference between Jakobson's and Šklovskij's notions of the device. For Jakobson, the material of verbal art was language and hence he conceived of poetic devices as linguistic by their very nature. Šklovskij did not deny that in poetry language itself is de-familiarized. "But," he hastened to add, "there are works of art in which the aesthetic perception of divergence rests outside the word, where the word is disregarded, is not felt, or has ceased to be felt."[16] These are, obviously, works of literary prose—the main field of Šklovskij's expertise. In this literary form, the source of de-familiarization is the deformation not of language but of events and happenings in the process of their verbal representation. Accordingly, the devices that Šklovskij studied most closely were those pertaining to prose composition and narrative.

The difference between literary narrative and the events it narrates in Šklovskij's understanding is that between the device and the material. A prose work is an intentional construction, whereas the events represented in it are merely the material for this construction. The corresponding terms in the sphere of narratology are "plot" and "story," the two modes in which events "occur" in literature. Story was understood as the series of events ordered according to their temporal succession (as they would have occurred in reality) and, as Tomaševskij stressed, according to causality.[17] Plot, on the other hand, was the liberation of events from temporal contiguity and causal dependency and their teleological redistribution in the literary text. The story, equated with material, served the artist as a mere pre-text for plot construction, a process governed not by external causes but by internal, formal laws. Here form, conceived "as the law of construction of the object,"[18] was opposed to "motivation" defined by Šklovskij as the "extraliterary [*bytovoe*] expla-

16. *Ich nastojaščee* (Moscow, 1927), p. 8.
17. *Teorija literatury* (Leningrad, 1925), p. 136.
18. Šklovskij, "Svjaz' priëmov sjužetosloženija s obščimi priëmami stilja," *O teorii prozy*, 2d ed. (Moscow, 1929), p. 60.

nation of plot construction."[19] Motivation was seen as playing only a secondary role in the literary construction, for "the forms of art are explained by their artistic regularity and not by extra-literary motivation."[20]

By relegating material to a mere ancillary position, the mechanistic Formalists ascribed value to it only insofar as it contributed to the technique of the work itself. Material was deprived of any emotional, cognitive, or social significance. Thus, a literary construction was nothing more than "pure form—a relation of materials."[21] Or, even more radically, "values became artistic material, good and evil became the numerator and the denominator of a fraction and the value of this fraction equaled zero."[22]

The position of the mechanistic model in the overall picture of Russian Formalism is rather peculiar. Perhaps the term "teaser" (*probnik*), which Šklovskij used to describe his own existential predicament, best characterizes the role this model played in the history of the movement.[23] From the vantage point of hindsight, the mechanistic metaphor represents a transitory stage in Formalism. Šklovskij's *The Resurrection of the Word* was, without any doubt, the first attempt at formulating some of the basic principles of literary study that later acquired the name of the Formal method. But in marking the beginnings of the Formalist enterprise, over the course of time this text inevitably became marginal in view of further developments. A historical marker, it seems, plays a double role. It is not only the boundary that separates two successive developmental stages, but also the point of their contact. Thus, while Šklovskij's 1914 manifesto revolutionized

19. *Literatura i kinematograf* (Berlin, 1923), p. 50.
20. Šklovskij, "Parodijnyj roman," *O teorii prozy* (1925), p. 161.
21. Šklovskij, "Literatura vne 'sjužeta,'" p. 162.
22. Ibid. p. 169. Šklovskij was far from consistent in his arguments, and though his position in general was that form determines material, sometimes he was willing to argue precisely the opposite. It is interesting for this study that his concessions to material were also couched in a simile from the realm of technology: "If a mechanic wished to substitute a steel part of a machine for a bronze or an aluminum one, this new part cannot be a copy of the old one. A new material requires a new form" (*Literatura i kinematograf*, p. 18).
23. *Zoo, ili pis'ma ne o ljubvi*, 2d ed. (Leningrad, 1924), pp. 66–67.

literary studies by injecting into them principles of the avant-garde artistic practice of Russian Futurism, at the same time it carried over a large remnant of the older critical tradition.

As I shall illustrate later, mechanistic Formalism was in some respects a mirror image of Veselovskij's poetics. We have already seen how its key term, "de-familiarization," was derived from its predecessor by reversing Veselovskij's criterion of poetic style. But Šklovskij was able to do so because he was brought up on Veselovskij's system and shared some of its postulates. While subverting some of Veselovskij's principles, Šklovskij covertly borrowed others from the nineteenth-century philologist. He was certainly aware of the perils that this inverse parallelism posed to his own theorizing. "I am afraid of the negative lack of freedom," he complained. "The negation of what others are doing ties me to them."[24] And it was this link to nineteenth-century philology that at least in part was responsible for the quick aging of the mechanistic model. In fact, most of the subsequent developments of Russian Formalism might be seen as a series of corrections of and departures from the original Šklovskian metaphor.

In his perceptive study of Veselovskij's poetics, Boris Èngel'gardt described it as consisting of two integral components: the history of literature in the strict sense of the word, and the theory of the genesis of poetry from extra-aesthetic phenomena.[25] The great Russian philologist conceived of literature, first of all, as part of the larger cultural context. According to his famous formula of 1893, the history of literature is the "history of social thought in imagistic-poetic experience and the forms that express it."[26]

The role of the literary historian, then, is to recover the causal relations among successive elements of social thought. "When

24. "Boduèn-de-Kurtenè, Blok, Jakubinskij," *Tret'ja fabrika* (Moscow, 1926), p. 52.

25. *Aleksandr Nikolaevič Veselovskij* (Petersburg, 1924), pp. 90–91.

26. Veselovskij, "Iz vvedenija v istoričeskuju poètiku: Voprosy i otvety," *Istoričeskaja poètika*, p. 53.

studying a series of facts," Veselovskij argued, "we observe their successivity, the relation of what follows to what precedes it. If this relation recurs we begin to suspect a certain regularity. If it recurs often enough we cease to speak of preceding and following and substitute the terms cause and effect." To establish the true regularity of the phenomena studied, however, historians must extend their research to the series contiguous to the one under investigation, to discern whether the cause of change does not lie outside it. They must also test knowledge gained from one series on other similar series to discover whether a causal relation obtains there as well. "The more such tested recurrences," Veselovskij concludes, "the more probable it is that the resulting generalization will approximate the precision of a law."[27]

The history of literature for Veselovskij is an incessant interaction between two factors: the passive artistic form and the active social content. What differentiates literature from other intellectual practices (philosophy, religion, and so forth), and hence what makes it possible to speak about the history of literature, is the repertoire of elementary poetic forms that express thought. These forms—various types of imagery, parallelisms, or plot constructions—which Veselovskij outlined in his genetic studies of poetry, are passed from generation to generation in the same way as every national language and are recombined in every literary work.

From this perspective it might appear that literary history is simply the permutation of the same forms without any actual change, but Veselovskij claims that literature does evolve, that the constant poetic forms are continuously imbued with new content. This content does not come from literature itself but from developments in social life and corresponding transformations in the human spirit. Thus, the engine of literary history according to Veselovskij lies outside literature and the task of the historian "is to study how new life content, this element of freedom that rushes in with every new generation, fills the old

---

27. "O metode i zadačach istorii literatury, kak nauki," ibid., p. 47.

molds, those forms of necessity in which the entire previous development has been cast."[28]

This short presentation of Veselovskij's views on literary history should suffice to explain Šklovskij's attitudes toward him. Šklovskij's radical separation of literature from other spheres of social life, his rejection of the causal explanation in literary studies—all of this can be seen as resulting from his negative relation to Veselovskij. Yet it must be stressed that despite this, Šklovskij did not banish diachrony from literary studies, and in fact affirmed the historical dimension of verbal art. As Jurij Striedter has observed, de-familiarization, the key concept of mechanistic Formalism, as the juxtaposition of old and new, definitionally presupposes some form of temporality.[29] Nevertheless, Šklovskij's notion of literary history deviated radically from Veselovskij's.

At the outset it must be said that Šklovskij's treatment of literary diachrony is not altogether consistent. The charismatic Formalist leader did not study this topic systematically, and in the course of time changed his mind about some important issues. The concept of de-familiarization is a case in point. In his *Resurrection of the Word*, Šklovskij argued that what art modifies above all is our habitual perception of the world. Art develops in order for us to regain a feeling for objects (and language) that have become automatized in our perception. This notion of de-familiarization is the direct reverse of Veselovskij's idea of literary change. For him it was the evolution of life that revitalized petrified artistic forms, whereas for Šklovskij the evolution of art revitalized the automatized forms of life. Nevertheless, this reversal still proceeds from an inevitable relationship between literature and everyday life, which Šklovskij's mechanistic model denied. The value of art is a function of its utility for *byt*, and hence cannot be separated from it.

For this reason Šklovskij subsequently modified his notion of

28. Ibid., p. 52.
29. "Zur formalistischen Theorie der Prosa und der literarischen Evolution," quoted from English tr. by M. Nicolson, "The Russian Formalist Theory of Literary Evolution," *PTL* 3 (1978), 1.

de-familiarization. As early as 1919, in the OPOJAZ collective volume *Poetics*, he declared that the development of art is totally immanent. New works come about to change our perception not of *byt* but of the artistic form itself, which has become automatized through our acquaintance with older works. "The work of art is perceived against the background of and through association with other works of art. Its form is determined by its relation to other forms that existed prior to it. . . . *A new form appears not to express a new content but to replace an old form that has lost its artistic quality.*"[30]

The admission that the work of art is peculiar because it differs not only from everyday reality but from earlier works as well introduces an element of chaos into the two-term system of mechanistic Formalism. Though Šklovskij still upheld the original opposition of art and *byt*, he was forced to complicate the category of art with a secondary dyad, canonized/noncanonized art. He took this step in his short booklet on Vasilij Rozanov. "In every literary period," Šklovskij wrote, "not one but several literary schools may be found. They coexist; one of them is the canonized apex and the others are a noncanonized [lower stratum]. . . . While the forms of the older art become as little perceptible as grammatical forms in language—from elements of artistic intention [*ustanovka*] turning into ancillary, nonperceptible phenomena—the new forms of art that substitute for the older ones are produced in the lower stratum. A younger school bursts into the place of an older one. . . . However, the defeated school is not destroyed, does not cease to exist. It is only displaced from the top to the bottom . . . and can rise again."[31]

This model of immanent literary history, however, begs certain questions. First of all, what is the ontological status of noncanonized literature? Within the framework of mechanistic Formalism this category is a conceptual bastard, in that it is composed of artworks whose form, paradoxically, is not percep-

30. Šklovskij, "Svjaz' priëmov sjužetosloženija," *Poètika: Sborniki po teorii poètičeskogo jazyka* (Petersburg, 1919), p. 120.

31. *Rozanov: Iz knigi "Sjužet, kak javlenie stilja"* (Petersburg, 1921), pp. 5–7.

tible. One might also inquire whether this model, which treats literary history as an "eternal return" of the same artistic forms, does not preclude the possibility of any actual developmental novelty. Earlier I argued that a similar problem had existed for Veselovskij when he insisted that every literary work is a recombination of the same elementary poetic forms. But because he did not conceive of literary history as an immanent process, formal repetition nevertheless implied for him novelty in content. This avenue was closed for Šklovskij, however, who programmatically refused to deal with the issue of literary content.

Locked in his mechanistic metaphor, Šklovskij could provide no viable answer to the ontological status of noncanonical art. It was only in another Formalist model, the one advanced by Jurij Tynjanov, that this issue was addressed. Tynjanov's studies of the change that Russian literature underwent in the eighteenth and nineteenth centuries refuted the basic premise of mechanistic Formalism, the strict separation of art from *byt*. As he illustrated convincingly, the line separating literature from nonliterature is flexible. What bursts into the place of canonized art may not be noncanonized art at all, but extra-artistic phenomena; moreover, the deposed canonized art may not only descend to lower strata in the artistic hierarchy but leave the sphere of art entirely and become extra-artistic.

Though Šklovskij admitted in a letter to Tynjanov that he was impressed by this argument, his overall reaction was ambivalent. On the one hand, Šklovskij seemed to reject the concept of immanent literary development to which he earlier subscribed: "We claim, it seems, that the literary work can be analyzed and evaluated without leaving the literary series. . . . However, the notion of literature changes all the time. Literature extends and absorbs extra-aesthetic material. This material and those changes which it undergoes while in contact with the material already aesthetically transformed must be taken into account." On the other hand, Šklovskij insisted that once this material becomes a part of art it loses its original ties with life and becomes a component of artistic form. "Literature lives while extending over nonliterature. But the artistic form accomplishes a peculiar rape of the Sabines. The material ceases to recognize its master. It is deformed by the law of art and is perceived outside of its original context."[32]

Because of the rule of exclusion underlying the binary model of mechanistic Formalism, the approach was unable to provide a description of literary change that would adequately account for the interplay of the literary and nonliterary spheres. Šklovskij's position was inevitably contradictory. He was aware of the historical relativity of the concept of literature, but could not take full advantage of his knowledge without destroying his conceptual frame. Caught in this paradox, he was unable to offer any solution. The conclusion of his letter is an example of what Richard Sheldon termed "the device of ostensible surrender," that is, an overt surrender hiding covert intransigence.[33] "Answer my letter but do not drag me into the history of literature," pleaded Šklovskij. "I will study art, realizing that all its dimensions [veličiny] are historical."[34]

While evading the problem of the interaction between literature and byt, Šklovskij's immanent literary history did offer a solution to the second problem: artistic novelty. In a succinct history of the novel, Šklovskij depicted artistic change as follows. Like all narratives, the novel's artfulness lies in the transformation of a lifelike story (fabula) into a literary plot (sjužet). This task is complicated by the composite nature of the novel, by the fact that it is a concatenation of several short stories. The history of the novel from this perspective is a succession of different motivations for the device of fusing short stories into larger wholes. In the most elementary novels (for example, Don Quixote), it was the protagonist who strung the pieces together. After this method became automatized, the psychology of the hero was used as the connecting thread. The works of Stendhal, Tolstoj, and Dos-

32. "Pis'mo Tynjanovu," Tret'ja fabrika, p. 99.
33. "Viktor Shklovskij and the Device of Ostensible Surrender," Slavic Review 34, no. 1 (1975), 86–108.
34. "Pis'mo Tynjanovu," p. 100.

toevskij provide ample variations on this psychological *motivi-rovka* (motivation). Eventually even this mode of fusion wore out. The audience's interest in connecting individual pieces waned and the segments themselves began to attract attention. At this moment, motivation itself turned into a device. The individual segments were brought together in a negative way to show the reader that they had nothing in common, that their connective tissue was simply a technical device enabling the writer to make them into a novel. This is the method of modern novels, Šklovskij claims, most notably of his own epistolary novel *Zoo*.[35]

It is instructive to compare this history of the novel with the earlier account of literary development found in Šklovskij's booklet on Rozanov mentioned before. Both proceed from an immanent notion of literary history driven by the opposition, defamiliarization/automatization. But whereas the Rozanov booklet presents literary change as an infinite permutation of the same poetic forms, Šklovskij's history of the novel adds something new to this scheme. The master device of this genre—the fusion of the constituent stories into a larger whole—remains the same, but different literary periods introduce different *motivirovki*. What the source of these new motivations is, Šklovskij does not say, and one might intuitively surmise that it is *byt*. This assumption does not contradict his two-term model, for as I showed earlier, the motivation of a device for him is merely an auxiliary component of the literary construction.

Šklovskij's foray into the history of the novel is noteworthy for yet another reason: its conception of historical process. According to this conception, the development of a literary genre is not an uninterrupted continuum, a chain of works successively defamiliarizing each other, but instead a qualitative leap, an abrupt ascent to a higher level of literary consciousness. There seems to be a qualitative difference between the way elementary or psychological novels are produced and the way their modern counterparts are. The earlier works presuppose a "naive" attitude

35. *Zoo, ili pis'ma ne o ljubvi* (Berlin, 1923), pp. 83–85.

toward writing. The author portrays characters and their psychic lives without being aware that all of this is nothing but an excuse for fusing short pieces into a novel. The modern novel is based on a self-conscious attitude toward writing on the author's part, a deliberate debunking of "deceptive" artistic practices. The modern novelist says that the emperor is naked, and by eliminating "fictitious" motivations lays the devices of his trade bare.

This ironic attitude toward literary production stems in turn from the writer's historical self-awareness, his or her reflexiveness about the logic of literary history. For example, the "naive" novelist creates characters and events without realizing that in fact he is complying with the historical demand for de-familiarizing artistic form. The "cunning" modernist, conscious of his historical role, proceeds differently. He analyzes the present state of literature and designs his writings in such a way as to achieve the maximal artistic effect. He does not merely deviate from previous conventions, but shows that they are mere conventions. By stripping bare the very process of literary creation, the modernist de-familiarizes artistic form anew, thus reaffirming the logic of literary history.

By merging literary theory and practice, its *istoria* and *poeisis*, Šklovskij also effectively subverted Veselovskij's objectivist literary history. For Veselovskij, the literary historians's task was to reconstruct the causal chain of the literary series. From Šklovskij's point of view such an approach to history writing was a mirror image of the "naive" novelist's attitude toward literary production. Not only were novelists unaware of their actual role in the historical process, but objectivist historians seemed equally ignorant of the aesthetic presuppositions involved in their practice. Because the literary series is virtually an infinite continuum, objectivist historians had to focus on only certain works, authors, or periods. And because they were dealing with literary phenomena, the ultimate criterion for this selection was their own literary sensibility. Thus, despite its claims, objectivist historiography never actually recaptured the literary past "as it was" but always provided varying, distorted pictures of it. The remedy

Šklovskij proposed was the same one he put into practice in his creative writing. Literary history should turn in upon itself and lay bare the devices of its trade. Instead of the pretended reconstruction of the literary past, literary history should become "the gay business of [its] destruction," a self-conscious "misreading" of history according to modern artistic principles.[36]

Hence, the job of the literary historian in Šklovskij's view was complementary to that of the artist. The artist revitalizes literature by creating new poetic forms that replace old, automatized ones; the literary historian does so by recycling these old forms through a de-familiarizing recreation of them. "We are losing the living perception of Puškin," Šklovskij argued, "not because our *byt* and language are far removed from his, but because we did not change the standard (the criterion) to which we compare him." Aiming at his own camp, Šklovskij continued, "the study of literary traditions, the Formal study of art in general, would be utter nonsense if it did not provide us with a new perception of the work." Therefore, he concludes, "the task of the Formal method or at least one of its tasks is not to 'explain' the work but to impede its perception, to renew the 'set toward the form' that is characteristic of the work of art."[37] He put this call into practice in the same article by presenting a new Puškin—a master parodist, a Russian follower of Laurence Sterne—whose *Evgenij Onegin* lays bare the devices that created its literary form.

This program for a new literary history, however, did not receive much of a welcome from the Formalists. The Muscovite Grigorij Vinokur, for example, in his review of the anthology on Puškin in which Šklovskij's essay had appeared, declared that its author "lacks any—even the most elementary—sense of history."[38] This negative reaction was in part conditioned by the fact that most of the other members of this movement did not share Šklovskij's passion for mingling scholarship with art. Even those

36. "*Evgenij Onegin:* Puškin i Stern," *Očerki po poètike Puškina* (Berlin, 1923), p. 220.

37. Ibid., p. 205.

38. "*Očerki po poètike Puškina*," *Russkij sovremennik* 3 (1924), 264.

who, like Tynjanov, applauded the artistic boldness of *Zoo* and its highly unusual blend of literary theory and creative writing,[39] refused to go the full route with Šklovskij and radically relativize their notion of literary history. They viewed Šklovskij's approach as a manifestation of aesthetic egocentrism, an ahistorical "imposition upon the past of current modes of poetic production," for which they had already blasted the older generation of literary scholars.[40]

The rejection of Šklovskij's approach to literary history by his comrades-in-arms had a certain justification. His reading of *Evgenij Onegin* was arbitrary, insofar as it was motivated by his idiosyncratic literary sensibility rooted in the iconoclastic poetics of Russian Futurism. Such an orientation was clearly unacceptable to the young theoreticians striving to establish an "objective" science of literature. Yet, at the same time, one might ask whether the Formalists in their campaign against historical relativism were not blind to the historical relativity of their own enterprise. As Jurij Striedter argues, most of the later Formalist reconstructions of the literary past "did not reflect on what was principally the historical character of their own school and its system, nor did they incorporate it in any way into their theory and analysis."[41] Of the Formalists, only Èjchenbaum was willing to take Šklovskij's challenge seriously and translate it into a more cogent scholarly program for a self-reflexive historiography. "In its essence," he wrote, "history is a discipline of complex analogies, a discipline with a dual vision: the facts of the past are discerned as significant and enter the system invariably and inevitably under the aegis of contemporary problems. . . . History, in this sense, is a particular method for studying the present through the facts of the past."[42] Ultimately, one may speculate that such a stance could have developed into what modern critical theory calls the history of

---

39. Tynjanov, "Literaturnoe segodnja," *Poètika, istorija literatury, kino* (Moscow, 1977), p. 166.
40. Roman Jakobson, *Novejšaja russkaja poèzija*, p. 5.
41. "The Russian Formalist Theory of Literary Evolution," 11.
42. "Literaturnyj byt," p. 49.

literary reception. But before this happened, Russian Formalism itself was transformed into a historical phenomenon.

Šklovskij's concept of literary history constitutes a programmatic rejection of Veselovskij's poetics. It either reversed or subverted all the crucial notions of its nineteenth-century predecessor concerning the development of literature. This is not to say that Šklovskij's relationship to Veselovskij was purely negative. According to Èngel'gardt, whose account was quoted earlier, Veselovskij's system involved not only literary history but also a theory of the genesis of poetry from extra-aesthetic phenomena. To this latter domain, in my opinion, mechanistic Formalism is very closely linked indeed.

Let me briefly characterize this aspect of Veselovskij's theory. In his genetic studies Veselovskij strove to establish which phenomena of primitive culture evolve into the simplest poetic forms. In order to do so, he dissected the literary work into its smallest elements—motifs, epithets and formulas—which he then pursued across the entire range of literatures of different nations and periods. Thus, aside from its historicity, Veselovskij's poetics can be described as genetic, inductive, and comparative.

The main thrust of mechanistic Formalism is also decidedly genetic. It tries to establish how a literary work arises from extra-literary phenomena. Šklovskij revealed his bias toward a genetic explanation when he wrote, "Phenomena can be grasped best when we can understand the process of their origin."[43] Because the most basic premise of mechanistic Formalism was never to seek an explanation for the facts of art among the facts of *byt,* its adherents disregarded all general cultural preconditions. Works of art were seen as intentional artifacts, and to grasp them meant to explain how they were made. The titles of some essays, for example, Šklovskij's "How *Don Quixote* Is Made," or Èjchenbaum's "How Gogol's 'Overcoat' Is Made," bear witness to this genetic approach.

The titles of these essays might, however, be misleading. They

---

43. "V svoju zaščitu," *Chod konja,* p. 74.

seem to suggest that by focusing attention on the genesis of particular literary texts, the mechanistic Formalists were studying their actual origins as individual and unique creative acts. Nothing would have been more alien to the Formalists and the tradition that they continued. The sober positivist Veselovskij had already waged a war against the Romantic myth of the literary work as a totally subjective expression of a strong individual. Assessing the state of his discipline in 1870, he wrote, "contemporary scholarship has taken the liberty of looking at the masses, which until now have stood behind [the heroes], deprived of any voice. It has discerned a life and movement in them which, like everything else that takes place on a grand spatiotemporal scale, is imperceptible to the naked eye. It is here that the hidden springs of the historical process ought to be sought. . . . The great individuals now appear as reflections of this or that movement prepared for among the masses."[44] The author, in Veselovskij's view, is merely a crystallization of poetic traditions and social currents existing independently of the author, and it is precisely these general preconditions of literary creation rather than any unique creative act that form the true object of scholarship.

The Formalists followed in Veselovskij's footsteps, though instead of attacking Carlyle and Emerson they attacked more recent psychological critics. Pointing a finger at the Freudian method, Šklovskij wrote: "Least of all should one become involved with psychoanalysis. It analyzes the mental trauma of only a *single* man. But the *single* man does not write; it is the time, the school-collective that writes."[45] As Osip Brik put it: "OPOJAZ thinks that there are *no poets and literati but poetry and literature.* Everything written by a poet is significant only as a part of his work in the common enterprise and is absolutely worthless as an expression of his 'I.' . . . *The devices of the poetic craft must be studied on a grand scale*, along with their differences from contiguous spheres of human work and the laws of their development. Puškin did not

---

44. "O metode i zadačach istorii literatury, kak nauki," p. 41.
45. "Ornamental'naja proza: Andrej Belyj," *O teorii prozy*, 2d ed., p. 211.

create a school; he was merely its head." And to make his point stick, Brik declared: "If there were no Puškin, *Evgenij Onegin* would have been written anyway. America would have been discovered even without Columbus."[46]

Given such a strong Formalist aversion to the individual aspect of the literary process, it is obvious that Šklovskij and Èjchenbaum were aiming at something other than a simple description of two disparate creative acts. Replying to a self-imposed question, "what is significant about the Formal method?" Šklovskij wrote in his characteristic staccato style: "What is significant is that we approached art as a production. Spoke of it alone. Viewed it not as a reflection. Found the specific features of the genus. Began to establish the basic tendencies of form. Grasped that on a large scale there is a real homogeneity in the laws informing works. Hence, the science [of literature] is possible."[47] What the Formalists subscribing to the mechanistic model set out to investigate, therefore, was the general technology of literary production and the laws that govern it, rather than the genesis of some randomly chosen texts. Both Šklovskij and Èjchenbaum utilized Cervantes's and Gogol's works as case studies to outline the broader principles that generate prosaic works in two different genres: the novel, and the short story oriented toward oral delivery.

The genetic approach was not merely a heuristic device for the mechanistic Formalists; they believed that the process of making art is intimately connected to the process of its perception. As Šklovskij wrote, "*art is the way to experience the making of a thing while what was made is not really important in art.*"[48] The perception of the work is thus nothing but the re-presentation of the intentional creative process which gave birth to the perceived work. And because the device is the "main hero" of this process, it should be the focus of attention for the student of literature. It is here that the inductive and comparative methods enter the scene. The

46. "T. n. 'formal'nyj metod,'" 213.
47. "Večera u Brikov," *Tret'ja fabrika*, pp. 64–65.
48. "Iskusstvo, kak priëm," p. 12.

literary work is dissected into such elementary devices as repetition, parallelism, gradation, and retardation, and the existence of these devices is ascertained through a comparison of the most heterogeneous materials—folksongs, tales, high literature, even film stories. The results then serve as a verification of the original premise of mechanistic Formalism about the heteromorphism of art and *byt*.

Earlier I noted the unenthusiastic response that Šklovskij's theory of literary history elicited among the Formalists. The same applied to his poetics. The first disagreement with the mechanistic model concerned the ontological status of the device. According to Šklovskij, the device was the smallest universal and virtually independent element of artistic form migrating from work to work. Viktor Žirmunskij objected that it does not exist independently but only as a part of the work and its actual value is always determined by the immediate whole in which it belongs: "The poetic device is not an independent, self-valuable, quasi-natural-historical fact. The device as such—the device for the sake of the device—is not an artistic element but a conjuring trick. . . . The same device, from the formal point of view, very often acquires a different artistic meaning depending on its *function*, i.e., on the unity of the entire artistic work and on the general thrust of all the other devices."[49]

Žirmunskij's comment implies a second objection to inductive poetics, namely, its disregard for the holistic nature of the literary work. The mechanistic model conceives of the work as a mechanical aggregation of its parts. This seems to be the gist of Šklovskij's slogan that the "content (soul) of the literary work equals the sum total of its stylistic devices."[50] The critics of this notion pointed out that the literary work is not a mere aggregate, but that it possesses a certain inward quality which belongs to it only as a whole and which is lost when it is mechanically dissected into its parts. "The search for the minimal atom of the text betrays a

49. "Zadači poètiki," *Voprosy teorii literatury: Stat'i 1916–1926* (Leningrad, 1928), p. 52.
50. *Rozanov*, p. 8.

materialistic quasi science," wrote Boris Larin condescendingly. "Every adolescent can dissect a frog believing that he is Harvey. In the same way it is easy for everyone to follow a little matrix and list on file cards the words in a pre-Petrian tale, the epithets of Puškin, or 'sound repetitions' in verse, or to separate the speeches from conversations in *Don Quixote*. The results of such an analysis can, of course, be utilized in many ways, but what I am aiming at is the inadmissibility of these oversimplified methods in obtaining the material of study itself. In stylistics we must not for a moment lose sight of the interrelation of elements, the wholeness of the artistic text."[51]

Indeed, though at times Šklovskij appears to be aware of the *Gestaltqualität* in the work of art, he has difficulty in finding its locus. As Victor Erlich has pointed out, Šklovskij's confusion over the word "form" has its roots in this problem. "The Russian Formalist leader seemed to fluctuate between two differing interpretations of the term: he could not make up his mind as to whether he meant by 'form' a quality inherent in an esthetic whole or an esthetic whole endowed with a certain quality."[52] It is thus not surprising that Šklovskij's work is riddled with contradictory statements concerning the holistic nature of the literary work. He insists upon its integral nature, stating that "nothing can be subtracted from a literary work,"[53] but then declares that "the unity of the literary work [is] . . . a myth."[54] Though most of the Formalists probably would have subscribed to the first statement, only a very few would have agreed to the second. To see the literary work not as a conglomerate of devices but as an intrinsically unified whole required another perspective—a metaphor quite unlike that offered by the mechanistic Formalists.

51. "O raznovidnostjach chudožestvennoj reči," p. 62.
52. V. Erlich, *Russian Formalism: History—Doctrine*, 3d ed. (The Hague, 1969), p. 187.
53. Šklovskij, *Literatura i kinematograf*, p. 16.
54. "Ornamental'naja proza," p. 215.

The Organism

The spirit of poetry, like all other living powers [. . .]
must embody in order to reveal itself; but a living
body is of necessity an organized one,—and what is
organization, but the connection of parts to a whole,
so that each part is at once end and means!
                —COLERIDGE, *Shakespearean Criticism*

Zweck sein selbst ist jegliches Tier, vollkommen entspringt es
Aus dem Schoss der Natur und zeugt vollkommene Kinder.
Alle Glieder bilden sich aus nach ewgen Gesetzen,
Und die seltenste Form bewahrt im geheimen das Urbild.
                —GOETHE, "Metamorphose der Tiere"

A belief in the holistic nature of the literary work compelled
other Formalists to seek a different conceptual frame for their
study of literature. As the mechanistic Formalists, drawing their
inspiration from the realm of technology, probed into the clock-
work of devices in the literary work, another group of Formalists
turned to biology and its subject matter—the organism—as their

Epigraph: Every animal is a purpose in its own right, perfect it rises / From
Nature's womb and deliveres perfect children. / All the limbs are developed
according to eternal laws, / And the rarest form guards in secret its proto-image.

model. In a methodological article, "The Boundaries of Literary Theory as a Science," Boris Jarcho, a member of the Moscow State Academy for the Study of Arts, noted three similarities between the literary work and the biological organism: (1) both are complex wholes composed of heterogeneous elements; (2) both are unified wholes; (3) in both the constitutive elements are hierarchically differentiated, in that some are essential to the unity of the whole and others are not.[1]

The literary work may be compared to the biological organism in other respects as well. Just as each individual organism shares certain features with other organisms of its own type, and types that resemble each other belong to the same species, the individual work is similar to other works of its form (for example, the sonnet), and homologous literary forms belong to the same genre (for example, the lyric). As a result of this organization, the work and the organism can be conceived generatively. New configurations both similar and dissimilar to previous ones are constantly arising, so that individual structures appear not as discrete entities but as the momentary stages of an ongoing morphogenetic process of transformation. This generative character of the organism, along with the holistic one mentioned earlier, was exploited by these literary scholars in what I shall call the morphological trend in Russian Formalism.

The name for this trend, morphological Formalism, is drawn from the writings of the Formalists themselves. For this reason we must scrutinize the name closely. The Formalists used the term in a variety of ways. Even the arch-mechanist Šklovskij sometimes referred to the Formalist movement as a "morphological school" to avoid the pejorative connotations of the label "Formalism."[2] However, this usage did not imply that Šklovskij had consciously explored the parallel between art and the organism. Of the Formalists who did use "morphology" in its biological sense, some

1. "Granicy naučnogo literaturovedenija," *Iskusstvo* 2 (1925), 59.
2. Cf., for example, *Literatura i kinematograf,* p. 40, or "Viktor Chovin: Na odnu temu," *Knižnyj ugol,* no. 8 (1922), 59.

did so in order to emphasize the holism of the literary work and others its generative nature.

The first group cannot be defined with any precision. It includes some Formalists who subscribed fully to the organic model (Žirmunskij and A. Skaftymov), others who resorted to this metaphor only occasionally (Èjchenbaum), and still others for whom the holistic study of the literary work was just a step to the generative model (M. Petrovskij). Consequently, the term "morphology" subsumed a wide range of meanings. For Žirmunskij it was equivalent to taxonomy, which "describes and systematizes poetic devices" prior to the study of their "stylistic functions in the typologically most essential poetic works."[3] For Èjchenbaum, morphology meant something akin to formal anatomy,[4] whereas for Petrovskij it included both the anatomy of the work (static description) and its physiology (dynamic functioning).[5] In general, the term "morphology" was not as crucial for these Formalists as other terms, such as "organism." But for the Formalists emphasizing the generative nature of the work—above all Vladimir Propp and Michail Petrovskij in his later writings—"morphology" was a key term and they used it in a very restricted sense. To understand this as well as the concept of "organism" we must examine the biological theories underlying morphological Formalism.

Emanuel Rádl has stated that "in biology, from the eighteenth century onwards it has been believed that the quintessence of an organism is revealed by its form and structure."[6] There were two opposing theoretical views explaining the actual forms of organic bodies. Georges Cuvier (1769–1832), the father of paleontology and comparative anatomy, described the organism by proceeding from the parts to the whole, the latter conceived as the

3. "Zadači poètiki," *Voprosy teorii literatury: Stat'i 1916–1926* (Leningrad, 1928), p. 55.
4. *Molodoj Tolstoj* (Petersburg, 1922), p. 8.
5. "Morfologija puškinskogo 'Vystrela,'" *Problemy poètiki*, ed. V. Ja. Brjusov (Moscow, 1925), p. 182.
6. *The History of Biological Theories*, tr. E. J. Hatfield (London, 1930), p. 129.

"correlation of parts." An organism was a functional system in which each element acquires a specific position according to its function. The holistic nature of the organism and the functionality of its parts were accepted as premises by Johann Wolfgang Goethe (1749–1832), the pioneer of morphology. Goethe, however, did not proceed from the individual organism but instead from the general whole—the a priori "ultimate phenomenon"—to the individual organism, an actual transformation of this phenomenon. He envisioned morphology as a science concerned "with organic shapes . . . their formation and transformation."[7]

Because of their different points of departure, Cuvier and Goethe emphasized two aspects of the concept of the type. For Cuvier, organisms belonging to a specific type could vary from one another only in their peripheral parts. He believed, as William Coleman has observed, that "the functionally integrated animal, a specific *type*, could not significantly vary in any of its parts or operations without abruptly perishing."[8] Goethe's notion of nature as a continual transformation produced an opposite view of the type. He saw biological wholes as *Dauer im Wechsel* (continuity in change), as creative forms or processes rather than static correlations. Ernst Cassirer succinctly summarized the difference between these two great biologists, whom he called "morphological idealists." According to Cassirer, "Cuvier advocated a static view of organic nature; Goethe a genetic or dynamic view. The former laid its stress upon the constancy, the latter on the modifiability of organic types."[9]

With these two notions of organism in mind we may return to the Formalists. Let us begin with those who shared Cuvier's static notion of the organism. Some of their isolated criticisms of the mechanistic model have already been mentioned. The general disagreement between the mechanistic and morphological ap-

7. "Vorarbeiten zu einer Physiologie der Pflanzen," *Goethes Werke* (Weimar, 1887–1912), sec. 2, vol. 6, p. 293.
8. *Georges Cuvier: Zoologist* (Cambridge, Mass., 1964), p. 3.
9. "Structuralism in Modern Linguistics," *Word* 1 (1945), 106.

proaches, however, is determined by their opposing notions of teleology, which must be examined more fully. In his introduction to the Russian translation of Oskar Walzel's book, *The Problem of Form in Poetry*, Viktor Žirmunskij pointed out the ambiguity inherent in Šklovskij's programmatic slogan "art as device." On the one hand, the device provides a purposive explanation of art—as a means of affecting the perceiver's reception (the principle of de-familiarization). On the other, it provides a functional explanation of art—as a means of affecting the teleological organization of the work (the manipulation of extra-artistic material).

Žirmunskij unequivocally rejected the purposive explanation of art. He argued that the aesthetic effect of the work is a bundle of multifarious consequences which cannot be reduced to de-familiarization alone. The perception of the work is not limited to the pure enjoyment of self-centered devices but "implicitly it includes cognitive, ethical, or religious elements."[10] This is especially valid for literature, Žirmunskij continues, because its material—language—is not purely formal as is the material of music, but always carries meaning. In addition to this linguistic meaning, literature as a thematic art employs translinguistic meanings which it shares with other thematic arts such as painting. Thus, Žirmunskij concludes, the strictly formalistic approach to art practiced by the theoreticians of OPOJAZ is incapable of dealing with literature in its totality and must be augmented by thematic studies. "The study of poetry as art requires attention to be paid to its thematic aspect, to the very *selection* of the theme as well as to its *construction*, compositional elaboration, and combination with other themes."[11]

The inclusion of thematics into literary studies provided Žirmunskij with further ammunition against the definition of art as an effect upon the perceiver. Thematics links literature not only to other thematic arts but to the extra-artistic sphere as well, and hence to general culture. Because the cultural configuration and

10. "K voprosu o 'formal'nom metode,'" reprinted in *Voprosy teorii literatury*, p. 161.

11. Ibid., p. 169.

the place of literature within it are in constant flux, to seek the essence of literature in the reaction of readers would be futile. Their reactions change as the culture changes, and each new reading in a shifting cultural milieu will bring about a new perception of the work. Therefore, to study literature from the reader's point of view would lead the student of literature to a relativism that would threaten the very identity of the work. Curiously, Žirmunskij stated his distaste for *Rezepzionsästhetik* most clearly in his refutation not of Šklovskij but of Tynjanov. "Further research in this direction leads to a theory according to which in different periods different elements can become the dominant of the same work, i.e., can acquire 'constructive' relevance. . . . In other words: the work of art is not 'formed' by the author but by the reader and the history of criticism and readers' taste replaces historical poetics as the study of the change in literary forms and styles."[12]

This statement, however, should not lead us to conclude that Žirmunskij identified the teleology of the artistic device with the intention of the artist. Despite his disagreement with the mechanistic Formalists, Žirmunskij shared their rejection of psychologism. "Every work of art," he wrote in the introduction to his *Byron and Puškin*, "has a special kind of ideal existence—fully autonomous and independent of the subjective processes in the creator's and perceiver's consciousness." Following this precept, Žirmunskij concentrated "above all on the study of *works themselves*. The writer's 'personality' and in particular his empirical, biographical personality, his human—all too human—psychology are thus excluded, as well as the study of the milieu that educated and formed him."[13]

Nevertheless, Žirmunskij did not subscribe to the extreme social determinism advocated by Brik. *Evgenij Onegin*, in Žirmunskij's opinion, demonstrates a certain degree of poetic indi-

---

12. "Vokrug *Poètiki* Opojaza: *Poètika: Sborniki po teorii poètičeskogo jazyka*. Pgrd. 1919," ibid., p. 356.
13. *Bajron i Puškin: Iz istorii romantičeskoj poèmy* (Leningrad, 1924), p. 8 and pp. 197–98.

viduality in relation to the works of other authors, which is undoubtedly related to the idiosyncrasies of Puškin's personality. Yet this differential quality, he insisted, is the property of the literary text, and the critic must infer it from the work itself and not from circumstances that are external to it. Thus, without denying the importance of the author for the work, Žirmunskij was not interested in the artist as a concrete psychophysical entity. Rather, he conceived of the artist as a specific final cause who gave rise to the work as a unified whole. Instead of speaking of the writer's intentions, Žirmunskij spoke of the "unity of the artistic task" or the "general form-giving principle," which he even called "entelechy"[14]—the Aristotelian term used by the neo-vitalists at the beginning of this century.

Though he rejected the purposive implications of the formula "art as device," Žirmunskij did endorse its functional meaning. The teleology of the device rests in the function it performs within the work. "Poetics studies the literary work as an aesthetic system determined by the unity of the artistic goal, i.e., as a *system* of devices [my italics]. Thus, in the study of the artistic work we consider metrical construction, verbal style, plot composition, and the selection of a particular theme as devices, i.e., as aesthetically relevant facts determined by their artistic teleology."[15]

Although Žirmunskij believed that this interpretation of the device was inherent in Šklovskij's slogan, there is a substantial difference between the two theorists' views of the role of the device within the work. For Šklovskij the device simply transformed the nonartistic material into an artistic form; for Žirmunskij the device helped to meet certain requirements within the work in which it occurred. Šklovskij spoke of the work as a "sum of devices"; Žirmunskij called it a "system of devices." Within an additive whole, it is the presence or absence of a device that matters; within a system, the presence of the device is taken

14. *Valerij Brjusov i nasledie Puškina: Opyt sravnitel'no-stilističeskogo issledovanija* (Petersburg, 1923), p. 6.
15. "K voprosu o 'formal'nom metode,'" p. 158.

for granted and it is its interrelatedness to other devices that counts.

The concept of the literary work as a system necessitated a redefinition of the concept of the device. It could no longer be seen as a purposive manipulation of material, but instead must be viewed as a functional exploitation of this manipulation. A poetic device, for example rhyme, was not to be described as a particular sound repetition but as a functional element within the literary whole. To define rhyme as "a sound identity occurring at the end of a line from the last stressed vowel on" would be to treat it nonfunctionally. This definition is inadequate, according to Žirmunskij, because it concerns the sound aspect of rhyme and virtually ignores its compositional role as a marker of the rhythmic series and the strophic organization. Rhyme, said Žirmunskij, is "every sound repetition which carries an organizing function in the metrical composition of a poem."[16]

The redefinition of the device introduces a further complication into the binary model of mechanistic Formalism. Šklovskij's opposition of material to device does not allow for the functionality of the device, because it does not posit any source of unity for the functional elements of the work. Therefore, Žirmunskij decided to augment this opposition with a third term, "the *teleological* concept of *style* as the unity of devices."[17] This notion would account for the interconnectedness of the devices of a text as well as the essential wholeness of every work of art. "Only if the concept of 'style' is introduced into poetics," Žirmunskij argued, "can we consider the basic conceptual framework of this discipline (*material, device, style*) complete."[18]

Žirmunskij's critique of the mechanistic model and his emphasis on the functional interrelatedness of elements within the work inspired several contemporary literary scholars. Among them, the one closest to his position was Aleksandr Skaftymov—a pro-

16. *Rifma, eë istorija i teorija* (Petersburg, 1923), p. 9.
17. "Zadači poètiki," p. 23.
18. Ibid., .p. 51.

fessor of Russian literature at the Saratov University. Though actually quite remote from the mainstream of Formalism, Skaftymov's writings during the early twenties bear the clear stamp of what I term the morphological metaphor. His embracing of this model was most likely the result of personal contact with Žirmunskij, who was conducting a course in theoretical poetics at the Saratov University at this time. Yet, despite their sharing of the organicist view, Žirmunskij and Skaftymov reacted against two different theoretical positions. Žirmunskij argued against the relativism of *Rezepzionsästhetik*, whereas Skaftymov's target was the genetic method which attempted to explain the literary work through the extraliterary phenomena surrounding its origin. As I showed earlier, this method had already been criticized by the mechanistic Formalists, who argued that the composition of a work is not determined by the factors of *byt* present during its creation but instead by the general laws of literary production. For the organicist Skaftymov, however, the key to understanding the literary composition lay in its inner teleology.

Skaftymov treated the work as a totality unified from without by an artistic intention which within the work becomes a form-giving dominant. "A study whose aim is to reveal the nature of a teleologically formed object must inevitably conceive of this object as a unity. This concept is then expressed in the description of the relations between the constitutive elements and the general system of coordinations and subordinations which exist within the [artistic] whole."[19] All the components of the work are drawn into this system of relations, including those thematic components that in some respects may exceed the limits of the work. "Elements of psychology, history, sociology, and so forth, fragmentarily contained in the work, are not interesting in themselves but only in the teleological thrust they obtain in the general unity of the whole."[20]

19. "Tematičeskaja kompozicija romana *Idiot*," *Tvorčeskij put' Dostoeveskogo*, ed. N. L. Brodskij (Leningrad, 1924), p. 135.
20. Ibid.

Skaftymov applied his teleological approach most successfully to the study of *byliny*—Russian oral heroic epics. In his monograph, *The Poetics and Genesis of Byliny*, he presented a theoretical alternative to the genetic study of folk poetry elaborated by Veselovskij and his followers.[21] This so-called ethnographic school had aimed at establishing a link between the elements of the *bylina* and the historical events that supposedly gave rise to individual compositions. The "original" *bylina* was presumably diluted and transformed in later renditions, so that it was difficult to discover. Nevertheless, Veselovskij's school believed that a thorough study of the variants would ultimately lead to the kernel of the *bylina* which would directly reflect an actual historical situation. Against this conception, Skaftymov posed his opposite view that *byliny* are literary compositions unified from within, their elements determined by their functions within these wholes and only secondarily by their extraliterary significance.

In opposing the "ethnographic" school, Skaftymov offered an all-encompassing critique of the inductive approach in literary studies. He rejected it on two grounds. Epistemologically, he claimed, a pure induction is a fiction: "It is no secret that every observation and classification of a multiplicity of varied facts is always performed according to some a priori principle." From a practical standpoint, he argued that the inductive method is incapable of dealing with the organic wholeness of *byliny*. Poking fun at the inductivists, he quipped, "we walked around it, we discerned some of its features, and without grasping their internal significance or their essence, we began to explain their growth and development. Comparing random bits and pieces of the *bylina*, we fragmented it, and then we combined those pieces, believing that we had recreated the extinct forms of the past. Out of a living organism we made mechanics."[22]

According to Skaftymov, any analysis of *byliny* as functionally integrated organisms would reveal a single, dominant, composi-

21. *Poètika i genezis bylin* (Moscow, 1924).
22. Ibid., p. 49; p. 43.

tional goal: the effect of surprise, which all the elements of the *bylina* help to establish. The basic binary structure of the *bylina* is conditioned by this goal, consisting of two parts and portraying two main protagonists. It begins with an introduction in which the hero and his adversary are contrasted, the hero as a rather inept figure (too young, in fragile health, and so on) and the villain as the possessor of a superhuman power. The second part of the *bylina* depicts the fight between the hero and his enemy. From the introductory description of the two it appears that the hero does not stand a chance. Indeed, the actual fight is very short and the vanquished party gives up with only a token resistance. The appeal of the *bylina*, however, rests in the fact that the loser is not the underdog of the introduction—the hero—but the villain, whose success seemed to be guaranteed. The hero's victory ends the *bylina*, for "immediately after the decisive moment, the progression of the plot ends; the singer has nothing more to speak about."[23] Only a brief formulaic conclusion expressing the gratitude of those saved by the hero or the general joy over his victory is attached to the finished story.

All the elements of the *bylina*, whether formal or thematic, are subordinated to the goal of creating an unexpected solution. For example, narration and description alternate in order to reinforce the *bylina*'s binary articulation. In the introduction description prevails; in the fight narration does. Moreover, the description focuses solely on the two main protagonists. All the secondary characters remain underdeveloped since they serve merely as the background against which the two main characters operate.

The total subordination of elements to a single structuring principle provides Skaftymov with a base from which to attack the genetic method, which had concentrated on thematic details—the names of characters and localities, the social organizations depicted, and so on—in order to reconstruct the origins of the *bylina*. However, as Skaftymov convincingly argued, these

23. Ibid., p. 61.

details are utterly secondary in the teleological structure of Russian heroic epics. For this reason, names are freely altered from one performance to another even by the same narrator, and the social interactions among the characters do not reflect the ideology of their time but the requirements of the plot structure. Skaftymov's conclusion that "every genetic study of the *bylina* requires a preliminary description of the inner constitutive meaning of its parts" epitomizes not only this study but the works of "morphological" Formalism in general.[24]

Although both Žirmunskij and Skaftymov understood the literary work as a functionally integrated organism, there was a slight difference in the way they conceived of this organism. Žirmunskij saw it above all as a harmony of functional parts, whereas Skaftymov saw it as a hierarchically organized whole in which the function of some parts was determined by other, dominant ones. This divergence results from the different aspects of Cuvier's zoological theories emphasized by each Formalist. To Žirmunskij, paleontology seemed the more valid metaphor. If the work was a system of parts whose functional correlations constituted a harmonious and unchangeable whole, it resembled more a dead fossil animal than a living, changing organism. Indeed, Žirmunskij compared the task of the student of style (the crucial concept of his art theory) to that of the paleontologist. "Just as a paleontologist can reconstruct from a few little bones of an unearthed animal—provided he knows their function—the entire structure of the animal, the student of artistic style . . . can reconstruct in general terms an organically integrated structure, 'predict' its presupposed forms."[25]

On the other hand, Skaftymov's treatment of literature, especially the *bylina*, was more like Cuvier's comparative anatomy and theory of the biological type. Skaftymov was keenly aware that there was considerable variability among the individual *byliny*, but he saw this variability as limited to secondary elements

24. Ibid., p. 127.
25. "Zadači poètiki," p. 51.

which were functionally insignificant. Cuvier's notion of the variability of the individuals of a given species was quite similar. As William Coleman has observed, "Cuvier did not deny the existence of variation. His plan was to reduce variation to its proper limits, and the anatomical rules provided the initial key to the problem. From the primary fact of the integral harmony of the organism it was recognized that certain organs were more important to the animal than others: heart, lungs, nervous system were more important than hair, skin, color, or size. These circumstances demanded a certain stability or invariability of the central organs and permitted the almost unlimited variation of peripheral features."[26] In like manner, the essential elements of the *bylina*—its two main protagonists and two narrative sequences—would correspond to the indispensable parts of the organism and its secondary features—the names, social status of the heroes, societal mores present in it—would correspond to the hair, skin, coloring, and so on.

It is interesting to note that Skaftymov's concern with the variability of the individual compositions belonging to a genre helped to prepare the way for another brand of morphological Formalism, which I shall discuss presently. This approach was inspired by Goethe's transformational concept of organic form. Skaftymov's characterization of the *bylina*, for example, has a distinctly Goethean ring: "Everything in the *bylina* is in flux. Its existence always was and will be in an uninterrupted creative process begun no one knows where, when, or by whom. The *bylina* is not something ready-made, but is always in a state of becoming."[27] Despite this assertion, however, Skaftymov's study pursues not the process of becoming per se, but rather what was stable and unchangeable in it. As a search for the functional invariant in a genre, it is quite different from those Formalist genre studies searching for transformational rules.

Vladimir Propp and Michail Petrovskij were the two most

---

26. *Georges Cuvier*, p. 143.
27. *Poètika i genezis bylin*, p. 36.

prominent Formalists to transfer Goethe's morphology from the organic to the literary form. Although the relationship between the "static morphologists" and Cuvier was only implicit (his name is absent from their writings) the "transformational morphologists" proclaimed their spiritual indebtedness to Goethe openly through the epigraphs in both Propp's *Morphology of the Folktale* and Petrovskij's "Morphology of the Short Story." The importance of these epigraphs for a proper understanding of their conceptual framework cannot be overstated. Propp himself made this clear in his answer to Lévi-Strauss's review of the 1958 English edition of his book, claiming that the omission of Goethe's epigraphs in the English version had caused Lévi-Strauss to misunderstand his method.[28] The historical context surrounding the publication of the two "morphologies" is also noteworthy, for they followed very closely on the publication of *Goethes morphologische Schriften* by Wilhelm Troll. According to Horst Oppel—the historian of the morphological method in German literary studies—this publication "paved the way for the acceptance of morphology *as method*."[29] Troll's edition of Goethe appeared in 1926, Petrovskij's "Morphology of the Short Story" in 1927, and Propp's book in 1928.[30]

Besides the external signs of kinship between Goethe's method and those of Propp and Petrovskij, there is an essential similarity in their epistemological presuppositions. Goethe constructed morphology as a science on the assumption that despite

28. Propp wrote, "Professor Lévi-Strauss knows my book only in the English translation. But its translator allowed himself an unpermissible liberty. Not understanding the function of the epigraphs which at first glance do not seem to be explicitly connected with the text, he considered them useless ornaments and barbarously omitted them . . . all these epigraphs . . . had the purpose of expressing what was left unsaid in the text of my book . . ." ("Strukturnoe i istoričeskoe izučenie volšebnoj skazki," *Fol'klor i dejstvitel'nost'* [Moscow, 1976], p. 135). Lévi-Strauss's "L'Analyse morphologique des contes russes," *International Journal of Slavic Linguistics and Poetics* 3 (1960) reviews the first English edition of Propp's *Morphology of the Folktale*, ed. S. Pirkova-Jakobson, tr. L. Scott (Bloomington, Ind., 1958).

29. Horst Oppel, *Morphologische Literaturwissenschaft* (Mainz, 1947), p. 13.

30. Petrovskij, "Morfologija novelly," *Ars Poetica*, vol. 1, ed. M. Petrovskij (Moscow, 1927), pp. 69–100; Propp, *Morfologija skazki* (Leningrad, 1928).

all the heterogeneity of organic phenomena a single underlying principle unites them. This idea occurred to him during a trip to Italy in 1786, where he encountered new and exciting plants. "In this new manifold I encountered here the following idea became more and more vivid to me: namely that all the forms of plants perhaps developed from a single form. This in itself would enable us to define species and genera correctly. . . ."[31] His search for the archetypal plant or animal (*Urpflanze* or *Urtier*) of which all the actual forms of a given species were metamorphoses is paralleled by Propp's and Petrovskij's search for the archetypes underlying all the actual forms of the two genres that they dealt with—the fairy tale and the short story, respectively. And just as Goethe conceived of organic forms as processes rather than products, the two Formalists defined their genres in terms of transformations, not as sets of fixed features. Significantly, each quoted Goethe's statement, "Gestaltenlehre ist Verwandlungslehre" (the theory of forms is the theory of transformations), Propp choosing it as the epigraph for his eighth chapter and Petrovskij as the motto for his entire study.[32] This Goethean principle was the basis for their literary inquiries.

Propp's book is well known so I shall deal with it only briefly. It is noteworthy that his motives for studying fairy tales were similar to Skaftymov's for oral heroic epics: dissatisfaction with the genetic approach previously used. We can even catch an

31. *Italienische Reise: I*, in *Goethes Werke*, sec. 1, vol. 30, p. 89.

32. "Paralipomena II," ibid., sec. 2, vol. 6, p. 446. The epigraphs of other chapters of Propp's book are from the following writings of Goethe: "Introduction"—"Vorarbeiten zu einer Physiologie der Pflanzen," ibid., pp. 298–99; "1st chapter"—"Versuch einer allgemeinen Knochenlehre," ibid., vol. 8, pp. 221–22; "2nd chapter"—*Tag- und Jahreshefte 1780*, ibid., sec. 1, vol. 35, p. 16; "9th chapter"—"Brief an Frau Stein, 9. Juni 1787," ibid., sec. 4, vol. 8, pp. 232–33. It is noteworthy that Skaftymov too uses a quotation from Goethe as the epigraph for his essay on Dostoevskij's *Idiot* (see note 19). However, in contrast to Petrovskij and Propp he does not quote from Goethe's scientific works or diaries but from *Faust* and the two lines used, "Willst du dich am Ganzen erquicken, / So musst du das Ganze im Kleinsten erblicken" ("If you want to enjoy the whole / You must learn to see the whole in the smallest part"), do not pertain to transformation but to the relationship of the parts and wholes.

echo of Skaftymov's stress on descriptive over genetic investigation in Propp's claim that the discussion of the morphology of the fairy tale must precede the question of its historical roots. "Historical studies may appear more interesting than morphological investigations . . . but the general question of where a tale comes from remains, on the whole, unsolved, though even here laws of genesis and development undoubtedly exist that are still awaiting elaboration. . . . However, we maintain that as long as there is no correct morphological study there can be no correct historical study. If we do not know how to dissolve the tale into its constituent parts we cannot carry out a comparative study. . . . [And] if we cannot compare one tale with another how can we study the relation of the tale to religion or myth?"[33]

This quotation is indicative of the unique direction Propp took in his morphological study of the fairy tale. Unlike all the other Formalists employing the biological model, he accepted the challenge of inductive poetics, attempting to isolate the smallest constituent of the genre he studied. In fact, he accused Veselovskij—the main representative of inductive poetics—of not being analytic enough, pointing out that the motifs he advanced as the minimal elements of narrative were readily divisible into smaller units.

Propp was not merely more analytic than Veselovskij; the real difference between them was the manner in which they tackled the problem of the minimal unit. This difference resembles the contrast between the "mechanistic" and "morphological" concepts of literature. Veselovskij, a true inductivist, believed that the part is prior to the whole, not only for the sake of the descriptive procedure but in the genesis of the work as well. For this reason, in describing individual motifs he paid no attention to their relationship to the wholes they composed, since the latter were posterior combinations. Propp's organicism prevented him from being an inductivist of this type. He agreed with Veselovskij that the "part is prior to the whole for descriptive pur-

33. *Morfologija skazki*, p. 26.

poses," but he would not claim that it was prior in an absolute sense. His definition of the minimal unit of the fairy tale treated it teleologically in terms of its role within the whole. On the most abstract level, he conceived of the fairy tale as a narrative about actions performed by certain characters. And it is the actions, and not the interchangeable characters, that count. Characters, as carriers of these actions, are functionally indispensable, but what is important is not their individuality but their function, that is, their "action defined from the point of view of its relevance for the course of action." Thus, Propp's definition of the minimal unit of the fairy tale as the "function of acting characters" differs from Veselovskij's notion of the motif as minimal unit, not so much in that the former is smaller than the latter, but that it is a part of a functionally integrated whole, whereas the motif is a part of a mechanical aggregate.[34]

From what was just said, it might seem that Propp's notion of the functionality of organic parts matches Cuvier's, but in fact it is quite close to Goethe's. Goethe insisted upon the functional definition of parts over the static description. "Function correctly grasped is the being conceived in activity." Thus, when "we are concerned with the human arm, [we are in fact dealing] with the front legs of an animal."[35] The variety of forms these limbs can attain is almost unlimited, but by acknowledging their functional similarity a morphologist can study and compare them. It was through just such a functional reduction that Propp succeeded in establishing thirty-one elements as the basic units of every fairy tale. These elements do not exist in isolation but are interlocked in a configuration—the compositional scheme of the fairy tale. The final test of Propp's method is not only to prove that all fairy tales are composed of the same elements but of the same elements in an identical sequence. By comparing the schemes of various tales Propp arrives at the invariant—the ultimate *Ur-Typ* of which all fairy tales are transformations.

34. Ibid., p. 22; pp. 30–31; p. 29.
35. "Principes de philosophie zoologique: II Abschnitt," *Goethes Werke*, sec. 2, vol. 7, p. 200.

After discovering the generic invariant of the fairy tale (what Propp called the composition), he might have been expected to outline the laws governing its transformations. This aspect of morphology is conspicuously missing from his book, however. Instead, he discussed transformation in an article in the fourth volume of *Poètika* published by the State Institute for the History of the Arts. "Transformations of the Fairy Tale" appeared separately from *The Morphology of the Folktale,* for reasons that I shall soon discuss. First let us consider the morphological theories of Michail Petrovskij.

Petrovskij's attempt at a morphology of the short story differs from Propp's, despite their common model. Petrovskij shows not the slightest interest in proceeding inductively from the minimal units of the short story. The elements of narrative with which he operates are defined functionally, but are certainly not the simplest possible. Moreover, the material the two morphologists consider differs. Propp analyzed a genre that was no longer a vital art form. Petrovskij's object of study, on the other hand, was very much alive at the moment he attempted to describe it. Consequently, his definitions are much less formalized than Propp's. The two genres also differ in their structures. In the short story there are two temporal sequences—that of the narrated event itself and that of its presentation. In the fairy tale both the number of elements and their sequence are fixed. The only thing that can vary is the appearance of the performers of the functions. Therefore, while Propp could present a single sequential formula for all fairy tales, Petrovskij had to account for two levels—the "disposition" or temporal sequence of events, and the "composition" or narrative sequence of these events.

The pair, disposition–composition, does not coincide precisely with Šklovskij's opposition of story and plot. Petrovskij, unlike Šklovskij, did not believe that the material of a prose work was life as such. Instead he emphasized that life as the material of literature "is always restructured life . . . it is always a selection."[36] Literary material is a semantically unified configuration, a life endowed with specific meaning. For this reason Petrovskij often used the term "plot" to designate what Šklovskij meant by "story." In general, the terms "plot" and "disposition" are interchangeable in Petrovskij's system.

The place of the short story as a genre, according to Petrovskij, exists between the anecdote and the novel. What distinguishes it from the novel is that it contains only a single event. It differs from the anecdote in treating this single event not in isolation but as part of a larger context. Conceived in this way, the minimal scheme of a short story's disposition contains three parts: the "kernel of the plot" (that is, the event itself), and the two connectors that link it to its larger context—the *Vorgeschichte* or as Petrovskij hesitantly translated it in a footnote, "the plot prologue," and the *Nachgeschichte,* "the plot epilogue." The composition of the short story, or the presentation of its plot, has a corresponding three-part scheme. First is an introductory "exposition" which leads toward the "climax" of the story (*naprjaženie*) and culminates in what Petrovskij calls the *pointe,* the moral of the story. The middle term of both the disposition and the composition of the short story, the "kernel of the plot" and the "climax," can be further subdivided into the "complication" (*zavjazka*), the "climax proper" or "knot of the plot" (the moment of highest tension), and the "resolution" (*razvjazka*). This scheme can be visualized as shown in the diagram.

Kernel of the Plot

DISPOSITION	*Vorgeschichte*	Knot of the Plot	*Nachgeschic*
		Complication ———— Resolution	
COMPOSITION	Exposition	Climax Proper	*Pointe*

Climax

In the second part of his study Petrovskij illustrates the trans-

36. "Morfologija novelly," p. 72.

formations of the basic scheme of the short story through specific examples. The fourth tale of the first day of the *Decameron* is the simplest story analyzed. Its content is rendered succinctly in the short synopsis that introduces the tale. "A monk, having fallen into a sin deserving a very grievous punishment adroitly reproaching the same fault to his abbot, quitteth himself of the penalty."[37] The complication of this story arises when the abbot surprises a young monk with a girl in his cell *in flagrante*. To escape the punishment the monk pretends to leave his cell and go to the forest to collect some wood, hoping that the abbot himself will fall into sin with the girl. This indeed happens and is secretly witnessed by the young monk. The moment of the highest tension follows when the abbot calls the young monk and threatens him with prison for his deed. The crisis ends in a happy resolution for the monk, who reveals to the abbot that he knows as much about the abbot as the abbot knows about him and thus "quitteth himself of the penalty."

Because this tale is a short story and not a simple anecdote, the event does not appear in isolation, but is introduced by the *Vorgeschichte* in which the situation of the event and its two main protagonists are described. In the composition of the tale, this description functions as the exposition of the event, preparing the way for the climax. Symmetrically, at the end of the tale the event is concluded by the *Nachgeschichte* consisting of a single sentence which describes the new relationship among the members of the triangle after the event: "Accordingly, [the abbot] pardoning him and charging him to keep silence of that which he had seen, they privily put the girl out of doors and it is believed that they caused her return thither more than once thereafterward."[38] This sentence, Petrovskij argues, is not only the *Nachgeschichte* of the plot but also the *pointe* of the composition. The phrase "and it was believed . . ." goes beyond merely connecting the event with a larger context but involves the pre-

---

37. *The Decameron of Giovanni Boccaccio*, tr. J. Payne (New York, n.d.), p. 30.
38. Ibid., p. 32.

sentation of this event by the narrator. In general the morphology of this tale follows closely the basic scheme of the short story without any transformations. All the parts of the scheme are present and there is no discrepancy between the disposition and composition. For this reason, Petrovskij calls this tale, using Goethe's terminology, the *Urphenomenon* of the short story.[39]

In contrast to the simplicity of Boccaccio's tale, de Maupassant's short story "Le Retour" represents a radical transformation of this basic genre scheme. Šklovskij once observed that this story is a variation of the famous plot, "a man at the wedding of his wife," which differs from the others of its type by presenting this surprising plot in a rather low-key manner.[40] Petrovskij's analysis amplifies this impromptu observation. He characterizes the kernel of the plot as the "return of the husband who disappears without a trace after his grass widow marries someone else and starts a new family."[41]

The striking feature of this story is that its composition differs from its disposition. The narration begins with an exposition describing the seaside, the cottage of the family Martin-Levesques, and its inhabitants. The complication starts when one of the girls notices the reappearance of a stranger three times in one day. After the exposition, comes the first part of the *Vorgeschichte* telling why the family has a hyphenated name. But immediately afterwards, the narration returns to the present and describes a hostile dialogue between the stranger and Mrs. Martin-Levesques. In the evening when Mr. Levesques returns, the stranger disappears. The event recurs the second day but now the complication changes into the knot of the plot. Mr. Levesques, who that day remained home, speaks to the stranger and finds out that he is no other than Mr. Martin. The second part of the *Vorgeschichte* which follows explains that he did not die in a shipwreck as was believed, but was captured instead by savages

39. "Morfologija novelly," p. 76.
40. "Svjaz' priëmov sjužetosloženija s obščimi priëmami stilja," *Poètika: Sborniki po teorii poètičeskogo jazyka* (Petersburg, 1919), p. 120.
41. "Morfologija novelly," p. 81.

who held him for twelve years. The two husbands decide to solve their problem by going to the priest. On the way they stop at a cafe for wine and the story ends with the following dialogue: "And the tavern-keeper, three glasses in one hand and a carafe in the other, approached, large of paunch, ruddy, fat, and asked with a quiet air: 'What, you here, Martin?' Martin replied: 'I am here.' "[42]

This abrupt ending seems to leave out some basic parts of the short story scheme—the resolution, *pointe,* and *Nachgeschichte.* Petrovskij argues that Maupassant's story represents a radical transformation of this scheme rather than a truncation of it, however. He compares the resolution of "Le Retour" to a draw in a game of chess. "A game of chess can end with the victory of the white or of the black side, but can also end in a draw. The meaning of the draw arises from the entire preceding game but it in turn provides the game with meaning. After a great dynamic tension everything results in zero."[43]

The *pointe* of the story rests precisely in this "incomplete resolution." It forces the reader to "shift retrospectively the semantic center of the story from the *facts* to the *attitude* toward them. . . . The irony of the story consists in the fact that in this ordinary fishermen's milieu an unusual conflict loses its unusualness, becoming colored by the gray, indifferent light of its heroes' psyche."[44] But in addition to this "incomplete resolution" Petrovskij argues that the story does contain the equivalent of a resolution which suggests the outcome of the event. This is the conversation of the two male protagonists before they go to the priest. There Martin proposes to keep the house and in return not to press any demands for his wife's return. Although readers are left in suspense as to whether this proposal is the actual resolution, it presents them at least with a plausible possibility. This "equivalent of the resolution" then serves as a functional

---

42. "Le Retour" is published under the title "A French Enoch Arden" in *Works of Guy de Maupassant,* vol. 17 (Akron, Ohio, 1903), p. 137.
43. "Morfologija novelly," p. 85.
44. Ibid.

equivalent of the *Nachgeschichte* linking this single event to the larger context of life.

Though Petrovskij goes on to analyze two other short stories, the two examples discussed so far are sufficient for a general understanding of his method. As I pointed out earlier, the main difference between the static and transformational morphologists was the latter's intention to go beyond a discovery of the invariant of a genre to outline the rules governing the transformations of the invariant in individual literary works. It is important to ask whether they were successful. Goethe had outlined a basic "double law" governing the formation and transformation of all organic wholes: "(1) the law of internal nature according to which plants are constituted, and (2) the law of external circumstances according to which plants are modified."[45] Petrovskij completely ignores the relation of the literary work to external circumstances. He is even more radical than Šklovskij in purging extraliterary phenomena from literary studies. Though the relation of literature to *byt* in Šklovskij's system was secondary, it was at least implicitly present, since life was considered the material of literature. But Petrovskij cut even this link to extraliterary phenomena by declaring literary material pre-poetic, that is, structured according to the requirements of literature. The *spiritus movens* of transformations must therefore lie in the internal nature of the genre itself. What it is, however, we may only guess. It is not the tension between what Šklovskij termed canonized and new forms, a notion that would explain a particular transformation at a particular time, nor can it be an inner necessity stemming from the basic scheme of the short story that Petrovskij had outlined. Instead of a theory of transformations we are presented with ad hoc rules which pertain to individual transformations within the stories analyzed but are far from constituting the *Verwandlungslehre* of the genre.

Propp's attitude toward the transformational rules of the fairy tale is more complex than Petrovskij's. As we have seen, he does

---

45. "Vorarbeiten zu einer Physiologie der Pflanzen," p. 286.

not discuss it in *The Morphology of the Folktale*, though he mentions in the introduction that the original manuscript had contained a section on this issue that was dropped (together with some other parts of the manuscript) for stylistic reasons.[46] In the same year that the book appeared, Propp published the article mentioned earlier dealing with the topic he had omitted in the book.

Yet after reading this "spin-off" article one begins to doubt that mere stylistic reasons had led Propp to omit it from the larger text. More likely it was his failure to elaborate any general transformational theory that prompted his decision. For a Goethean morphologist, the elaboration of transformational rules is as important as the isolation of the generic invariant. To eliminate this issue "for the sake of brevity and a more vivid presentation" seems a rather high price to pay, especially by someone who otherwise demonstrates little consideration for his reader. The omission casts considerable doubt on the legitimacy of the term "morphology" used in the title of the book. And from his remarks addressed to Lévi-Strauss (quoted earlier) it is obvious that the author himself was not unaware of this fact. "To be absolutely precise," he wrote, "I should not have spoken of 'morphology' but used the much more restricted concept of 'composition' and called the book *The Composition of the Folkloric Fairy Tale*."[47]

Propp's article "The Transformations of the Fairy Tale" in conjunction with his book shows that, unlike Petrovskij, he takes into account both aspects of Goethe's "double law." The book discusses the constitution of the genre as a particular configuration of functional elements, whereas the article deals with the external circumstances that modify this generic invariant. As

---

46. Propp explained, "For the sake of brevity and a lively presentation we were forced to omit many things that a specialist would like to keep. In addition to those parts appearing below, the original draft of the work contained a study of the rich sphere of the acting characters' attributes. . . . it dealt in detail with the questions of metamorphosis, i.e., of the transformations of the tale" (*Morfologija skazki*, pp. 6–7).

47. "Strukturnoe i istoričeskoe izučenie volšebnoj skazki," p. 140.

Propp argues in the latter, "the causes of transformations often lie outside the tale, and without taking into account comparative material from the environment of the tale, we shall not grasp its evolution." Propp hastens to add that the external causes do not modify the whole fairy tale but only some of its parts: "There is a great difference between organic formations and the fairy tale. Whereas in the first, the change in one part or feature causes a change in another, in the fairy tale every part can change independently of the other parts."[48] Instead of offering general rules explaining the particular modifications of the basic scheme in different milieus, Propp provides four criteria for distinguishing the variants of a part of a fairy tale from the original one (a fantastic treatment is prior to a rational one, a heroic to a humorous one, and so on) and twenty modifications which a single element might undergo (reduction, amplification, corruption, and so on).

Propp's search for the transformational rules of the genre led him into problems with the biological metaphor, because unlike other morphological Formalists, he overextended it. Despite many similarities, there is obviously an essential difference between a literary and a genuine organic whole: literary works are intentional objects endowed with an immaterial meaning but organisms are empirical objects whose proper existence is in the realm of material reality. The other morphologists were keenly aware of this difference. In fact one of their main arguments against the mechanists was that they reduced the literary work to a mere formal construction and paid little if any attention to literary semantics. Instead of such a monistic notion of the literary work, the morphological Formalists conceived of it in a dualistic manner—as a unity of the formal construction (we might say, of the material vehicle) and theme (semantics in the broadest sense of the word). Propp did not accept this dualistic vision. In pursuing the organic metaphor, he conceived of the fairy tale

48. "Transformacii volšebnych skazok," *Poètika: Vremennik Otdela slovesnych iskusstv* 4 (1928), 72–73.

as an empirical object and analyzed it not as a semantic but a formal construction.

Whether this division of a work into formal and thematic components is justified is another matter. Nonetheless, this distinction is a handy way of discussing the category of the "function of an acting character," which Propp found so crucial. The monist Šklovskij had treated characters as primarily a part of the formal construction. For example, he claimed that Don Quixote was a device for stringing disparate motifs together into a narrative whole. Don Quixote's characteristics per se were irrelevant; Šklovskij shows that they actually change as the narrative unfolds. What remains constant is Cervantes's use of that character in his manipulation of the material. On the other hand, the dualist Skaftymov argued that the formal aspects of the prose work are subordinate to its thematics. Therefore, he analyzed the way in which the characters of Dostoevskij's *Idiot* function within the overall unity of its theme. He was especially interested in the traits of literary figures, examining their actions and interactions as contributions to their characterization. He considered the deep inner conflicts within Dostoevskij's characters and the discord among them as supporting the general theme of the novel, the dialectic resolution of contradictions through forgiveness. It is obvious that Propp's conception of the function of a character is closer to Šklovskij's than to Skaftymov's. Šklovskij and Propp do differ, of course: in Šklovskij's opinion, the character of Don Quixote links disparate motifs; in Propp's view it is the fairy tale characters' actions that create linkage by necessitating the actions of other characters. But both theorists treat the character as merely a part of the formal construction.

I began this discussion by accusing Propp of overextending the biological metaphor, for in treating the literary work as a formal construction, he was reducing it to an empirical object. This assertion requires some clarification, because Propp selected only certain empirical characteristics of the fairy tale as crucial for his morphological analyses of the genre. The most important of these was its temporal extension. Propp conceived of the fairy tale as a narrative unfolding in time as a string of events. All the constitutive parts of the fairy tale that he considered relevant are related to the temporal flow of the narrative, whereas all static or atemporal features are dismissed as secondary.

In his morphological analyses Propp operates with two types of formal units—the simple and the complex—which he terms "functions" and "composition," respectively. The functions, that is, the functions of an acting character, participate in the temporality of the narrative because when one appears, the other necessarily follows, until their entire sequence (the composition, the basic generic scheme) is complete. The other type of simple unit in the fairy tale does not contribute to the narrative flux; this is what Propp calls the static element. "A motif like 'Baba-Jaga gives Ivan a horse' consists of four elements of which only one represents a function [the verb]; the others are static."[49] The static elements are the attributes of the acting characters which make up what we might call the thematic aspect of the tale. Because they do not influence the narrative flux, however, Propp treats them as accidental embodiments of the functions, irrelevant to the morphology of the tale. The static elements combine in actual fairy tales with functions, or better, provide the latter with flesh and blood, and in the predetermined sequence they create the "unique" plot or the variants of the fairy tale. Propp does not pay any attention to what might be called the overall theme of the tale. Whether it is Baba-Jaga who gives the horse to Ivan or Ivan who gives it to Baba-Jaga, the temporality remains the same. For Propp, the plot of the fairy tale is nothing but an actualization of the fairy tale's composition—the narrative flux itself. As a result, Propp was indignant when Lévi-Strauss in the review referred to "plot" as "theme": "For a folklorist and a literary scholar, the 'plot' is the center of attention. In Russian the word 'plot' as a literary-theoretical term has acquired a very specific meaning: the totality of the actions and

49. Ibid., p. 71.

events which are unfolded in the course of narration. . . . However, for Professor Lévi-Strauss the plot is uninteresting. He translates it into French as 'theme.' He most likely prefers it because 'plot' is a category pertaining to time whereas 'theme' lacks this feature. There is, however, no student of literature who would accept such a substitution. We can understand these two terms in many ways but never can we identify them or substitute one of them for the other."[50] Needless to say, the term "theme" does not appear in Propp's morphological investigations of the fairy tale.

Propp's conception of the fairy tale as an empirical, temporally extended object led him to stress the formal units that constitute narrative flux and to disregard the fairy tale's semantics. Admittedly, this radical reduction paid off in his search for a generic invariant, for the wealth of semantic nuances had blinded earlier students of folklore to the formal regularity of the fairy tale. As soon as transformation is the issue, however, all those features, all the semantic nuances that differentiate one tale from another, become crucial. Indeed, Propp's genre definition disregarded these very features. As Lévi-Strauss jokingly observed, "Before formalism we were certainly unaware of what these tales had in common. Since formalism, we have been deprived of any means of understanding how they differ."[51] Propp cannot have his cake and eat it too. One cannot have transformational rules without treating semantic features as elements of a system. Because a fairy tale is not an empirical but an intentional object, the static elements and their relations must be taken into account if we are to grasp the unity of the fairy tale in its process of transformation.

Lévi-Strauss convincingly showed that the semantics of the fairy tale is crucial. The specific acting characters that fulfill a function are not altered arbitrarily. For example, three birds may fulfill a function in a certain tale: an eagle, an owl, and a

50. "Strukturnoe i istoričeskoe izučenie volšebnoj skazki," pp. 145–46.
51. "Structure and Form: Reflections on a Work by Vladimir Propp," *Structural Anthropology*, vol. 2, tr. M. Layton (New York, 1976), p. 133.

crow. Though on the formal level it makes no difference which bird fulfills the function, from the semantic point of view these birds are opposed to each other in significant ways. The eagle is diurnal, whereas the owl is nocturnal; as predators both are opposed to the scavenger crow.[52] From this example it follows that the acting characters are not accidental embodiments of minimal functions but partial meanings whose dynamic interplay encompasses the overall structure of the meaning of a given fairy tale. They are interconnected, and a change in one leads to a change in all the others.

The Formalists who were inspired by Goethe's concept of morphology actually failed to realize their goal—to isolate the transformational rules of a literary genre. Despite their claims, they were ultimately quite close to the "static morphologists." Even though they attempted to grasp literature as a process, they succeeded only in pinning down the invariants of the genres they studied. By conceiving of these invariants as a functional correlation of parts they arrived at the same organic metaphor as the morphological Formalists who were proceeding from Cuvier.

The application of the biological metaphor to literature demonstrated that the literary work is not a conglomerate of devices but a functionally integrated whole whose elements are determined by the role they fulfill in the literary organism. When they attempted to cross the boundaries between literature and extraliterary phenomena, however, the morphologists did not fare well. Though they criticized the mechanistic Formalists for their radical separation of art and *byt*, they themselves were unable to bridge this gap. Instead they replaced the mechanistic opposition of art and *byt* with the regular versus the accidental. In other words, they admitted that the internal organization of a literary work is subject to influences from the nonliterary world, but they saw these influences as random and secondary to an understanding of the inherent regularities of literature.

52. Ibid., p. 135.

The inability to bring literature and life together quite strongly affected the morphological Formalists' attitude toward literary history. They rejected the mechanists' immanent approach, but as long as they saw the extraliterary sphere as incidental to the internal constitution of literature they could not develop a systematic explanation of literary change. Concerned with the identity of literature in its internal regularity, they had no place in their theories for the vicissitudes of history. Thus they willingly traded the insecurity of change for the certitude of identity, diachrony for synchrony. For them the theory of literature was independent of and prior to its history.

In his 1922 inaugural lecture at Saratov University, Skaftymov separated the theoretical and historical aspects of literary studies, giving precedence to theory. "I contrast the theoretical to the historical view on the following points: (1) A theoretical knowledge grasps the object in its inner constitution; a historical study views the object in the process of its becoming. (2) A theoretical study takes into account the holistic correlation of the constitutive elements of the object; a historical knowledge is concerned with cause and effect relations (causality)."[53] The theoretical approach alone, Skaftymov believed, is adequate for the treatment of a literary work as an aesthetic object and all historical facts play a merely auxiliary role in it. Moreover, a history of any phenomenon can be studied fully only after its identity is established theoretically. Quoting Žirmunskij—another Formalist relying on the morphological metaphor—Skaftymov declared, "Only a 'theoretical poetics' can construct the system of scholarly concepts which the historian of literature needs for solving his concrete historical problems."[54] This notion surfaces six years later in Propp's book on the fairy tale in a passage quoted earlier: "Historical studies may appear more interesting than morphological investigations. . . . However, we maintain

53. "K voprosu o sootnošenii teoretičeskogo i istoričeskogo rassmotrenija v istorii literatury," *Učënye zapiski Gosudarstvennogo saratovskogo universiteta*, vol. 1, pt. 3 (Saratov, 1923), pp. 55–6.
54. Ibid., p. 67; see Žirmunskij, "Zadači poètiki," *Načala* 1 (1921), 51.

97

that as long as there is no correct morphological study there can be no correct historical study."[55]

The rift between theory and history and the privileged position the morphologists accorded synchronic studies were not, however, shared by all Formalists. It was in response to these issues that a third Formalist model arose which sought to treat literature as a strictly historical phenomenon.

55. See note 33.

The System

> No poet, no artist of any art, has his complete
> meaning alone. His significance, his appreciation is
> the appreciation of his relation to the dead poets
> and artists. You cannot value him alone; you must
> set him, for contrast and comparison, among the
> dead. I mean this as a principle of aesthetic, not
> merely historical criticism.
>
> —T. S. Eliot,
> "Tradition and the Individual Talent"

I call the third Formalist model "systemic" because it uses the metaphor of the system as its primary frame of reference. The role of systemic Formalism was to fill the gaps left by the other two metaphors: to describe the relationship between art and *byt* and provide an account of literary history capable of explaining the dynamic interplay between these two domains.

The name "systemo-functional" was chosen by Jurij Tynjanov, the main proponent of the model, to designate his approach to literary studies.[1] It points aptly to the holistic and

---

1. "O parodii," *Poètika, istorija literatury, kino* (Moscow, 1977), p. 295. Unfortunately, the adjective "systemic" that I use for this Formalist model carries certain biological connotations (relating to the body as a system) that I do not intend. Its only possible replacement, "systematic," is even less felicitous, however, because of its primary meaning of "methodical" or "thorough." I have chosen "systemic" therefore, in its sense of "relating to a system," and hope that the reader will not be distracted by the specifically medical or biological usage of the term.

relational nature of the approach. These features, too, indicate the link between the systemic metaphor and new developments in such other disciplines as psychology, logic, and linguistics. I would like to outline briefly the way advances in these areas helped to shape the systemic metaphor of Russian Formalism.

One of the leading Gestalt psychologists, Kurt Koffka, devoted part of his *Zur Analyse der Vorstellungen und ihrer Gesetze* (1912) to the distinction between "descriptive" and "functional" concepts in psychology.[2] Descriptive concepts like "color" or "image" are those which involve direct experience and "derive from simple perception and the descriptions of experiences."[3] Functional concepts, such as "distortion of memory" go beyond simple perception. They are used "to put experience into relation with other objects, either with other experiences or with stimuli."[4] Koffka concludes that "all functional concepts have as their basis experiences that have somehow been made objective. This kind of concept formation is of the same type as the formation of concepts [in physics]."[5]

The literary scholar must also distinguish between concepts relating to the direct experience of literary texts and concepts that bring these into categorical relation. Tynjanov expressed this distinction as the opposition between "literary fact" and "literature." He noted that "whereas a hard *definition of literature* is more and more difficult to make, every contemporary can point his finger at what is a *literary fact*. He will tell you that this or that as a fact of *byt* or of the poet's private life" is not a literary fact, "while something else certainly is."[6] "Literature" is a notion of

2. Koffka's work seems to have been well known in the teens in Russia; the Formalists certainly were aware of it. It was the topic of Professor Georgij Čelpanov's seminar held at the Moscow University in 1915/1916. Roman Jakobson participated in this seminar (see Elmar Holenstein, "Jakobson und Husserl: Ein Beitrag zur Genealogie des Strukturalismus," *Tijdschrift voor Filosofie* 35 [1973], 562).

3. Koffka, "The Distinction between Descriptive and Functional Concepts," *Thinking: From Association to Gestalt*, ed. J. M. Mandler and G. Mandler (New York, 1964), p. 238.

4. Ibid.

5. Ibid., p. 242.

6. "Literaturnyj fakt," *Archaisty i novatory* (Leningrad, 1929), p. 9.

an order distinct from the literary fact. It is a functional concept relating notions of direct literary experience, Koffka's descriptive concept. This distinction, which at first glance might appear obvious, was quite important to the systemic Formalists. Until it had been elaborated, literary critics frequently identified literary facts with literature in general, confusing a particular literary sensibility, for instance, with the theory of literature itself.

The rise of the relationalist outlook at the turn of the century was obviously fostered by new advances in the sciences. But it would have been unimaginable without the support of the philosophers and logicians who provided its epistemological justification. In his influential book *Substanzbegriff und Funktionsbegriff* (1910) Ernst Cassirer declared that the "two chief forms of logic which are especially opposed to each other in the modern scientific development, are distinguished . . . by the different value which is placed upon *thing-concepts* and *relation-concepts.*"[7] The "thing-concept," whose origin Cassirer traces back to Aristotle, is characteristic of traditional concept-formation based on the process of abstraction. A general concept, it was believed, was derived from particulars by abstracting their similar feature. The fallacy of this approach, according to Cassirer, rests in the presupposition that similarities are not merely a principle of logical ordering but real properties of objects. Thus, in the process of abstraction what is nonessential to objects is eliminated in order to discover their unchangeable substance. With this substantialist view Cassirer contrasts the relationalist one, in which similarity is not considered a property of objects but a categorical tool that enables us to unite disparate objects in a single concept. Thus, similarity is one of many possible principles of logical

---

7. *Substance and Function and Einstein's Theory of Relativity*, tr. W. C. Swabey and M. C. Swabey (Chicago, 1923), p. 9. The Formalists made a few references to Cassirer's book. Èjchenbaum cites it in his diary in January 1919 as one of the books to be consulted on issues of methodology (see M. O. Čudakova's commentary in the collection of Tynjanov's articles, *Poètika, istorija literatury, kino*, p. 455). A passage from Cassirer's work is quoted by Sergej Karcevskij in *Système du verbe russe* (Prague, 1927), pp. 13–14. This passage is subsequently quoted by V. Vinogradov in his critique of Tynjanov's method, *O chudožestvennoj proze* (Moscow, 1930), p. 59.

ordering that give rise to "relation-concepts." As Cassirer explains the process, "all construction of concepts is connected with some definite form of construction of series. We say that a sensuous manifold is conceptually apprehended and ordered, when its members do not stand next to one another without relation but proceed from a definite beginning, according to a fundamental generating relation, in necessary sequence. It is the identity of this generating relation, maintained through changes in the particular contents, which constitutes the specific form of the concept."[8]

There are several clear points of contact between Cassirer's and Tynjanov's theories. Most important is their common use of the mathematical function as a model for concept-formation in general. Quoting the German logician Moritz Drobisch, Cassirer asserts, "Every mathematical function represents a universal law, which, by virtue of the successive values which the variable can assume, contains within itself all the particular cases for which it holds." Moreover, this concept of function "is not confined to mathematics alone," but "extends over into the field of the *knowledge of nature*."[9] Tynjanov, taking Cassirer's lead, crossed even this boundary and applied the notion of function to the study of cultural phenomena as well.

Concept-formation in literary studies is more complex than in psychology or the natural sciences. The task of a psychologist or a physicist is to match two sets of givens: Cassirer's "objects of the first order" (or Koffka's descriptive concepts) and "objects of the second order"—those concepts "determined by the form of the generating relation from which they proceed" (Koffka's functional concepts).[10] Besides these two givens, however, the student of literature must also deal with "objects of a third order"— socially shared sets of conventions which determine the existence and identity of the objects of the first order.

An awareness of this problem most likely came to Tynjanov

8. *Substance and Function*, p. 15.
9. Ibid., p. 21.
10. *Substance and Function*, p. 23.

through his acquaintance with the theories of Ferdinand de Saussure. The Swiss linguist had pointed out that speech phenomena are implementations of the underlying linguistic system shared by speakers of each particular language, a system he termed *la langue*. His example of the knight in chess illustrates this notion well. The identity of this piece is purely relational. If the physical piece is lost during the game the knight can be replaced by any object, even something as different as a matchbox. The equation of two such objects is not the same as bringing them together in the concept-forming mode I have just described. There the knight and the matchbox would be subsumed under a single concept through a logical relation introduced from outside the game. In the game, however, their relationship is generated from within because the matchbox, like the knight, becomes liable to the same set of rules—the game itself. The substitution of one object for another depends on "an unchangeable convention, the set of rules that exists before a game begins and persists after each move."[11] In the same way that a piece in a game of chess derives its identity from an underlying system of rules, the identity of a linguistic fact is a function of the underlying linguistic system—*la langue*. As Saussure argues, the socially shared linguistic code "is necessary if speaking is to be intelligible and produce all its effects."[12]

The analogy between language and literature is obvious. The identity of every literary fact is determined by sets of norms we call genres, schools, or historical styles. Significantly, even the fact that an utterance is considered literary is determined by the existence of a social habit we call "literature." Thus Tynjanov asks, "Is the so-called immanent study of a literary work . . . outside of its interrelation with the literary system possible?" The answer is negative: "Such an isolated study of a work is a mere abstraction similar to the abstracting of an individual element

11. F. de Saussure, *Course in General Linguistics*, tr. and ed. W. Baskin (New York, 1959), p. 88.
12. Ibid., p. 18.

from the work."[13] A literary work is inseparably linked to the literary system, and outside this context loses its identity.

Tynjanov's distinction between "literary fact" and "literature" and between both these concepts and "literary system," and his relational approach to concept-formation all show his affinity to the theories of Koffka, Cassirer, and Saussure. Tynjanov, however, departed from all these thinkers in two significant respects: he approached his material dialectically and historically. Perhaps it was the tradition of Hegelianism in Russian intellectual life that led him to conceive of literature as a dynamic hierarchy, an ongoing struggle for domination among parts and wholes. It is this intrinsic dynamism of literary structures that Tynjanov identified as the distinctive feature of literature. "Literature is a speech construction perceived precisely qua construction, i.e., literature is a *dynamic speech construction*."[14]

Here the concept of the "dominant" enters Tynjanov's system, which according to Jakobson's later assessment "was one of the most crucial, elaborated, and productive concepts of Russian Formalist theory."[15] But because of its wide currency among the Formalists, we must differentiate among its various usages. The term itself was borrowed from Broder Christiansen's *Philosophie der Kunst*. In discussing the perception of a work of art he wrote, "It happens only rarely that the emotive factors of an aesthetic object participate equally in the effect of the whole. On the contrary, normally a single factor or a configuration of them comes to the fore and assumes a leading role. All the others accompany the dominant, intensify it through their harmony, heighten it through contrast, and surround it with a play of variations. The dominant is the same as the structure of bones in an organic body: it contains the theme of the whole, supports this whole, enters into relation with it."[16]

---

13. "O literaturnoj èvoljucii," *Archaisty i novatory*, p. 34.
14. "Literaturnyj fakt," p. 14.
15. Jakobson, "The Dominant," *Readings in Russian Poetics: Formalist and Structuralist Views*, ed. L. Matejka and K. Pomorska (Ann Arbor, Mich., 1978), p. 82.
16. *Philosophie der Kunst* (Berlin, 1912), pp. 241–42.

The notion of the dominant as a skeletal, form-giving element in the static hierarchy of holistic correlations caught the fancy of some of the Formalists. Boris Èjchenbaum, who was responsible for this borrowing from Christiansen, occasionally used the term in this sense. In his analysis of Anna Achmatova's early poetry he tried to isolate the "essential dominant determining the major facts of a style," in this case, her "striving for laconicism and energy of expression."[17] This meaning of the dominant fit very well the conceptual frame of those morphological Formalists who discussed literature as an organism. Thus, according to Skaftymov, the role of the literary scholar was to "reveal the interrelations of the work's compositional parts, to point out the emerging dominants and among them the final concluding and all-embracing point which in turn was the basic form-creating intention of the author."[18] On a more empirical level, Žirmunskij spoke of metaphor as the "capital device, the stylistic 'dominant'" of Aleksandr Blok's poetry.[19]

For the systemic Formalists, however, it was Èjchenbaum's reinterpretation of Christiansen's term that was accepted instead. Èjchenbaum used "dominant" to refer to a specific element within a literary work which is brought into the foreground and "deforms" to its needs all the other elements. He saw the work not as a harmonious correlation of parts and wholes but as a dialectic tension among them. "The work of art," Èjchenbaum argued, "is always the result of a complex struggle among various form-creating elements; it is always a kind of compromise. These elements do not simply coexist and 'correlate.' Depending on the general character of the style, this or that element acquires the role of the organizing *dominant* governing all the others and subordinating them to its needs."[20] In

17. Èjchenbaum, *Anna Achmatova: Opyt analiza* (Petersburg, 1923), p. 63.
18. "Tematičeskaja kompozicija romana *Idiot,*" *Tvorčeskij put' Dostoevskogo,* ed. L. N. Brodskij (Leningrad, 1924), p. 24.
19. "Poèzija Aleksandra Bloka," *Voprosy teorii literatury: Stat'i 1916–1926* (Leningrad, 1928), p. 221.
20. *Melodika russkogo liričeskogo sticha* (Petersburg, 1922), p. 9.

the type of lyric poetry Èjchenbaum analyzed, the dominant was intonation, because it deformed the other aspects of the poems—syntax, word order, and so on.

Keeping in mind this notion of the dominant we may consider Tynjanov's definition of literature. The perception of a speech construction qua construction is based, according to Tynjanov, on our awareness of the hierarchical organization of such a construction caused by the tension between the dominant and the subordinated elements. "Art lives through this interplay, this struggle. Without the sensation of subordination, the deformation of all the factors by the factor fulfilling the constructive role, there would be no fact of art. . . . If the sensation of the interplay of factors (necessarily presupposing the presence of two elements—the dominating and the subordinated) vanishes, the fact of art is obliterated; it becomes automatized."[21]

This is Tynjanov's most basic definition of literature, but it omits one important point. For Tynjanov, the very identity of a literary fact rests in its relation to the underlying literary system: "Whether a fact is *literary* or not is a function of its differential quality (i.e., whether it is related either to the literary or the extraliterary series)."[22] This means that not every strikingly organized speech construction will be perceived by us as literary. It is rather the other way around: the special perceptibility of a speech construction comes about only through its comparison to other speech constructions considered by us literary. Thus, a construction that appears merely "usual" can, at one moment, become a literary fact because of the unusual nature of the immediately preceding literary tradition against whose background it is perceived, and vice versa. "Transrational language [*zaum'*] always existed in the language of children and mystics, but only in our time did it become a literary fact. And, on the other hand . . . charades, logographs are children's games for us, but in Karamzin's period [the 1790s] in which verbal trifles and

---

21. *Problema stichotvornogo jazyka* (Leningrad, 1924), p. 10.
22. "O literaturnoj èvoljucii," p. 35.

the play of devices were foregrounded, they were a literary genre."[23] Thus, not perceptibility per se but perceptibility vis-à-vis the literary system is, for Tynjanov, the opposite pole of automatization.

By applying the opposing values, perceptible/automatized, to the literary system, Tynjanov exposed the relativity of the notion of the literary fact. That the literary system is a social institution and as such liable to change means the literary facts of different periods might be quite dissimilar. How then is it possible to construct a literary series, to discover a relation that would encompass under the single category of literature all the disparate literary facts? Because the relativity of literary facts is historical, Tynjanov found the answer to this question in literary history. "Only in evolution," he claimed, "can we analyze the 'definition' of literature."[24] Literary facts of various periods, disparate in themselves, become related if they are placed within a concrete historical process and viewed according to the logic of this process.

Tynjanov conceived of the logic of literary history dialectically. To be meaningful, the perceptibility of a speech construction needed an opposite—the automatization of this perception. Literary change is triggered by the tension between these two. "Evolution is caused by the need for a ceaseless dynamics. Every dynamic system inevitably becomes automatized and an opposite constructive principle dialectically arises."[25] The life of a literary fact is the vacillation of a linguistic construction between these two poles. It is lifted from the sphere of automatization to replace some older constructions, which in the course of time have become automatized; for a longer or shorter period of time it is perceptible, only to become automatized again and replaced by some newer constructions.

Thus, the literary series conceived historically is an ongoing

---

23. "Literaturnyj fakt," p. 9.
24. Ibid., p. 14.
25. Ibid., p. 15.

struggle of dialectically opposed speech constructions. It is a succession of literary facts which exhibit contrastive principles of construction. From this perspective only a negative definition of literature is possible. The identity of the literary series rests in a constant negation of its identity by its members.

Literature as a concept did not, however, occupy a central position in the theories of the systemic Formalists. The true crux of their thought was the notion of the literary system—the ultimate arbiter of what is and what is not a literary fact. As I pointed out above, Tynjanov derived this concept from Saussure's *langue*—the linguistic system underlying the facts of speech. Certain critics of Tynjanov, such as Viktor Vinogradov, claimed that his theory was nothing but a "re-telling of Saussure in literary-historical terms."[26] In my opinion this judgment is a polemical exaggeration. It takes only a brief glance at Saussure's concept of *langue* to see how different it is from Tynjanov's literary system.

First of all, Saussure's *langue* is static, devoid of any evolutionary dynamics. In fact, he declared it incompatible with history, as his famous division of linguistics into synchronic and diachronic studies attests. Further, Saussure saw changes in *langue* as catastrophic. They are brought about at random from the outside, and once they penetrate the system they destroy it and establish a new system different from the previous one. For this reason the system of *langue* is absolutely autonomous. As the concluding words of Saussure's *Course* state: "*the true and unique object of linguistics is language studied in and for itself.*"[27]

Tynjanov's "literary system" differs from *langue* in every one of these respects. The separation of synchrony from diachrony was utterly alien to his historical orientation. "The juxtaposition of synchrony and diachrony," Tynjanov and Jakobson wrote in

---

26. *O chudožestvennoj proze*, p. 24. More recently, Fredric Jameson has asserted that "Tynjanov retains Saussure's basic model of change, in which the essential mechanisms at work are the ultimate abstractions of Identity and Difference," *The Prison-House of Language: A Critical Account of Structuralism and Russian Formalism* (Princeton, N.J., 1972), p. 96.

27. *Course in General Linguistics*, p. 232.

1928, "was the juxtaposition of the notion of system to that of evolution; it becomes meaningless as soon as we recognize that every system exists in evolution and on the other hand that evolution is necessarily systemic."[28] Tynjanov took to heart Šklovskij's notion that opposing literary schools—the canonized and noncanonized—coexist in every literary period. The literary system is not a balanced, harmonious structure like *langue* but is intrinsically unbalanced, torn by conflicting tendencies to preserve the status quo and to change it. Such a system simultaneously contains its past and points to the future. Its past is contained in constructions that have been literary facts; its future rests with the constructions negating this automatized past which are about to become literary facts. It is impossible to extract from this ongoing process an atemporal slice of the synchronic "present," Tynjanov declared. "The literary epoch, the literary present, is not at all a static system opposed to the dynamic, evolving historical series. The same historical struggle of different layers and formations which exists in the diachronic historical series goes on in the present."[29]

If the literary system at every moment contains developmental tendencies, Saussure's belief in the asystemic and catastrophic nature of changes in *langue* does not apply to it. The developmental character of the system also makes untenable Saussure's claim that the external impulses for change are totally random. They appear random only if viewed in separation from the literary system. From the perspective of the developmental regularity of the literary system there is no randomness. To underline this difference, the systemic Formalists divided Saussure's diachrony into two categories: "the genesis of a literary phenomenon" on the one hand, and "its evolutionary significance, its place in the evolutionary series" on the other.[30] The specific origin of a literary phenomenon is a cross-section of many im-

28. Tynjanov and Jakobson, "Problemy izučenija literatury i jazyka," *Novyj Lef*, no. 12 (1928), 36–37.

29. "Literaturnyj fakt," p. 11.

30. Ibid., pp. 12–13; see also Tynjanov, "O literaturnoj èvoljucii," p. 31.

pulses—biological, psychological, social—and so in its full complexity might be random. But the fact that this configuration of extraliterary factors was incorporated into the literary series, that it crystallized into a literary fact—an element of literary history—can always be explained in reference to the evolution of the literary system. Thus, while "it is impossible to construct a genetic history of literature," it is quite possible to write a history of the literary system.[31]

An especially clear illustration of Tynjanov's claim is Èjchenbaum's dispute with Lev Trockij. To discredit the Marxist approach to literary history Èjchenbaum shrewdly employed an example that Trockij himself had used against the psychobiological interpretation of art: can J. M. W. Turner's role in the evolution of Europoean painting be deduced from the fact that he suffered from astigmatism? For the young Trockij, this was an inadmissible reduction of a social to a biological phenomenon—a stance subsequently applauded by Èjchenbaum. But when Trockij later attacked the Formalist concept of literary history, he denied art its specificity by conceiving of its evolution as an extension of class struggle. There is, of course, a difference between treating art through a biological and a sociological frame of reference, and one could argue that sociology is the more relevant concern. But this answer would not satisfy the Formalists, for whom both biology and sociology were capable of explaining only the genesis of the work and not its evolutionary significance. "Art has its specific 'sociology' and its laws of evolution," Èjchenbaum argued in the tones of a literary historian. "If they tell us that a writer was psychologically a representative of a certain class, it is just as true as that Turner was an astigmatic, but 'it does not concern me' because these are facts of a different order [than artistic facts]."[32]

In other words, not every Russian nobleman born in the 1820s turned out to be a Tolstoj, nor did every astigmatic painter born

---

31. Tynjanov, "Tjutčev i Gejne," *Archaisty i novatory*, p. 386.
32. Èjchenbaum, "V ožidanii literatury," *Literatura: Teorija, kritika, polemika* (Leningrad, 1927), p. 286.

in the late eighteenth century produce work of Turner's quality. The reason for the systemic Formalists' rejection of the possibility of a genetic history of literature is that the number of extraliterary impulses instrumental in a literary change is limitless. Only those impulses that mesh with the developmental tendencies of the literary system have a chance of influencing the system. In Tynjanov's words, "An 'influence' can be successful at a time when there are literary conditions for it and in the direction indicated by those conditions."[33]

The belief in the immanent development of the literary system might seem to bring the systemic Formalists close to Saussure's view of the absolute autonomy of *langue*. If everything literary is determined solely by the preconditions of the literary system, this system would indeed be "in and of itself the unique object of literary studies." This similarity to Saussure is hard to deny and has a historical justification. Saussure and Tynjanov's emphasis on the autonomous character of their systems was meant to establish their respective fields of study as independent disciplines. It would be wrong, however, to see Tynjanov's position on this issue as absolutely set and inflexible. He effected a gradual relativization of the original Formalist position on the autonomy of the literary system.

Only at the very end of the movement, though, did the systemic Formalists succeed in advancing a coherent theory of the *relative* autonomy of the literary system. I refer here to Tynjanov's and Jakobson's nine-point thesis written in 1928. In this scheme, Tynjanov rejected his strictly deterministic conception of the literary system according to which the domination of one principle of construction necessarily and unequivocally causes the rise of a single contrastive principle, which in time becomes the new dominant. Instead he proposed a more pluralistic view according to which several new principles of construction different from the dominant emerge and struggle for control. Moreover, Tynjanov recast his entire concept of the relation between

33. "O literaturnoj èvoljucii," p. 46.

literature and extraliterary phenomena. He conceived of the entire culture as a complex "system of systems" composed of various subsystems such as literature, science, and technology.[34] Within this general system, extraliterary phenomena relate to literature not in a piecemeal fashion but as an interplay among systems determined by the logic of the culture to which they belong. Thus, among all the pretenders to dominance in the literary system, the one that converges with the developmental tendencies of the overall cultural system becomes the victor.

This, of course, is a highly abstract scheme which—because time ran out for the Formalists—they never put into action. Nonetheless, it indicates the road the systemic metaphor was taking to release literature from the social vacuum into which it had been forced by the Formalists' belief in the autonomy of the literary system. By the same token the theses demonstrate the deep-seated difference between Saussure's and Tynjanov's thought, making a simple equation of their theories impossible.

So far I have discussed systemic Formalism only in relation to other fields of knowledge, but it is also useful to compare it with the other two Formalist metaphors. Systemic Formalism is the most advanced stage of the movement. That it was qualitatively different from the other models was obvious to its contemporaries. In 1927 Viktor Žirmunskij, for example, felt compelled to add a footnote to his 1919 review article of the OPOJAZ anthology *Poetics*, in which he termed Tynjanov a "neo-Formalist" in order to distinguish his approach from the "original" Formalism.[35]

It is worth specifying precisely what that difference is. For example, at first glance it might appear that systemic Formalism approached the morphological model with its notions of system and function. In fact, the coincidence of vocabulary is a matter of homonymity and not a sign of any conceptual affinity between the two Formalisms. The morphological approach used

34. "Problemy izučenija literatury i jazyka," p. 37.
35. "Vokrug *Poètiki* Opojaza: *Poètika: Sborniki po teorii poètičeskogo jazyka*. Pgrd. 1919," *Voprosy teorii literatury*, p. 356.

these terms in a biological sense, whereas the systemic one used them in a mathematical-logical sense. For the former, "function" denotes the role an element performs within a whole; this whole is a system because it is an interplay of functional elements held together by what Žirmunskij once called the "unity of artistic goal." For the systemic Formalists, function was the relation of the interdependent variables, and system a hierarchical set of interdependent variables.

In general, these two Formalisms were mutually antipathetic. The systemic Formalists perceived the morphologists as mere fellow travelers, whereas for the morphologists those who considered literature a system were extremists and radicals. Žirmunskij, after his split with OPOJAZ in 1922, was the most hostile of the morphologists, and the systemic Formalists never tired of accusing him of academic ecclecticism. Žirmunskij quite properly objected to some of the extreme postulates of the systemic metaphor, such as the immanent development of the literary system and its strict determinism, which as I noted earlier was later abandoned by the systemic Formalists themselves. Žirmunskij's critique lacked effect because he was unable to offer a viable alternative hypothesis as to how literature is connected with the overall development of culture or what brings together all the disparate human activities of a particular historical moment. Instead of elaborating these problems Žirmunskij hid behind a smoke screen of vague terms such as "the uniform perception of life," "the psychological background of an era," or the "uniform life tendency," which he had borrowed from contemporary German aesthetics.[36]

The relation of systemic to mechanistic Formalism was quite different from its relation to morphological Formalism. Members of the two groups were personal friends and their theories tended to overlap. Tynjanov accepted many of Šklovskij's key concepts and freely acknowledged his debt. Such surface similarity should not obscure the important differences between the

36. Cf., for example, "Zadači poètiki," ibid., pp. 55–58.

two Formalisms, which transcend the metaphoric divergence to involve the mode of concept-formation underlying each model. Tynjanov did not passively borrow Šklovskij's terms but always reformulated what he borrowed, fitting it into a different conceptual frame.

In Cassirer's terms, one might say that the "thing-concept" dominated Šklovskij's thinking and the "functional concept" was crucial to Tynjanov's. Šklovskij proceeded from the assumption that an unchangeable literary essence—"literariness"—was intrinsic to every literary phenomenon. On the infraliterary level, that is, the level of elements composing the work, he isolated the device as a monad of literary form endowed with "literariness" regardless of its context. On the highest extraliterary level, the level of all human activities, Šklovskij drew a sharp line between phenomena with a literary essence and those without it. For him, the facts of literature were incompatible with the facts of *byt*.

The middle intraliterary level, the level composed of literary works themselves, played havoc with the mechanistic metaphor. If Šklovskij's theory had been ahistorical, this level would have posed no problem to him, for he considered all literary works to be essentially the same, differing only in the way they were made. Because, as I argued earlier, such was not the case, he encountered difficulties. To maintain the separation of literature and life he had to locate the source of this change within literature itself. For this reason, he introduced the new opposition of "canonized" and "noncanonized" literature. But this opposition was incompatible with the substantivist nature of mechanistic Formalism. If all literary works were literary, but some at a given moment were more literary than others, it is not an unchangeable essence but a changeable *relationship* among works that constitutes literariness.

This was the point of departure for systemic Formalism. Unlike Šklovskij, Tynjanov did not locate the differential quality of literary phenomena in the phenomena themselves. Instead he found them literary by virtue of the relation in which they participated at the level of a single work, literature in its totality, and the whole national culture of a given time.[37] Each of these was a system for Tynjanov, a set of interdependent *variables*, no element enjoying a privileged status prior to its incorporation into the appropriate system. Moreover, Tynjanov considered systemic not only the organization of each level but the interrelations among the levels as well. Thus, the minimal system—the literary work—was a variable in the higher literary system, and in turn this system was a variable in the ultimate cultural system.

At the infraliterary level, Tynjanov warns against the futility of any inquiry into the constitutive parts of a literary work that separates them from their context. "Analyses of the isolated elements of a work—plot and style, rhythm and syntax in prose, rhythm and semantics in verse—were enough to convince us that the abstraction of these elements is permissible to some extent as a *working hypothesis*, but that all these elements are *correlated* and interacting. The study of rhythm in verse and in prose revealed that the very same element performs a different role in a different system."[38] Thus, the literary purport of a device is derived solely from the context into which it is incorporated and the material of a literary work is not determined by its extraliterary substance but only by its place in the literary construction. Clearly aiming at Šklovskij, Tynjanov wrote: "It is self-evident that 'material' is not at all the opposite of 'form'; it is also 'formal' because there is no material which would be external to a construction. . . . Material is that element of the form that is subordinated for the benefit of the foregrounded constructive elements."[39]

Tynjanov follows the same pattern with the narrative aspect of the literary work, which Šklovskij had split into the literary "plot" and the lifelike "story." I have pointed out that some

37. The three-level scheme that I outline here simplifies Tynjanov's actual thought somewhat. The middle, intraliterary level in particular comprises several subsystems—genres, literary schools, and styles. Tynjanov did not provide any clear-cut picture of this level of system, however.

38. "O literaturnoj èvoljucii," p. 33.

39. "Literaturnyj fakt," p. 15.

Formalists expressed misgivings about the manner in which Šklovskij differentiated between these two notions. They argued that the story is not merely a sequence of events but a semantic structure—a sequence extracted from its context and endowed with meaning. Tynjanov agreed with this qualification. As he wrote, "story is the *entire* semantic scheme of the action" represented in the literary work.[40] But his conception of plot and how it is related to "story" was different from the other Formalists'. He did not see plot merely as a literary redistribution (composition) of the sequence of events but as something more intimately related to the overall structure of the work. "The plot of a work is defined as its dynamism comprised of the interplay among all the correlations of material . . . stylistic, story-related, and so on."[41] Story—the configuration of events depicted in the work—is only one among many variables in this process.

Story is thus related to plot as a partial configuration to the complex configuration encompassing the work as an overall system. However, this part/whole relation must not be viewed as static. As Tynjanov stressed several times, "the unity of a work is not a closed symmetrical whole but an unfolding dynamic integrity; among its elements stands not the static sign of equation and addition, but always the dynamic sign of correlation and integration."[42] The relation of the story and plot was no exception to this rule. In every literary work (lyrical poetry included) a struggle goes on between the two. In some works, for example the traditional novel, the semantics of events clearly dominates the overall structure of the work, whereas in others the plot unfolds outside the story. In both cases it is the relationship between them that exerts a decisive influence on the overall meaning of the work.

It is important to notice that as the systemic metaphor developed, its treatment of the infraliterary level underwent a gradual expansion. In the beginning Tynjanov was primarily in-

40. "Ob osnovach kino," *Poètika, istorija literatury, kino*, p. 341.
41. Ibid.
42. *Problema stichotvornogo jazyka*, p. 10.

terested in the relations among the textual elements themselves, but in the course of time he began to focus more and more on the vertical connections between this and higher levels and their impact upon the relations among the infraliterary elements. In the earliest stage of his career, "deformation" was the term he used to describe the makeup of a literary work.[43] It was a set of hierarchically related elements in which the dominant (or as Tynjanov often calls it, the "constructive factor") deforms to its needs the "material," that is, all the other subordinate elements. While the constructive factor and material are variables in the sense that any linguistic element can become the dominant of a work, the subordination/superordination relation is constant; it is precisely this hierarchical tension among the elements of a speech construction that renders it a literary fact.

It became obvious to Tynjanov that there was a constancy in the constructive factor and material of different literary works. Genre and any other systems larger than the work determine the hierarchical arrangement of elements within it. Thus, the simple notion of deformation was subsequently replaced by a more comprehensive concept, the "principle of construction," which denotes the deformation of a specific material by a specific constructive factor. Tynjanov's probes into the difference between prose and poetry, for instance, revealed that the "principle of construction in prose is the deformation of sound by meaning," whereas the "principle of construction in poetry is the deformation of meaning by sound."[44] As long as poetry is perceived as different from prose, the internal organization of every poetic work will be based upon the deformation of meaning by sound regardless of the specific form this deformation takes. In this way the principle of construction vertically integrates the system of a single work into the overall literary system

43. Apparently Tynjanov was not very happy about this term. He complained to Grigorij Vinokur in a letter of November 7, 1924: "My term 'deformation' is infelicitous; it should have been 'transformation'—then everything would be in its place," *Poètika, istorija literatury, kino*, p. 517.

44. "O kompozicii *Evgenija Onegina*," ibid., p. 55.

and renders the relations of the infraliterary elements a function of the next higher level.

In the last stage of his theoretical career, Tynjanov attempted to link the infraliterary textual elements to the extraliterary level as well. He introduced the notion of the "constructive function" of an element that consists of two simultaneous relations: infrarelations proper, which he called the "syn-function" or the relations of an element "to the other elements of a given [work-]system"; and intraliterary and extraliterary relations, which he termed the "auto-function" or the relations of an element "to the similar elements of other work-systems and even of other series."[45] This distinction resembles to some extent the Saussurean opposition between syntagmatic and associative relations in language, the first being *in praesentia* vis-à-vis the other elements of the syntagm in which they occur, and the second *in absentia*, "present" only in the linguistic system. The different modalities of these relations are reflected in the fashion in which Tynjanov links the syn- and auto-functions. The auto-function is potentially the precondition of the constructive function of an element within the work, but the syn-function determines its actual constructive function. Tynjanov offers the following illustration. An archaism appears in a literary work. Its existence there is determined by its auto-function, the relation of this word to the lexical system of a given language. But its syn-function—its incorporation into the work—determines whether the archaism serves as a lexical signal of high style (Michail Lomonosov's usage) or of an ironic standpoint (some of Fëdor Tjutčev's archaisms).

Tynjanov's treatment of the intraliterary level was equally relational. Šklovskij had set aside his substantivism in treating it, so it is no surprise to find here a confluence of the mechanistic and systemic metaphors. In particular, the concept of parody used in Šklovskij's studies of Sterne and Puškin is echoed in some of the earliest of Tynjanov's work.

---

45. "O literaturnoj èvoljucii," p. 33.

For Šklovskij, parody was above all a means of de-familiarizing automatized literary forms through the laying bare of automatized devices and the displacement and violation of customary literary norms, and its aim was to provide us with a new perception of literary form. "The appearance of *Tristram Shandy*," Šklovskij argued, "was motivated by the petrification of the devices of the traditional *roman d'aventure*. All of its techniques had become totally automatized. Parody was the only way to rejuvenate them. *Evgenij Onegin* was written . . . on the eve of the rise of a new prose. The molds of poetry were cooling off. Puškin dreamt of writing a prosaic novel; rhyme bored him."[46]

In his earliest studies, Tynjanov exhibited a keen interest in works oriented toward other works, especially parodies and stylizations. The similarity between the two lies in the fact that "both are leading a double life: behind the plane of the work stands the second plane, the stylized or parodied one."[47] Apart from this kinship there is an important dissimilarity between them. In a stylization the plane of the work is congruent with the background; in a parody there is an incongruity between the two planes. This notion of parody approaches Šklovskij's. It is this incongruity of the new and the old, the parodying and parodied, that shakes our perception and renders the literary form defamiliarized. Tynjanov differs from Šklovskij in his use of the concept of parody, however. As Jurij Striedter observes, "while for Šklovskij parody serves first and foremost as the testing and verification of his previously formulated thesis of art as estrangement, for Tynjanov the literary-historical analysis of parodistic texts and the subsequent 'theory of parody' are the starting point for a . . . theory of literary evolution."[48]

For literary evolution, conceived as a struggle for domination

46. "*Evgenij Onegin:* Puškin i Stern," *Očerki po poètike Puškina* (Berlin, 1923), p. 219.

47. Tynjanov, "Dostoevskij i Gogol': K teorii parodii," *Archaisty i novatory*, p. 416.

48. "Zur formalistischen Theorie der Prosa und der literarischen Evolution," quoted from English tr. by M. Nicolson, "The Russian Formalist Theory of Prose," *PTL* 2 (1977), 459.

of different elements, the "dialectical play of devices" in parody becomes an important vehicle of change.[49] Nikolaj Nekrasov's parodies of Lermontov's poems are a case in point. Nekrasov arrived on the Russian literary scene in the 1840s after the long domination of Romantic poetry which, in the works of Puškin (1799–1837) and Lermontov (1814–1841), established the canon of Russian verse. The clumsiness and prosaic quality of Nekrasov's poems contrasted sharply with this smooth and elegant tradition, although his role in the development of Russian poetry proved considerable. As Tynjanov put it, "The 'impossible,' unacceptable form of Nekrasov, his 'bad' verses, were good because they displaced automatized verse, because they were new."[50] Thus, Nekrasov's early parodies of Lermontov's poems were an important element in the process of literary change toward post-Romanticism. "The essence of his parodies does not rest," according to Tynjanov, "in the mocking of the parodied but in the very sensation of the displacement of the old form through the introduction of a prosaic theme and vocabulary" into poetry.[51] And although the mechanism of Nekrasov's parodies was quite simple, "the combination of elevated rhythmical-syntactic figures with 'low' themes and vocabulary," they marked a departure from the Romantic canon.[52]

As Tynjanov further elaborated the systemic metaphor, his view of the intraliterary level broadened and he eventually transcended the mechanistic model. He realized that not only parodies and stylizations but all literary texts are directed toward other works. The identity of a work in respect to genre, style, or school, indeed its very identity as literature, is based on its relations to other literary works through the underlying literary system. The principle of construction—a special relation between the dominant constructive factor and the subordinate ma-

49. Tynjanov, "Dostoevskij i Gogol'," p. 455.
50. "Literaturnyj fakt," pp. 11–12. See also Ejchenbaum's article "Nekrasov," *Literatura*, pp. 77–115.
51. "Stichovye formy Nekrasova," *Archaisty i novatory*, p. 401.
52. Ibid.

terial—was the means Tynjanov used to link the internal organization of a work to the appurtenant literary system. Tynjanov even went so far as to identify the principle of construction with the literary system itself. Every speech construction exhibiting a particular hierarchical organization of linguistic elements perceptible to us becomes by virtue of this a literary fact.

The connection between the principle of construction and the literary system is especially apparent from a developmental perspective. As soon as an automatized "principle" is negated by a new principle, its systemic existence becomes clear. For only if we conceive of the new principle as a dialectic negation of the old literary system can we perceive its implementation as a literary fact and not merely a mistake.[53] On the other hand, the new principle must be system-creating, must be implemented in more than a single "accidental" speech construction. Tynjanov's model of literary change thus contains four stages: "(1) the contrastive principle of construction dialectically rises in respect to the automatized principle of construction; (2) it is applied—the constructive principle seeks the easiest application; (3) it spreads over the maximal number of phenomena; (4) it is automatized and gives rise to a contrastive principle of construction."[54]

In 1928 Tynjanov replaced the principle of construction with the "literary function" in a wholesale revision of his terminology. He conceptualized the three literary levels I have discussed as three sets of functions: the constructive function corresponding to the infraliterary level, the literary function to the intraliterary level, and the social function to the extraliterary level. This shift was not a question of mere nomenclature; there were important conceptual differences between, for example, the principle of construction and the new "function." Tynjanov characterized

53. That is, it is a mistake from the point of view of the system, not from that of the creating subject. As I argue later in this chapter, the systemic Formalists considered the author's intentions irrelevant to literary change and claimed that it is an author's unconscious slips rather than conscious efforts that give birth to a new principle of construction.

54. "Literaturnyj fakt," p. 17.

the principle of construction as a "concept which changes and evolves constantly,"[55] whereas the literary function undergoes a much more gradual change, evolving "from epoch to epoch."[56]

It is probably wrong to find in this terminological shift the hint of a more static and restrained view of literary change. In fact, if we scrutinize the meaning of "system" in regard to each pair of terms, we discover that they are neither contradictory nor incompatible. Tynjanov uses "system" for entities as different as the works of one author, literary styles and schools, genres, and even prose and poetry in general. Naturally, each of these subsystems evolves at a different speed. To draw a parallel from social history—a favorite ploy of the Formalists—we must distinguish between recurring coups d'état, which simply recycle the ruling elite, and genuine social revolutions which establish new economic-political formations. Literary evolution has both frequent coups and rare genuine revolutions. Though Tynjanov fails to provide us with any clear picture of the hierarchy of literary subsystems or a timetable of their evolution, the principle of construction does seem to apply to more limited subsystems which change rapidly, whereas the literary function applies to more general and hence more stable subsystems.

The functional concept formation of systemic Formalism was also apparent on the extraliterary level. This level was inaccessible to the mechanists because they programmatically separated art from *byt*, literature from life. From very early in his theoretical career, Tynjanov questioned the rationale behind this artificial distinction. "I do not object," he wrote polemically, "to the 'relation of literature and life.' I only doubt whether this question is properly posed. Can we say 'life and art' when art is 'life' as well? Do we have to seek some additional utility of 'art' if we do not seek the utility of 'life'?"[57]

This assertion was not meant to deny literature an identity of its own. In fact, it was just the other way around. *Byt* is an

55. Ibid., p. 16.
56. "O literaturnoj èvoljucii," p. 41.
57. *Problema stichotvornogo jazyka*, p. 123.

amorphous conglomerate of the most disparate phenomena. Against the background of this nebulous domain the various specialized human activities stand out—the arts, science, technology—which in themselves are systems. These systems introduce specific functions among the heterogeneous phenomena by either incorporating their forms into a system in the course of its development or by rejecting them. Thus, when the fact of *byt* is rendered a function of a particular series it becomes a fact of that series (for example, a literary fact), or, on the other hand, after losing its affiliation with that series it turns into a fact of *byt*. As Tynjanov wrote, "*byt* is teeming with the rudiments of various intellectual activities. It is made up of a rudimentary science, rudimentary art and technology; it differs from a full-fledged science, art, and technology in the way that it deals with [phenomena]. The 'artistic *byt*' is thus different from art in the role art plays within it, but they touch upon each other in the form of the phenomena [they both deal with]."[58]

Defining literature as a "dynamic speech construction," Tynjanov saw "*byt* [as] *correlated with literature primarily through its speech aspect,*" since speech phenomena exist in both *byt* and literature. For this reason he termed the "most immediate social function" of literature its speech function.[59] Our language behavior is a complex structure of various forms, patterns, and modes of discourse—some of them well defined, others more fluid—which evolve alongside the entire structure of human communication. In every historical period these forms of discourse are differentiated according to which series they belong to: some are considered literary; others belong to *byt*. But from the developmental perspective, the boundaries between these two domains are far from being fixed and the forms of discourse vacillate between them. According to Tynjanov, "Every lin-

58. "Literaturnyj fakt," p. 19.
59. "O literaturnoj èvoljucii," p. 42. The concept of the "auto-function" discussed earlier, as a language link between literature and extraliterary phenomena, thus can be seen as one aspect of the overall "speech function" of literature.

guistic fact of *byt* has *multifarious* and complex functions which are interlocked in a struggle. Under certain conditions one of these functions—the literary—becomes foregrounded"; at this moment a linguistic fact turns into a literary fact.[60] The process works the other way round as well: a literary fact becomes automatized, its literary function recedes, and it turns into a neutral linguistic fact—a fact of *byt*.

Tynjanov called this intricate interplay of literary and extraliterary discourse *ustanovka*. The term is very resistant to translation or explanation. It has two common meanings in Russian, as Jurij Striedter has pointed out: "intention" on the one hand, and "orientation," on the other, "the idea of positioning oneself in relation to some given data."[61] From Tynjanov's point of view, these meanings have a serious drawback—they are teleologically founded. In both cases what is implied is a psychological subject of action who either projects his intentions into the object he creates or whose orientation (mental attitude) is instrumental in the act of perception. Neither the "intentional" nor the "affective" fallacy stemming from these meanings of *ustanovka* accords with the objectivist thrust of systemic Formalism. This model strove to replace the psychological subject of the literary process with transpersonal, self-regulating systems. Tynjanov emphasized several times that in his usage *ustanovka* is devoid of all its teleological, intentional connotations.[62]

Through this usage of the term Tynjanov tried to express an important feature of the literary system. In adjusting itself to extraliterary modes of discourse, the literary system exhibits a self-regulating quality characteristic of all teleological processes. This quality is not introduced from without through a psychological subject; it is an intrinsic property of the literary system.

60. "Predislovie," *Russkaja proza,* ed. B. Èjchenbaum and Ju. Tynjanov (Leningrad, 1926), p. 10.
61. "Zur formalistischen Theorie der Prosa und der literarischen Evolution," quoted from English tr. by M. Nicolson, "The Russian Formalist Theory of Literary Evolution," *PTL* 3 (1978), 2.
62. Cf., for example, "O literaturnoj èvoljucii," p. 43, or "Oda kak oratorskij žanr," ibid., p. 49.

The point Tynjanov intended to make in this rather clumsy way is grasped today in the distinction between "goal-intended" and "goal-directed" behavior, or between teleology and "telenomy." In discussing Jakobson's concept of linguistic change, Elmar Holenstein has provided a succinct summary of this distinction. "Goal-intended behavior is based on conscious ideas, convictions, wishes, and intentions. These act as the cause of a particular behavior." In contrast, "a process is designated as goal-directed when it evokes the appearance of goal-intended behavior but no consciously acting subject is discernible." The essential feature of a goal-directed or "telenomic" process, according to Holenstein, is its "directive correlation": "a process is regarded as telenomic when it is bound to another process in such a way that it not only causes it, but is in turn steered in its own course by the other process."[63]

In deciding whether Tynjanov's *ustanovka* is a directive correlation, let us look first at an application of this concept to some literary material. Perhaps the best illustration is Tynjanov's discussion of the transition from Classicism to Sentimentalism in Russian literature. There, the *ustanovka* of the dominant genre of Russian Classicism, the ode, was toward the rhetorical speeches delivered before large audiences. The techniques of this type of discourse are clearly echoed in the "oratorical" odes of Michail Lomonosov (1711–1765), the best-known poet of the period. Lomonosov's odes were persuasive in thrust, trying to sway the listener's opinion. His rhetorical stratagem was not to appeal to the listener's reason, but to his or her emotions. To achieve this goal, he structured his odes by combining distant and heterogeneous elements: the unusual nature of such combinations was calculated to have a maximal emotive impact.

Moreover, the *ustanovka* toward an oral delivery highlighted several other features of the ode. The intonational line aimed at the richest possible changes in vocal height, and the stanzaic

63. *Roman Jakobson's Approach to Language: Phenomenological Structuralism* (Bloomington, Ind., 1976), pp. 119–20.

structure was subordinated to this aim. Copious sound repetitions in euphonic and onomatopoetic constructions also forced the phonic aspect into prominence. And the "oratorical" ode achieved a semanticization of sound. Not only phonemes but meters were linked to particular meanings. In addition to accentuating the sound level, the *ustanovka* toward an oral delivery made possible the use of gestures as rhetorical means. These became semanticized through a secondary code of what Tynjanov called the "gestural illustrations" of odes.[64] Sometimes these "illustrations" actually became the main vehicle of meaning: words turned into stimuli for specific gestures. Finally, the imagery of Lomonosov's odes was also geared toward emotive persuasion. Here combinations of semantically distant words (motivated often by sound) resulted in a change in the habitual meaning of these words, in a semantic shift capable of affecting the listener's emotions.

By the end of the eighteenth century the ode had become automatized. It began to be used in nonliterary ways, as a salutory speech or supplicatory verse, for example, so that it gradually became a fact of *byt*. This transformation, Tynjanov points out, did not affect the genre of the ode alone: the entire canon of high Classicism was becoming automatized. A new principle of construction arose, and a "small emotion, small form came to the fore."[65] In fact, the entire system of social intercourse changed. The new environment of *salons* cultivated the art of conversation, a discourse light and personal, playful and sociable. The *ustanovka* of the literary system rendered many of the forms of social intercourse literary. Especially important among them, Tynjanov claims, was the epistolary form in which the new Sentimentalist principle of construction found its optimal implementation. "Implicit meaning, fragmentariness, the small 'household' form of the letter, all of this motivated the introduction of trifling subject matter and devices in contrast to the

64. "Oda kak oratorskij žanr," p. 61.
65. "Literaturnyj fakt," p. 21.

'grandiose' devices of the eighteenth century." From a fact of *byt,* the letter became an important literary genre. Karamzin's *Letters of a Russian Traveler* (1791) marked a new stage in the history of Russian prose and even the subsequent generation of Romanticists paid close attention to the epistolary form. Only in the course of further development did the letter revert to what it is today—a fact of *byt.*[66]

This example, I believe, provides some basis for terming literary *ustanovka* a directive correlation. It locates the cause of literary change not in a teleological subject but in the dynamic interaction among systems. "It is clear," Tynjanov wrote of the vicissitudes of literary history, "that what matters here are not individual psychic conditions, but objective ones, the evolution of the functions of the literary series in relation to the most immediate social series."[67] It is also possible to argue that in some of its aspects *ustanovka* is not, properly speaking, a directive correlation. The interaction between literature and the "most immediate social series" that it describes is somewhat one-sided. Tynjanov was spiritually still too close to Formalism to be able to abandon a belief in the autonomy of literature. He saw literary development as determined mainly by the internal conditions of the literary system and regarded the extraliterary context as secondary, merely complementing the internal developmental causes by providing literature with speech constructions fitting the needs of the de-automatizing principle of construction.

The concept of *ustanovka* appears to be perched somewhere between the theoretical frame of Formalist poetics and post-Formalist tenets. By rescuing literature from the social vacuum into which it was placed by Formalism, *ustanovka* clearly points beyond this literary-theoretical school of thought. By not providing any avenue for the active involvement of social systems in literary development, however, *ustanovka* remains rooted in the Formalist postulate of autonomous literature.

66. Ibid, pp. 21–23.
67. "O literaturnoj èvoljucii," p. 45.

That the concept of *ustanovka* was pointing toward the future is obvious from the nine-point thesis that Tynjanov wrote with Jakobson in 1928, quoted earlier. Only here was the literary system fully incorporated into the overall cultural system of systems and literary evolution conceived in terms of a directive correlation between these two systems. As the penultimate point of this interesting document states:

> The discovery of the immanent laws of literature (language) permits us to characterize every concrete change in literary (linguistic) systems but does not permit us either to explain the tempo of evolution or to determine the actual selection among several theoretically possible evolutionary paths. This is because the immanent laws of literary (linguistic) evolution are indefinite equations which, while limiting the number of solutions, do not necessarily leave only a single one. Which pathway or at least which dominant is chosen can be determined only through an analysis of the correlation among the literary and other historical series. This correlation (the system of systems) has its own structural laws which should be studied.[68]

The Tynjanov-Jakobson theses occupy a crucial position in the history of Slavic poetics. The fruit of a collaboration between a leading Formalist, who had earlier lectured before the Prague Linguistic Circle, and the Circle's vice-chairman, it represents a definite point of contact between Formalism and what later became known as Structuralism. The theses' boldly charted design transcends the Formalist mode of inquiry, yet there was no opportunity for the Formalists to apply them to concrete literary material. They served as a springboard for the earliest Structuralist literary-historical studies, which aimed at demonstrating that literary development cannot be studied in isolation from the overall development of society.[69]

Tynjanov's effort to eliminate the psychological subject from literary studies, to describe literary process in terms of objective,

---

68. "Problemy izučenija literatury i jazyka," p. 37.
69. Cf. for example, Mukařovský's study "Polákova *Vznešenost přírody:* Pokus o rozbor a vývojové zařadění básnické struktury," *Sborník filologický* 10 (1934), 1–68.

intersystemic mutations, is to a large extent a child of its time. As I indicated earlier, all the Formalists, regardless of the theoretical model to which they subscribed, argued vehemently against psychologism and subjectivism in literary study. The systemic model in general followed this pattern. It is true that Tynjanov included the subject (especially the author) among his theoretical topics, but by "de-psychologizing" and "de-subjectivizing" him, Tynjanov ended by fusing the subject with the literary system. The subject served the system in two capacities: first, as an unconscious generator of the varied principles of construction needed by the system for its constant rejuvenation; and second, as the system's vehicle of literary sensibility signaling the automatization of the dominant principle of construction and thus triggering its replacement by a contrasting principle. In each case the subject is completely subordinate to the system. What matters in literary process are not a subject's volitions, feelings, or actions but the internal conditions of the impersonal, self-regulating system.

Tynjanov's concept of the author was influenced by Tomaševskij, probably the first among the Formalists to succeed in separating the authorial subject—for Tomaševskij a legitimate object of literary study—from the author as a concrete psychophysical being, whose locus is outside of literature. Tomaševskij treats the concept of the author from a dual perspective: the production and the reception of the literary text. The reader's "struggle to comprehend the creative unity in a poet's works naturally entails an interest in the writer as a kind of concrete unity. Thus, the reader is not satisfied with comprehending the abstract unity of poetic works. This unity must be embodied, named, recognized. The life of the poet is the frame which conveniently and simply fits his creation." Such a conflation of *Wahrheit* and *Dichtung*, of an individual and a style, is, in Tomaševskij's opinion, one source of the conceptual confusion in which "poetic individuality is comprehended as personal individuality" and the "key to artistic unity is sought in the unity of a personality."[70]

70. Tomaševskij, *Puškin: Sovremennye problemy istoriko-literaturnogo izučenija* (Leningrad, 1925), pp. 56–57.

This confusion, however, can be introduced into the perception of the text deliberately by its author, who in one way or another establishes a link between his or her work and life. From the standpoint of literary production, Tomaševskij distinguished between two types of authors: those *with* a biography and those *without* one. It is the former who contribute to the confusion, for their texts acquire specific meanings and significance in connection with their author's biography. Tomaševskij sees Voltaire as the first author with a biography in the history of modern literature. "Voltaire's works were inseparably linked to his life. He was not only read; he was sought by pilgrims. The admirers of his oeuvre were also worshipers of his personality; the opponents of his works, his personal enemies. Voltaire's personality unified his oeuvre. His works are not the first thing that comes to mind when his name is mentioned. Even today when most of his tragedies and poems are completely forgotten, the image of Voltaire is still alive and these forgotten works still shine by the reflected light of his unforgettable biography."[71]

This distinction between the two types of authors does not mean that the literary critic should study an author as a concrete psychophysical individual. On the contrary, Tomaševskij's article specifically argues against this approach. For him the term "biography" has two senses. In one sense, it is a documentary narrative produced by traditional literary criticism, a collection of facts from the poet's private and public life. Tomaševskij claims that this kind of biography has very little to do with literary studies. "As far as 'documentary' biographies are concerned, they all fall into the sphere of the history of culture on a par with the biographies of generals and inventors. For literature and its history they are mere external, though necessary, sources of reference and auxiliary material."[72]

What *is* integral to literary studies is what Tomaševskij calls the artistic, "legendary" biography. It differs from the "docu-

71. "Literatura i biografija," *Kniga i revoljucija*, no. 4 (28) (1923), 6.
72. Ibid., p. 9.

mentary" biography in that it is not generated by literary critics but by writers themselves conscious of the fact that "their lives will be the permanent screen against which their works will be projected." Such reflexiveness affects authors in two ways. It "forces them, on the one hand, to stage the epic motifs in their lives, and on the other hand, to create for themselves an artistic biography—a legend with a well-calculated selection of real and fabricated events."[73] Despite the fact that in this type of biography it is impossible to demarcate with any precision where *Dichtung* ends and *Wahrheit* begins, or perhaps because of it, Tomaševskij finds the artistic biography proper to the sphere of literary studies. "This is because these biographic legends are literary interpretations of the poet's life, interpretations which are essential as the perceptible background of a literary work, as a premise taken into account by the author when he created his works."[74] In other words, the artistic biography presents us not with the author as a concrete psychophysical subject but with the authorial subject, that is, the author's image refracted through the literary medium.

Furthermore, the artistic biography is a literary matter because both the existence of "authors with biographies" and the contents of these biographies are conditioned by the literary conventions of a period. In Russian literature of the mid-nineteenth century, for instance, after a proliferation of authors with biographies in the Romantic period, "authors without biographies" became the norm. As Tomaševskij put it, "the poet-hero was replaced by the poet-professional, the entrepreneur. The writer wrote, sent his manuscripts to the printer, and did not permit any views into his private life." By the same logic, if there is a period of "authors with biographies" these biographies exhibit the characteristics demanded by the period's literary conventions. Describing a collection of biographies of fashionable belletrists of the turn of the century, Tomaševskij wrote: "They

73. Ibid., pp. 6–7.
74. Ibid., p. 8.

all scream over one another that they have not studied anything because they were kicked out of high schools and technical schools, that they have nothing but a pair of torn pants and a couple of buttons, and that all this is because they do not give a bloody damn."[75] Such examples illustrate how tenuously the artistic biography is linked with the "real" author. What emerges from it instead is the authorial subject—a figure whose birthplace and domicile are purely literary.

Tynjanov found Tomaševskij's concept of biography congenial for a simple reason. It softened the rigid Formalist opposition of literature to author, while at the same time, by separating the literary from the nonliterary side of the author, it preserved the Formalist belief in the autonomy of literature. Despite the fact that several of Tomaševskij's points turn up in Tynjanov, the latter approached the problem of the literary author from a different perspective, through the category of the proper name. It is the author's proper name, Tynjanov believed, that is primarily responsible for the confusion between literature and *byt*. The name simultaneously denotes an individual tangential to the literary system and entities as essentially connected to this system as texts, literary schools, genres, or periods.

Tynjanov's interest in the proper name was probably motivated by its importance in philosophical discussions of the late nineteenth and early twentieth centuries, discussed in the first chapter. In the argument between those who maintained that the proper name is a senseless mark and those who insisted that it a shorthand description, Tynjanov sided with the descriptivist camp. This position fit well with his overall relational outlook, in which the identity of phenomena is a function of their context. The descriptivist view also conformed to the peculiar status of proper names in literature, which of course was Tynjanov's central concern. As soon as we designate someone a literary author, we place that individual in a special context. He or she becomes a component of a literary process and the person's identity be-

75. Ibid.

comes circumscribed through the texts, genres, or periods with which he or she is associated. For example, the names of Puškin, Dostoevskij, or Tolstoj denote only indirectly the individuals Messrs. Puškin, Tolstoj, or Dostoevskij. Instead they refer to purely literary entities, particular stylistic features, sets of texts, and so on.

The peculiar status of the author's name is especially palpable in the reception of literary works. Here the name serves as a kind of bridge where impulses coming from the text meet with extratextual information. On the one hand, the name might arise from the text itself as the label of its stylistic individuality: "There are stylistic phenomena which lead to the person of the author . . . the particular vocabulary, syntax, and especially the intonational outline of the phrase; all of this more or less alludes to the ungraspable and yet at the same time concrete features of the narrator. . . . the *name* is the last limit of this stylistic person's literary concreteness."[76]

The name, on the other hand, is also attached to the text from the outside, and through its connotations it introduces specific information and expectations into the reading of the text. The case of the pseudonym is especially telling. "Taken in its extra-literary aspect," argued Tynjanov, "a pseudonym is a phe-nomenon of the same order as an anonym."[77] Its purport in literature, however, is completely different. "When a nine-teenth-century writer signed an article 'An Inhabitant of New Village' instead of using his name, he obviously did not wish to convey to the reader that he lived in New Village, because the reader does not have to know this at all. But precisely as a result of this 'purposelessness' the name acquires different features— the reader selects from the concepts [in the pseudonym] only what is *characteristic*, only what in some way suggests a character for the author, and applies these to the features that arise from the style, the peculiarities of the narrative [*skaz*], or the preexist-

76. "Literaturnyj fakt," pp. 26–27.
77. Ibid., p. 28.

ing stock of similar names. Thus, New Village is for him the 'frontier,' and the author of the article a 'recluse.'"[78]

According to Tynjanov, real proper names affect our reading of a literary text in the same manner as pseudonyms. The only difference is that the connotations of proper names are not derived directly from the words that make up the name but from the literary reputation of their bearers. Tynjanov uses Tomaševskij's concept of biography to clarify the notion of literary reputation in terms of Tomaševskij's "author's artistic biography"—the blend of real events, hearsay, and outright fabrication that constitutes the image of an author. This image carries the same proper name as the psychophysical individual existing behind it, but this is merely a case of homonymity and should not suggest that the two entities are identical. Tynjanov differentiates between the "author's individuality"—a set of personal characteristics irrelevant from a purely literary viewpoint—and "literary individuality"—a set of features representing the author in the reader's mind. Though there is always some partial overlap between the two, students of literature should keep them distinct in their minds. The structure of "literary individuality" is ultimately a function of the literary system, whereas the author's individuality is accidental from the standpoint of this system.

A careful differentiation between the author's individuality and literary individuality is necessary in the study not only of the reception but of the production of literary works. As Tynjanov wrote, "it is very common today to substitute the problem of the 'author's individuality' for the problem of 'literary individuality.' The problem of the psychological genesis of every phenomenon is thus substituted for the problem of evolution and literary change, with the suggestion that instead of literature we should study the 'creator's personality.'" Tynjanov points out the fallacy in this view using a parallel from social history. "To speak of the creator's personal psychology and to see in it the source of the originality of a phenomenon and its significance for literary

78. Ibid., p. 27.

evolution is like claiming in an interpretation of the origin and significance of the Russian Revolution that it happened because of the personal idiosyncrasies of the leaders of the fighting parties."[79]

The regularity of literary production can be studied only within its actual context, which is provided, Tynjanov believed, by the state of the literary system. Within this context, an author's individuality figures only as an accident. It is a conglomerate of haphazard activities in which some might become relevant for literature but only if required by the developmental needs of the system. All the author's intentions, originality, and so on play no role in literary change. The new "principle of construction" always "arises on the basis of 'fortuitous' results and 'fortuitous' deviations, mistakes," not because it was planned.[80] From the systemic point of view the authorial subject's role in literary production can be studied only within the framework of "literary individuality." This individuality, however, is a transformation of the "author's individuality." It is a configuration, a selection of certain of the subject's actions which became enmeshed in the history of the literary system. Here too the same name stands for both "individualities" but again this is not a sufficient reason to conflate them.

In addition to the author, of course, another subject participates in the literary process—the reader. Although the systemic Formalists at least paid lip service to the authorial subject, the perceiving subject was virtually ignored. Tynjanov discussed the reader in two contexts. In his discussion of verse language he employed several basic categories pertaining to the reader's consciousness, such as retention and protention, successivity and simultaneity, or mental attitude.[81] Tynjanov's goal was not the "phenomenology of reading" but the nature of poetic rhythm. Therefore, he did not treat these categories in a systemic fashion; they served him rather as heuristic devices to demarcate

79. Ibid., pp. 12–13.
80. Ibid., p. 18.
81. *Problema stichotvornogo jazyka,* esp. pp. 28–45.

verse language from prose. Tynjanov also includes the reader in his studies of literary change, as an accessory to the literary system, or more precisely, as the very self-consciousness of this system that prompts it to seek a new principle of construction.

In harmony with the overall thrust of systemic Formalism in both of these instances, the reader is purged of all possible subjectivity and accidentality. Readers are first reduced to the intersubjective basis of human consciousness. In the service of the system, moreover, they are as much present at the birth of a literary work as are the authors, and the readers' acceptance or rejection of the work as literary is an externalization of the current state of the literary system. At the time the work is produced there seems to be no doubt as to its literariness—"every contemporary can point his finger at what is a *literary fact*."[82] Yet at the moment the readers cease to be a part of the context from which the work arose, Tynjanov loses interest in them. Now chance prevails and the reading turns into a "misreading." "It is not true," Tynjanov argued, "that works cannot live 'through the centuries.' Automatized objects can be used. Each epoch focuses on certain phenomena of the past which are akin to it and forgets the others. But these cases are, of course, secondary phenomena, new work on old material. The historical Puškin differs from the Puškin of the Symbolists, but the latter is incompatible with the evolutionary significance of Puškin in Russian literature."[83]

How incompatible the study of literary reception was with systemic Formalism can best be illustrated by Tynjanov's 1929 article "On Parody." There he attempts to rebut Žirmunskij's charge that Tynjanov's neo-Formalism aims at replacing "historical poetics with the history of criticism and readers' tastes."[84] "It is utterly impossible to separate the author of literature from the reader because they are essentially the same. The writer is a reader too, and the reader carries on the writer's job of con-

---

82. "Literaturnyj fakt," p. 9.
83. Ibid., p. 12.
84. Žirmunskij, "Vokrug *Poètiki* Opojaza," p. 356.

structing the literary work. This contrasting of reader and writer is furthermore incorrect because there are different readers and writers. The writer of one cultural and social system is closer to the reader of the same system than to the writer of a different system. The issue of 'reader reception' arises only if it is approached from a subjectivist-psychologistic standpoint, and not if it is studied systemo-functionally."[85] In other words, for a systemic Formalist, the only legitimate object of literary studies is the self-regulating literary system. The perceiving subject is either treated as an appendix of this impersonal system or ignored.

85. Tynjanov, "O parodii," pp. 294–95.

3

A Synecdoche

The three metaphors of Russian Formalist theory, decisive as they were in their proponents' thinking, still do not account for perhaps the most fundamental Formalist conception: the notion of language as the material of poetry. "Insofar as the material of poetry is the word," Žirmunskij wrote, "the classification of verbal phenomena provided by linguistics should be the basis for a systematically constructed poetics. Because the artistic goal transforms each of these phenomena into a poetic device, every chapter of theoretical poetics should correspond to a chapter from the science of language."[1] Language thus generated a fourth Formalist model. But the trope underlying it was not a metaphor, as in the cases of the mechanistic, morphological, and systemic models. These posited a similarity between the literary work and a machine, organism, and hierarchical system, respectively, but the model described by Žirmunskij is a synecdoche, a *pars pro toto* relationship. It substitutes language—the material of verbal art—for art itself, and linguistics—the science of language—for literary studies.

The linguistic model, as this theoretical synecdoche might be termed, has its roots in the early Formalist preoccupation with

1. "Zadači poètiki," *Voprosy teorii literatury: Stat'i 1916–1926* (Leningrad, 1928), p. 39.

"poetic language." The importance of this notion for the entire Formalist enterprise cannot be overstated. Pavel Medvedev, a Marxist critic of the movement, quite correctly claimed that the "hypothesis of the distinctness of poetic language is the basis upon which the entire Russian Formalist method is built."[2] The Formalists themselves were aware of the privileged status of this concept. Indignant at the label of "Formalism" foisted upon them, these young literary scholars proudly presented themselves as students of poetic language and even as linguists. The names of their two original groups, the Society for the Study of Poetic Language and the Moscow Linguistic Circle, and the title of their first two collective publications, *Studies in the Theory of Poetic Language*, clearly indicate the image they strove to project at the inception of the movement.[3]

The acceptance of any concept among the whole Formalist membership was never a simple matter and "poetic language" was no exception. Because of the inherent heterogeneity of the movement and the fluidity of its concepts over time, the Formalists never reached a general definition of either poetic language or the linguistic frame of reference for its description. Moreover, as Formalist theorizing unfolded, the fortunes of the linguistic model in general and the notion of poetic language in particular fluctuated widely. OPOJAZ's initial infatuation with the two gave way to a sharp backlash in the early twenties. But just as the stock of the linguistic model was dipping in Petersburg, it was rising in Moscow. Obviously, the idea of a single theoretical synecdoche in Russian Formalism is an oversimplification. In fact, this fourth model encompasses several distinct theories, each of which treated literature as the art of language and used methods borrowed from linguistics. In the discussion that follows, I shall attempt to describe some of the most important currents among them.

2. *Formal'nyj metod v literaturovedenii: Kritičeskoe vvedenie v sociologičeskuju poètiku* (Leningrad, 1928), p. 111.

3. *Sborniki po teorii poètičeskogo jazyka* 1 (1916); 2 (1917) (both published in St. Petersburg).

Zaum'

The meaningless pursuit of *meaning* by our writers is quite astonishing.

Wishing to portray the incomprehensibility, the illogicality of life and its terror or mystery, they resort (as ever, as always!) to "clear, precise" common language. [. . .]

We were the first to say that for portraying the new and the future *completely new words and new combinations* are necessary.

This striking newness will come through the combination of words according to their own immanent laws revealed to the poet and not according to the rules of logic or grammar, as has been the case before us.

—ALEKSEJ KRUČĔNYCH,
"The New Paths of the Word"

"Poetic language" was already a loaded term by the time it entered Formalist discourse. Aleksandr Potebnja (1835–1891), the heir to the tradition of Humboldtian linguistics, was the first to introduce the distinction between poetic and prosaic language into Russian philology.[4] The Formalists' attitude toward their

4. Cf., for example, L. Jakubinskij, "O dialogičeskoj reči," *Russkaja reč': Sborniki statej*, vol. 1, ed. L. V. Ščerba (Petersburg, 1923), pp. 113–14; Victor Erlich, *Russian Formalism: History—Doctrine*, 3d ed. (The Hague, 1965), pp. 23–26; or W.-D. Stempel, "Zur formalistischen Theorie der poetischen Sprache," *Texte der russischen Formalisten*, vol. 2, ed. W.-D. Stempel (Munich, 1972), p. xiv.

"precursor" was rather ambivalent, however. Their willingness to borrow from him implied a respect extended to no other nineteenth-century Russian philologist but Veselovskij. Still they criticized Potebnja's work violently in order to differentiate themselves from him, and especially from his numerous epigones. The Symbolist literary critic D. Filosofov, the first reviewer of OPOJAZ's 1916 collective publication, described this dialectic relationship: "All the contributors to this new collection are in a sense Potebnja's pupils. They know him by heart; they live off the late scholar's ideas. But they are not arrested in them. They reexamine the mysterious correlations of sound and representation and in doing so they focus their entire attention on sound. But in the end they make clear that sound, even 'nonarticulated' sound, generates representation. They speak of the magic of sound, the magic of words."[5]

The Formalist departure from Potebnja should not be viewed merely as a struggle for recognition. Though a powerful and prolific thinker, Potebnja was often more suggestive than clear, and in his elaborate handling of topics he often multiplied the definitions of even his most cherished concepts. The opposition between prosaic and poetic language is a case in point. Sometimes it is presented as a simple formal dichotomy between prose and poetry, and at others, as a psychological antinomy between prosaic and poetic thought. In the latter case, the presence of a mental image is the essential feature of the poetic, and "poetic thinking" is defined as "thinking in which the image is important."[6] When the distinction is made on formal grounds, the differential feature is a matter of function; prose is thus "language oriented solely toward practical aims or serving as an expression of scholarship."[7]

Despite these inconsistencies, Potebnja's poetics did rest on certain basic assumptions. The word and/or poetic work consists of three parts: the outer form (the perceptible aspect), the

5. "Magija slov," *Reč'*, no. 265 (September 26, 1916), 3.
6. *Iz zapisok po teorii slovesnosti* (Char'kov, 1905), p. 98.
7. Ibid., p. 102.

meaning (the intelligible aspect), and the inner form or representation (the tropological link between the two). The crucial member of this triad is inner form, a notion heavily dependent upon certain ideas from psychology. In agreement with the atomistic theory of association so popular in his time, Potebnja treated mental life as an aggregate of simple sensory elements. For him, the perceptual identity of an object (what he termed its "image") was guaranteed by the persistence of a simple characteristic through whatever contextual modification the object undergoes. Language follows this model when a distinctive characteristic motivates an object's designation, that is, when the object is named according to this feature. But though thought and language coincide here, this is not a case of inner form proper. Only a single sensory image has provided the link between the outer form and meaning, whereas the inner form is an umbrella for a multitude of such images; in Potebnja's words, "it is not an image of an object but an image of an image, that is, a representation."[8]

As a metaconcept, inner form is endowed with the power that a single image lacks: it links outer forms and meanings that were originally connected to diverse sensory images. In this respect, the inner form of language is the crossroads of the old and the new. As the "nearest etymological meaning of a word," it stands for the linguistic past, but as the *tertium comparationis* that generates the figurative transformations of a word, it is the agent of the future.[9] Because of this creative potential, the inner linguistic form became the central category of Potebnja's poetics. Without denying salience to the other two components of the word, Potebnja found the *eidos* of poetic language in its polysemy, the capacity of its inner form to evoke multiple meanings. Stated in quasi-mathematical terms, "the general formula of poetry (or art) is: 'A (image) < X (meaning)'; that is, there is always an inequality between image and meaning because A is smaller

8. *Mysl' i jazyk*, 3d ed. (Char'kov, 1913), p. 117.
9. Ibid., p. 146.

than X. To establish an equality between A and X would destroy poeticity; i.e., it would either turn the image into a prosaic signification of a particular phenomenon devoid of relation to anything else or it would turn the image into a scientific fact and the meaning into a law."[10]

The Formalist redefinition of poetic language represents a considerable departure from Potebnja's basic position. This departure, however, was not solely motivated by theoretical concerns but also by the current poetic practice. Some of the early Formalists entered the Russian intellectual scene not as disinterested observers or commentators, but as proponents and interpreters of Futurism, the most flamboyant artistic movement of their generation. The rise of Futurism in the early teens was directly linked to the decline of another movement that had dominated Russian letters for nearly two decades—Symbolism. The great poet-theoreticians of this movement had exploited Potebnja's philology as the theoretical springboard for their own poetics. In Roman Jakobson's words, "the Symbolists canonized Potebnja."[11] Thus, the Futurist onslaught against Symbolism involved at the same time a "de-canonization" of Potebnja, a search for new theoretical foundations upon which to construct their poetics.

Of the various groups in Russia calling themselves Furturists, the most iconoclastic was known as Hylaea, and it was with this group that the Formalists were most closely allied, both personally and in terms of a shared artistic sensibility. Hylaea's membership included the Burljuk brothers, Chlebnikov, Kručënych, and Majakovskij. In the unceasing stream of public appearances, manifestos, and joint publications, all orchestrated to *épater les bourgeois*, the Hylaeans declared the art of the past dead and presented themselves as the only true champions of the artistic future. Their incompatibility with Potebnja's system is obvious at first glance. Disdaining the cognitive function of art ("thinking

10. *Iz zapisok,* p. 100.
11. "Brjusovskaja stichologija i nauka o stiche," in Akademičeskij cèntr Narkomprosa, *Naučnye izvestija* 2 (1922), 223.

in images"), the Futurists insisted on the shock effect. Artworks, according to Chlebnikov and Kručënych, ought to be "as if written with difficulty and read with difficulty, less comfortable than blacked boots or a truck in a sitting room," their language "resembling if anything a saw or a savage's poisoned arrow."[12] Against the historicism of Potebnja's poetic word (that is, its etymological meaning), the Hylaeans' manifesto, "A Slap in the Face of Public Taste," proclaimed the poet's right to an "insuperable hatred for the language that existed before him."[13] They ridiculed the entire psychologistic bias of the previous poetics. Poetry, they insisted, is not a mirror of the soul but "the unfolding of the word as such." Or in more epigrammatic form, "The work of art is the art of the word."[14]

This conception of verbal art was obviously reflected in the earliest, mechanistic model. Key notions such as de-familiarization or the absolute split between art and *byt* are direct projections of Futurist poetics onto Formalist literary theory. The notion of poetic language was most profoundly influenced by the Futurist concept of *zaum'*. Coined by Kručënych, the term designated a special tongue that defied the rules of common sense: transrational language. *Zaum'* attacked the very heart of Potebnja's aesthetic system—the identification of poeticity with the inner form of language, since this "ultimate" language of verbal art was without inner form. Its two main exponents among the Hylaeans, Kručënych and Chlebnikov, disagreed about which of the remaining parts of the verbal parcel—outer form or meaning—was instrumental in *zaum'*. As Vladimir Markov has observed, "for Kručënych [*zaum'*] was a free, but often emotionally expressive, combination of sound, devoid of full meaning; for Chlebnikov, it was basic meaning expressed in the purest and most direct way."[15]

---

12. *Slovo kak takovoe*, repr. in *Manifesty i programmy russkich futuristov*, ed. V. Markov (Munich, 1967), pp. 53 and 56.
13. "Poščečina obščestvennomu vkusu," repr. in ibid., p. 51.
14. A. Kručënych and V. Chlebnikov, a draft of *Slovo kak takovoe*, repr. in ibid., p. 59.
15. *Russian Futurism: A History* (Berkeley, Calif., 1968), p. 303.

If, as in traditional aesthetic discourse, the term Formalism applies to theories asserting the primacy of artistic form over content, Kručënych's *zaum'* would seem to be distinctly Formalist. "A new content," he proclaimed, "*is born only* when new expressive devices, new forms, are achieved. Once there is a new form, the new content follows. Thus, the form determines the content."[16] Consequently, it was not the ideas or things presented by the literary work that were important, but the mechanism of this presentation itself. Because this mechanism is above all linguistic, Kručënych spoke of two types of language: rational *common language* governed by extralinguistic requirements, a vehicle of meaning; and self-sufficient *transrational language* governed by its own rules, "whose words do not have a definite meaning."[17]

This indefiniteness of meaning in *zaum'* is quite different from Potebnja's poetic polysemy. The quantitative imbalance occurs not between the inner form of the word and its meaning, but between the meaning and the word as such, that is, its outer form. Moreover, transrational language reverses the ratio of Potebnja's formula: in *zaum'* sound always is greater than meaning. Kručënych wrote, "We declared in art: THE WORD IS BROADER THAN ITS MEANING. The word (and the sounds composing it) is not merely curtailed thought, not merely logic, but above all the transrational (its mystical and aesthetic components)."[18] Hence, transrational language is literally language that goes beyond reason, that addresses the nonrational human faculties. To achieve this objective, the poet is free to dissolve language into elements that lack any logical meaning, or to combine these elements into nonsensical neologisms. The poet can also emulate the types of *zaum'* existing outside verbal art. One especially favored by Kručënych was the glossolalia of religious sectarians speaking the "language of the holy spirit." There was

16. "Novye puti slova," repr. in *Manifesty i programmy*, p. 72.
17. *Pomada*, repr. in A. E. Kručënych, *Izbrannoe* (Munich, 1973), p. 55.
18. "Novye puti slova," p. 66.

also children's language[19] or the sound patterns of foreign languages unknown to the poet.[20]

If Kručënych's *zaum'* privileged the outer form of the word, Chlebnikov's privileged the meaning. To those familiar with the impenetrable hermeticism of Chlebnikov's texts, this might come as a surprise. But understanding was never an issue for him. "Verses," he wrote, "may be comprehensible or incomprehensible, but they ought to be good, ought to be truthful [*istovennyj*]."[21] To be transrational for Chlebnikov meant to go beyond ordinary reason, but only to express the higher reason that he believed language inevitably embodied. Potebnja's notion of inner form was thus suspect, for it posited merely a figurative link between sound and meaning. Chlebnikov's *zaum'*, in contrast, was a quest for the direct, unmediated meaning of sound.

In his study of Chlebnikovian *zaum'*, Ronald Vroon has identified four such linguistic structures: the languages of the "stars," "Gods," and "birds," and "sound-painting." He maintains that each of these tackles the issue of pure meaning in a different way.[22] For instance, the "language of the stars"—Chlebnikov's favorite—is based on the same kind of argument for the natural origin of names that Plato credits to Cratylus. It assigns a distinct spatiogeometric meaning to virtually all Russian consonants. This *zaum'*, Chlebnikov believed, was not an arbitrary construction but a faithful reconstruction of the original language of mankind, of which our present-day tongues are mere shadows.

In rough terms, the rift between Kručënych and Chlebnikov over *zaum'* corresponds to the conflicting theories of poetic language in the Formalist movement. OPOJAZ's early concern for poetic sound and its emotive qualities betrays Kručënych's influ-

19. According to the title page and a note inside, Kručënych's 1913 collection *Piglets (Porosjata)* was coauthored by an eleven-year-old, Zina V.

20. Another 1913 collection of Kručënych's works, *Explodity (Vzorval')*, contains three poems written in "Japanese," "Spanish," and "Hebrew."

21. "O stichach," *Sobranie proizvedenij*, vol. 5 (Leningrad, 1933), p. 226.

22. *Velimir Xlebnikov's Shorter Poems: A Key to the Coinages* (photocopy, Ann Arbor, Mich., University Microfilms International, 1978), esp. pp. 30–34 and 266–99.

ence, whereas the Moscow Linguistic Circle's insistence on the meaningfulness of linguistic sound reflects the logocentrism of Chlebnikov's *zaum'*. We shall now look more closely at the earlier of these two tendencies, those of OPOJAZ. In 1916, Viktor Šklovskij undertook the first direct critique of Potebnja's poetics. "Imagery, or symbolism," he insisted, "is not what differentiates poetic from prosaic language. Poetic language differs from prosaic language in the perceptibility of its structure."[23] Šklovskij's strategy here is quite obvious: he is revising Potebnja's dichotomy between poetic and prosaic language according to the specifications of his mechanistic model. The special perceptibility of poetic language drains our mental energy and de-familiarizes our perception of language in general. This essential feature of poetic language is explained by its artistic *telos*. "If we study poetic speech . . . we encounter the same symptom of the artistic everywhere: that it was created intentionally to de-automatize perception and that the author's goal was to call attention to this; that it was made 'artificially' in such a way that perception lingers over it, thus reaching its greatest possible intensity and duration." The direct opposite of this "hampered and tortuous" speech is automatized prosaic language. "Prose is normal speech: economical, easy, regular (the *dea prorsa* is the goddess of regular, uncomplicated delivery)."[24]

It is significant that while Šklovskij's treatment of poetic language rejects Potebnja's, it retains his fundamental dichotomy of poetic and prosaic language. Here we witness yet another example of the peculiar contradiction in the mechanistic model mentioned earlier; namely, its propensity for merging the most radical stance with a traditional conceptual framework. This marriage of the old and the new tends to generate problems. The opposition between poetry and prose would appear to coincide with Šklovskij's distinction between art and *byt*. But if this were the case, poetic speech, with its patent goal of de-familiarization,

23. "Potebnja," *Poètika: Sborniki po teorii poètičeskogo jazyka* (Petersburg, 1919), p. 4.
24. "Iskusstvo, kak priëm," ibid., pp. 112–13.

would be the only discourse to use language purposively, and prosaic speech, as a phenomenon of *byt*, would be governed purely by causality. As Šklovskij himself showed, "economical, easy, and regular" speech might also be used for the sake of defamiliarization. This is the case of artistic prose that renders extraliterary reality strange in the process of its verbal representation. In this way, one is forced to speak of not two but three types of language: the poetic, which makes strange our perception of language itself, the prosaic-artistic, which does the same to the perception of reality, and the prosaic proper, that is, normal everyday language. Yet according to the logic of Šklovskij's model, the first two types are clearly different from the third. Whereas the two differ in what they de-familiarize, they are united through their common artistic goal. Normal everyday language, in contrast, belongs to *byt*. This fact, however, is completely lost in the simple opposition of prose and poetry that Šklovskij inherited from Potebnja. Thus, it was necessary to readjust Potebnja's original opposition in such a way that the line between literature and nonliterature would be drawn more clearly.

This task was performed by another OPOJAZ member, the linguist Lev Jakubinskij, who was responsible for introducing the distinction between poetic and practical language into literary theory. In linguistics, Jakubinskij argued, the opposition between the teleological and the causal can be suspended, because every utterance, whether poetic or not, pursues some objective. From this perspective, language can be conceptualized as a means–end structure serving particular goals. This view of language is similar to the functional classification of linguistic sounds advanced by the Kazan' School to which Jakubinskij's teacher, Baudoin de Courtenay (1845–1929), belonged.[25] It is also parallel to the thesis propounded by Franz Brentano's fol-

---

25. Cf., for example, R. Jakobson, "The Kazan' School of Polish Linguistics and Its Place in the International Development of Phonology," *Selected Writings*, vol. 2 (The Hague, 1971), p. 399; and "Efforts toward a Means–Ends Model of Language in Interwar Continental Linguistics," ibid., p. 524.

lower, the philosopher Anton Marty (1847–1914), concerning the teleological origin of language as a means of human communication. Jakubinskij, however, avoided the psychologism of Marty's teleology, which treated intention in terms of a conscious subject. For Jakubinskij, it was not the subjective intentions of the speaker but the objective correlation of linguistic means and ends that distinguished poetic from practical language.

"Linguistic phenomena," Jakubinskij argued, "should be classified, among other ways, from the standpoint of the goal for which the speaker exploits the verbal material in a given case. If he uses it for the purely practical goal of communication, we are dealing with the system of *practical language,* in which linguistic representations (sounds, morphemes, etc.) have no value in themselves but serve merely as a *means* of communication. Other linguistic systems are conceivable (and exist) in which the practical goal retreats into the background and linguistic combinations acquire a *value in themselves.* . . . I conditionally call this system verse [*stichotvornyj*] language."[26]

Jakubinskij's distinction between language as a means of communication and language as a self-valuable end should remind us of Kručënych's distinction between common language and *zaum'.* This parallel becomes even more pronounced when Jakubinskij goes on to discuss the difference between practical and poetic language in terms of the opposition between sound and meaning. "In *practical* language the semantic aspect of the word (its meaning) is more prominent than its sound aspect. . . . details of pronunciation reach our consciousness only if they serve to differentiate the meaning of words. . . . Thus, various considerations compel us to recognize that *in practical language sounds*

26. "O zvukach stichotvornogo jazyka," *Poètika,* p. 37. It is important to stress that Jakubinskij himself conceived of "verse language" simply as a "special case of poetic language" ("Skoplenie odinakovych plavnych v praktičeskom i poètičeskom jazykach," ibid., p. 54). As I shall show later, this seemingly subtle difference developed into an important argument against the entire linguistic model.

do not attract our attention. It is the other way around in verse language. There, one can claim that sounds enter the bright field of consciousness and do attract our attention."[27]

This foregrounding of sound profoundly affects the structure of poetic language. Kručěnych's statement that *zaum'* combines words "according to their immanent laws . . . and not according to the rules of logic and grammar" is relevant. Jakubinskij too claims that poetic and practical language are demarcated by antithetical combinatory laws. He states that the liquid consonants (*r*, *l*) tend to cluster in poetic language, whereas in practical language they are almost always randomly dispersed. If in practical language adjacent syllables contain the same liquid, this consonant will either be dropped altogether in one of them or replaced by another liquid. For the "clustering of the same liquids *impedes* pronunciation (even causing stammering) and *violates the usual tempo of speech,* thus willy-nilly directing the attention of the speaker toward the phonic aspect of the utterance. . . . [It] violates the *automatism* which is so essential to practical language."[28] Poetic language, on the other hand, which aims at focusing attention on sounds themselves, not only tolerates the clustering of the same liquids but deliberately produces such clusters.

Jakubinskij's equation of poetic language with *zaum'* goes even further. In his 1921 essay, "Where Does Verse Come From?" he argues that the concern for the sound of an utterance to the neglect of its content links poetic language to other types of discourse that defy normal reason. For example, "first of all, [in] the *dream* . . . the association of words according to their sound may determine the dream content. Second, in *mental illness* some patients utter entire tirades that are relatively unconnected in their content (as they ought to be) yet obviously linked in their sound, and often in meter. Third, in states of *ecstasy,* for instance among religious sectarians," utterances often contain "sound

27. "O zvukach stichotvornogo jazyka," p. 38.
28. "Skoplenie odinakovych plavnych," p. 52.

repetition and meter."[29] In a rather startling move, Jakubinskij invoked Freud's authority to claim that verse as well as the other three kinds of abnormal language are in fact the first stage of infantile language emerging from the subconscious in moments of weakened rational control. Thus, he answers the question raised in the title of his article by claiming that "verse comes from infantile babble," providing a psychoanalytic explanation for Kručënych's transrational language.

Jakubinskij was not the only Formalist to conceive of poetic language as a particular manifestation of *zaum'*, though the others usually did not invoke a psychoanalytic frame of reference. Not surprisingly, Viktor Šklovskij was one of the most powerful voices advocating the exclusion of semantics from verbal art. "We must ask," he wrote, "whether words have meaning even in language that is not overtly transrational but simply poetic, or whether this belief is a mere fiction—the result of our inattentiveness."[30] In a speech to the Futurists at the Stray Dog, a Petersburg cabaret, Šklovskij spoke of transrational experiments in terms borrowed from Potebnja and the Symbolists. He compared *zaum'*, for example, to the foreign languages used in liturgical services. "The religious poetry of almost all nations was written in such a semiunderstandable language: Church Slavonic, Latin, Sumerian (which died out in the twentieth century B.C. but was used as a religious language until the third century), and the German of the Russian Pietists [*štundisty*]."[31] Later Šklovskij dropped such "metaphysical" explanations and preferred to speak instead of the "sweetness of verse on our lips," the de-automatized movement of our speech organs producing unusual phonic patterns.[32] "Maybe," he mused, "the greatest part of the pleasure caused by poetry lies in its articulatory aspect, in the peculiar dance of the speech organs."[33]

29. "Otkuda berutsja stichi," *Knižnyj ugol* no. 7 (1921), 23.
30. "O poèzii i zaumnom jazyke," *Poètika*, p. 25.
31. This speech was published separately in 1914 as *The Resurrection of the Word*; see *Voskrešenie slova*, repr. in *Texte der russischen Formalisten*, vol. 2, p. 14.
32. *Literatura i kinematograf* (Berlin, 1923), p. 8.
33. "O poèzii i zaumnom jazyke," p. 24.

The metaphor of dance employed by Šklovskij is telling. Once poetic language is purged of meaning, verbal art can quite conveniently be described in terms of another nonthematic art. Music—the art of pure sound—is an obvious parallel; that is, if literature is nothing but a striking organization of phonic material, the poetic text is very much like a musical composition. Osip Brik, another contributor to the early OPOJAZ collections, declared that "poetic language is musical language" and attempted to describe a major principle of the phonic organization of verse that had so far escaped the attention of other investigators.[34]

Brik proceeded from the same assumption as Jakubinskij, namely, that poetic utterances are composed according to certain combinatory rules that are phonic in nature. For Jakubinskij, this was the clustering of liquids, but Brik went beyond this in two respects. First of all, he did not stop with liquids, but included all the consonants. Second and more important, he was not interested merely in isolated consonantal patterns but in the reiteration of these patterns throughout the poetic text. Traditional literary studies, according to Brik, merely paid lip service to the phonic aspect of poetic language and recorded only the most obvious cases of speech sound repetition: rhyme, assonance, alliteration, onomatopoeia. But these are merely an "obvious manifestation, a special case of fundamental euphonic laws," and there are other cases that follow these laws but remain unnoticed.[35] Brik's essay studied one of these—the recurrence of consonantal patterns—as it appeared, for example, in this Puškin line:

> *Vezuvij zev* otkryl . . .
> (Vesuvius opened its gorge)[36]

Brik termed this type of consonantal reiteration "sound repetition" and attempted not only to provide a typology of such repe-

---

34. "Zvukovye povtory: Analiz zvukovoj struktury sticha," ibid., p. 62.
35. Ibid., p. 60.
36. Ibid., p. 80.

titions but also to relate them to the overall outer form of the poetic text (verse, stanza, rhythm). Using literally hundreds of lines from Puškin and Lermontov Brik demonstrated that sound repetition permeates even the most canonical of Russian poetry.

Another contributor to the early OPOJAZ volumes, Boris Kušner, argued that the treatment of poetic language in terms of the other arts, for example, dance and music, is natural because their materials have something in common. They are temporal rather than spatial media. "But," Kušner warns, "despite their shared sound material, one can speak of verse music only metonymically. Here the term music no longer signifies a given art but the basic material of its works—sound."[37] This figure of speech is therefore not productive for poetics, Kušner argues, for musical and poetic sounds are incompatible phenomena. The former are tones (*tonirujuščie zvuki*), sounds correlated according to precise scales and intervals, whereas the latter are merely sonorous sounds (*sonirujuščie zvuki*) whose actual phonic values are largely arbitrary. Music and poetry can, however, be related metaphorically, through the similarity of their artistic forms, that is, the precisely calculated organization of sound material. These "sonorous chords"—the repetitions of particular sounds and their groups in a poetic work—are what Kušner sets out to study.

But how do Kušner's "sonorous chords" differ from Brik's "sound repetitions"? First of all, in the way they are described: Brik presents his repetitions as objective phonic structures, whereas Kušner is concerned with the constitution of the "chords" in the perceiver's consciousness. Second, Brik's treatment of the poetic sound stratum is quite atomistic: he deals with a couple of isolated lines each time. For Kušner, on the other hand, the "sonorous chords" are the property of an entire poem. Of all the factors that create a rhythmical impression on the perceiver, Kušner focuses on two: the articulation of speech

---

37. "O zvukovoj storone poètičeskoj reči," *Sborniki po teorii poètičeskogo jazyka*, vol. 1, p. 43.

into syllables, and the segmentation of the continuous utterance into verse lines. In this way each speech sound is assigned a precise place within a two-dimensional grid based on its position vis-à-vis the other syllables of the line and vis-à-vis corresponding syllables in other lines. The resulting grid of verse positions accounts for the distribution of all speech sounds in the poetic text, thus enabling Kušner to detect any patterns that they might form—the sonorous chords.

The Formalists discussed so far tackled the category of poetic language as a primarily phonic phenomenon. Their preoccupation with poetic sound was chiefly inspired by Kručěnych's concept of *zaum'*—language contemptuous of everyday rationality and semantics. It must be stressed that even though Kručěnych scoffed at language that merely conveys thought, he conceived of transrational language as something more than mere sound. The unfolding of the "self-valuable word" was only one aspect of *zaum'*, for the destruction of syntax and grammar still served a particular objective. A normally structured utterance, Kručěnych reasoned, contains a logical meaning that transmits thought into words. The deformed *zaum'*, on the other hand, lacks such a definite meaning, but precisely because of this its words can express directly the noncognitive components of the poet's consciousness. "The clear and decisive evidence for the fact that until now the word has been in shackles is its *subordination to sense.* Until now it has been maintained that 'thought dictates laws to the word and not the other way around.' We have pointed out this mistake and provided a free language, transrational and ecumenical. The path of previous artists led through thought to the word; ours leads through the word to direct apprehension."[38]

Kručěnych, however, failed to explain in any cogent way either the mechanism for this immediate apprehension or its object. His point might be expected to carry rhetorical weight within a poetic manifesto but certainly not elsewhere. Yet it caught

38. "Novye puti slova," pp. 65–66.

the fancy of the Formalists, who argued against Potebnja's identification of poetic language with inner linguistic form. From their point of view, Kručënych's *zaum'* was the best evidence that verbal art can do quite well without any images. To sustain this argument they had to translate Kručënych's statements about the direct expressivity of outer poetic form into more scholarly terms.

Here they could turn to a theory of another member of the Kazan' School, Mikołaj Kruszewski (1851–1887). In studying the universal laws of association operating in language, Kruszewski had argued that "the coexistence of the two aspects of the word—its external appearance and its meaning—rests on an association based on contiguity which binds these two aspects 'into an inseparable pair.' But to our memory 'such a binding seems weak and insufficient; it must be supported by an association to another word based on similarity.'" This dual linkage of each verbal unit is the engine that drives linguistic change. Kruszewski depicts the process of linguistic evolution as "an eternal antagonism between a progressive force determined by associations based on similarity and a conservative one determined by associations based on contiguity."[39]

Kruszewski's two types of association correspond in turn to two figures of speech: metaphor and metonymy. The ingenious Šklovskij used this tropological distinction in attacking Potebnja. He claimed that not only poetic but prosaic language might involve inner linguistic form, that is, the figurative transference of meaning. But it is necessary to distinguish between two different figures of speech: the "conservative" metonymy, based on contiguity, and the "progressive" metaphor, based on similarity. Given the bias of Šklovskian aesthetics toward novelty in art it is not surprising that he considered the metaphor as the only truly poetic trope. Metonymy is merely the "practical means of thinking, of conceptualizing objects" and as such it

39. R. Jakobson, "Značenie Kruševskogo v razvitii nauki o jazyke," *Selected Writings*, vol. 2, pp. 436–37.

characterizes prosaic language, but metaphor is the "means for intensifying perception" and hence the essence of poetic language. To illustrate, calling someone "a hat" simply because he happens to wear one is to evoke a prosaic image-trope, whereas the same designation for a helpless, languid fellow would be a poetic figure.[40]

Despite Šklovskij's criticism, however, he was still operating with Potebnja's concept of inner form. The metaphoric designation that he described involved a cognitive *tertium comparationis*— a mental construct linking the outer form of the word with its figurative meaning, as in "helplessness" and "sloppiness" in his "hat" example. But the Formalists inspired by Kručěnych's *zaum'* were not much concerned with traditional poetic tropes. Rather, they looked for cases of what Roman Jakobson aptly termed "negative inner form," that is, "words which so to speak seek their meaning," or, put differently, words with a directly expressive outer form.[41]

One hypothesis about the immediate emotive value of poetic sound was enunciated by Lev Jakubinskij. He approvingly quoted the observation of the famous French Indo-Europeanist Antoine Meillet (1866–1936) that in "practical language there is no *inner link* between the sound of the words and their meanings. Their link is determined by an *association based on contiguity* and is *factual*, not natural."[42] This is so because in practical language sounds merely serve to differentiate meaning. The foregrounding of sound that is proper to poetic language, however, changes the picture. In such language, "because our attention is attracted by sounds, an emotive attitude is aroused toward them. This circumstance," Jakubinskij stressed, "is very important for determining the interrelations of the phonic and semantic aspects of speech in verse language."[43] Here the two are linked by the relation of similarity. Jakubinskij's notion of similarity is, howev-

---

40. "Iskusstvo, kak priëm," p. 103.
41. *Novejšaja russkaja poèzija: Nabrosok pervyj* (Prague, 1921), p. 67.
42. "O zvukach stichotvornogo jazyka," p. 44.
43. Ibid.

er, somewhat different from that of Kruszewski: what is similar in poetic language is the emotive charge belonging to the phonic and semantic aspects of the word. "The emotions evoked by certain sounds and their combinations can take various courses: 'pleasure-displeasure,' 'arousal-satisfaction,' 'tension-resolution.' It is also absolutely clear that the emotions triggered by sounds *should not take a course antithetical to the emotions triggered by the 'content'* of the poem (and vice versa). . . . Thus, the poet selects sounds and combinations that emotionally correspond to images valued by him for some reason, or, vice versa, he selects images that emotionally correspond to *sounds* and combinations that are significant for some reason in the given circumstances."[44]

In addition to the emotive charge of sounds, the similarity of the phonic and semantic aspects of poetic language is provided by what Jakubinskij called the "capacity of the speech organs for expressive movements."[45] There is, he believed, a curious juncture of emotions and language in our facial expressions. The movement of our facial muscles can be caused on the one hand by our emotions, and on the other, by the articulation of speech sounds. In practical language, where the *phonè* is just a means, speech sounds can be modified to accommodate the emotions. This is impossible, however, in language dominated by sound. Thus, in verbal art the poet is forced to "select words whose sounds are pronounced through movements of the speech organs corresponding roughly to given expressive movements. . . . Broadly speaking, if the poet experiences emotions pertaining to a smile (a stretching of the lips sideways), then he naturally will avoid sounds articulated by pushing the lips forward (e.g., *u, o*)."[46]

Another theory of the direct expressiveness of linguistic sound was formulated by a specialist in Far Eastern languages, Evgenij Polivanov, in an essay dealing with a phenomenon that he termed "sound gesture." This essay constituted a partial dis-

44. Ibid., p. 45.
45. Ibid.
46. Ibid., p. 48.

putation of Jakubinskij's views. Polivanov began by dividing all
the means of linguistic expression into two by now familiar categories: the one completely arbitrary and conventional, for example, the phonic structure of the Russian word for table—
$s+t+o+l$—which in itself does not suggest its meaning; the other
motivated and natural, such as the intonation that expresses
emotional states and seems to be immediately understandable to
anyone, even to animals. Gestures—nonlinguistic means of expression that often accompany emotive language—are prime
examples of the latter category. They convey emotions in the
most direct fashion.

Very soon, however, Polivanov undercut this simple opposition. As he argued, both motivated and arbitrary linguistic expressions are in fact conventional—deriving from the relation of
contiguity between expressions and their meanings. "If we know
that a given extralinguistic phenomenon is expressed through a
particular intonation or gesture, the origin of this knowledge
can be simply explained by the fact that we have always or often
observed such an emotion accompanied by the given intonation
or gesture. Thus, we have learned this link in precisely the same
fashion as we learned the link between the phonic sequence
$s+t+o+l$ and the representation of table, for this sequence was
always used by the speaker when the thought of table was present."[47] Therefore, the difference between so-called natural and
conventional linguistic expressions is not absolute but rather a
matter of degree, an admixture of the two principles.

If all means of expression were placed on a scale from "conventional" to "natural," the closest to the natural, in Polivanov's
opinion, would be mimetic gestures that copy objects or actions
and seem spontaneously comprehensible to everyone. Well
aware that the process of reproduction is always conventional,
Polivanov calls these gestures "potentially natural." The question, then, is whether language contains any "phonic sequences
(combinations of vowels and consonants in a certain order)

47. "Po povodu 'zvukovyx žestov' japonskogo jazyka," ibid., p. 30.

whose role is analogous to that of potentially natural gestures."[48]

The answer is yes, as Polivanov illustrates with numerous Japanese onomatopoetic words imitating sounds, and reduplicative words imitating the repetition of an action or the recurrence of a phenomenon. By analogy with "mimetic gestures," Polivanov termed these imitative linguistic expressions "sound gestures."

Polivanov departed from Jakubinskij both in denying that emotions are the vehicle of the direct expressiveness of linguistic sounds, and in not considering the connection between sound gestures and verbal art.[49] In some respects, however, the two Formalists shared common ground. First of all, Polivanov claimed that sound gestures and children's language were related. "Japanese 'sound gestures' can be regarded in general as the principle of a special, childish morphology that has retained its right to existence in the language of adults."[50] In addition, both Jakubinskij and Polivanov believed that a substantial phonic difference, which has its roots in pronunciation, existed between poetic language and sound gestures on the one hand, and practical or normal language on the other. For Jakubinskij, the clustering of liquids impedes pronunciation, thus attracting attention to the sounds themselves. Polivanov observed that in Japanese onomatopoetic and reduplicative words the phoneme [p] occurred, which has disappeared from contemporary Japanese except in loan words; the "nasal g" [ŋ] is also found in initial position in these words, though otherwise it occurs only medially or finally. Such aberrations, Polivanov believed, are

---

48. Ibid., p. 31.

49. Nevertheless, this connection is implied by the fact that Polivanov's essay appeared in the OPOJAZ *Studies in the Theory of Poetic Language*. Viktor Šklovskij wrote, "The observation that in Japanese poetic language there are sounds which do not exist in practical Japanese was most likely the first actual indication that these two languages are divergent" ("Iskusstvo, kak priëm," p. 104). Still, it seems far-fetched to claim, as Ladislav Matejka does, that Polivanov wrote about Japanese poetry ("The Formal Method and Linguistics," *Readings in Russian Poetics: Formalist and Structuralist Views*, ed. L. Matejka and K. Pomorska [Ann Arbor, Mich., 1978], p. 282).

50. "Po povodu 'zvukovych žestov,'" p. 36.

caused by the fact that the "value of the particular phonic structure [of sound gestures] is greater than in other words. In normal words, as a matter of fact, it does not make any difference
which phonic complexes express a particular idea. . . . But obviously for 'onomatopoetic' words, some links between the expressed representations and particular sounds are important."[51]
Thus, Polivanov concludes, the *p* in normal language can easily
be replaced by any other speech sound, but it must be retained
in words imitating, for example, the puffing of tobacco smoke or
the sound of a flute.

The Formalists, to be sure, did not claim originality in discovering the importance of oral articulation in language and
verbal art. They referred to such nineteenth-century scholars as
the German psychologist Wilhelm Wundt (1832–920) or the
Polish classical philologist Tadeusz Zieliński (1859–1944), who
had made similar observations about pronunciation as the
bridge between sound and meaning.[52] But the Formalists' interest in the articulatory aspect of language was most likely triggered by the rise of *Ohrenphilologie* in the German literary studies
of Eduard Sievers (1850–1932), his pupil Franz Saran (1866–
1931), and others. In contrast to traditional *Augenphilologie*,
which analyzed the text primarily as a visual or graphic manifestation, Sievers's "aural philology" emphasized the acoustic
aspect of the text. Of particular interest were the involuntary
motor reactions (movements of the diaphragm, bodily motions,
facial expressions, and gestures) accompanying an utterance,
which, in their opinion, were decisive in articulating the phonic
substance of language.

There are several reasons that *Ohrenphilologie* was so attractive
to the OPOJAZ Formalists. First of all, even though its overall

51. Ibid., p. 34.
52. In an appendix to the first volume of the OPOJAZ *Sborniki* appeared a
Russian translation of segments of M. Grammont's *Le vers français* and K.
Nyrop's *Grammaire historique de la langue française* that discussed the expressive
quality of linguistic sound stemming in part from its articulatory properties (see
Sborniki po teorii poètičeskogo jazyka, vol. 1, pp. 51–71).

outlook and goals were incompatible with those of the Russian Futurists whom the Formalists found so congenial, their respective views of literature coincided on one important point, namely, that sound is central to poetry. Earlier I mentioned that Kručënych attributed poetic value to foreign languages unknown to him as one source of his *zaum'* (see note 20). In a striking correspondence Saran wrote: "the theoretician of verse . . . ought to adopt toward verse the attitude of a foreigner who listens to it without knowing the language in which it is written."[53] Jakobson considered this statement an epitome of the Ohrenphilological outlook.

Like *Ohrenphilologie*, OPOJAZ was essentially positivistic, attempting to establish a new science of literature that would "turn to the facts and push aside general systems and problems."[54] In this "new fervor of scientific positivism," sound was considered the only concrete reality of verbal art, for meaning, in its ephemerality, was only a subjective mental construct that could not be pinned down with any certitude. An earlier linguist and teacher of some of the OPOJAZ members, Lev Ščerba (1880–1944), had expressed this view in his introduction to a "linguistic commentary [*tolkovanie*]" on one of Puškin's poems that was primarily a directive for the proper oral delivery of this text.[55] In it, Ščerba argued that "all semantic observations can only be subjective," whereas the analysis of poetic sound, especially in the oral reading of a text, can attain to some degree the objectivity of a laboratory experiment.[56] This claim to scientific objectivity is reflected in the title of an informative article on *Ohrenphilologie*

53. Saran, quoted in R. Jakobson, *O češskom stiche preimuščestvenno v sopostavlenii s russkim* (Berlin, 1923), p. 21.
54. Boris Èjchenbaum, "Teorija 'formal'nogo metoda,'" *Literatura: Teorija, kritika, polemika* (Leningrad, 1927), p. 120.
55. It was from Ščerba's monograph on Russian vowels, *Russkie glasnye v kačestvennom i količestvennom otnošenii* (St. Petersburg, 1912), that the Formalists drew their conclusions about the nature of sound in practical language (see, for example, L. Jakubinskij, "O zvukach stichotvornogo jazyka," p. 38; or R. Jakobson, *Novejšaja russkaja poèzija*, p. 9).
56. "Opyty lingvističeskogo tolkovanija stichotvorenij. I: 'Vospominanie' Puškina," *Russkaja reč'*, vol. 1, p. 17.

by Šklovskij's brother Vladimir, which appeared in the second
volume of the OPOJAZ *Studies:* "The Rhythmical-Melodic Experiments of Professor Sievers."[57] This esteem for the methods
of "aural philology" extended beyond the early stage of Formalism.[58] Aside from the German literary theorist Oskar Walzel
(1864–1944), Sievers and Saran were the only honorary members of the Section for Verbal Arts at the State Institute for the
History of the Arts, the institution that absorbed OPOJAZ in the
twenties.[59]

Of the contributors to the OPOJAZ *Studies,* the closest to
Ohrenphilologie was Boris Èjchenbaum. His affinity to this approach was most likely a function of his age. Born in 1886,
Èjchenbaum began his literary studies before the advent of Formalism. Thus, he did not always share the Bohemian proclivities
of some of the younger members of OPOJAZ, apparently more
impressed by sober scholarship than the vague notions of Futurism. The scientism of *Ohrenphilologie* coincided with Èjchenbaum's own orientation, as recorded in his diary entry of January 1919: "Proceeding from Rickert, one realizes that the
methods of the natural sciences must be applied to the history of
the arts . . . when we deal with the 'nature' of the material from
which the work is made. In [this field] the construction of laws
and definitions is quite conceivable."[60] Moreover, Èjchenbaum
held that the material of verbal art is the oral word.

> We always speak about literature, the book, the writer. Written-
> printed culture has inculcated the letter in us. . . . We often totally
> forget that the word has nothing to do with the letter, that it is a
> living, ongoing activity created by the voice, articulation, and into-

57. "O rytmiko-melodičeskich èksperimentach prof. Siversa," *Sborniki po teorii
poètičeskogo jazyka,* vol. 2, pp. 87–94.
58. For a list of Formalist articles pertaining to Sievers's school, see M. R.
Mayenowa, "Rosyjskie propozycje teoretyczne w zakresie form poetyckich,"
Rosyjska szkoła stylistyki, ed. M. R. Mayenowa and Z. Saloni (Warsaw, 1970), p. 18.
59. "Otčët o naučnoj dejatel'nosti Otdela slovesnych iskusstv GIII s l/l 1926 g.
po l/l 1928 g.," *Poètika: Vremennik Otdela slovesnych iskusstv* 4 (1928), 155.
60. Quoted in M. O. Čudakova's commentary to Jurij Tynjanov's *Poètika,
istorija literatury, kino* (Moscow, 1977), p. 455.

nation and joined by the gesture and facial expression [*mimika*]. We think that the writer *writes*. But it is not always so, and in the realm of the artistic word it is more often just the opposite. The German philologists (Sievers, Saran, et al.) began to argue a few years ago that the philology of the "eye" (*Augenphilologie*) must be replaced by its "aural" counterpart (*Ohrenphilologie*). This is an extremely fertile idea which has already yielded interesting results in the domain of verse. . . . Such an "aural" analysis, however, is also fruitful for the study of artistic prose. The bases [of this form] are also marked by its origin in the oral *skaz* which influences not only its syntactic structure and the selection and combination of its words, but its very composition.[61]

The untranslatable term *skaz* (akin to the Russian verb *skazat'*, to tell) subsequently gained wide currency in Slavic literary studies. It was the focal point of Èjchenbaum's Formalist debut, his analysis of Gogol's short story, "The Overcoat." *Skaz* designated a particular narrative technique in which the elements of oral delivery play a crucial role. The structure of Gogol's story, Èjchenbaum claimed, in not organized according to the laws of the plot but rather by a "certain system of varied expressive-articulatory facial gestures."[62] In a later study devoted to the Akmeist poet Anna Achmatova, Èjchenbaum applied the notion of the articulatory gesture to poetry as well. His thesis was that Achmatova's poetry "is oriented toward the process of pronunciation, of expressive [*mimičeskij*] pronunciation."[63] This orientation is manifested in the frequent occurrences of what Èjchenbaum termed the "*expressive quality of speech [rečevaja mimika]*." He showed how the repetition of the same or similar vowels or the juxtaposition of contrasting ones forces the reader to move his lips in a particular way so that the "words come to be perceived not as 'sounds' and not as articulation in general but as an expressive [*mimičeskij*] motion."[64]

61. "Illjuzija skaza," *Knižnyj ugol*, no. 2 (1918), 10.
62. "Kak sdelana 'Šinel'' Gogolja," *Poètika: Sborniki po teorii poètičeskogo jazyka*, p. 151.
63. *Anna Achmatova: Opyt analiza* (Petersburg, 1923), p. 87.
64. Ibid., p. 86.

The years separating Èjchenbaum's study of Gogol' and his monograph on Achmatova mark an important period in the development of OPOJAZ. As Èjchenbaum himself observed, the teens for the Petersburg Formalists were "years of struggle and polemics," so that "many of the principles [they] advanced during these years of intensive struggle with their adversaries were not merely scholarly principles but paradoxical slogans exaggerated for polemical and contrastive purposes. The failure to take this into account, to treat the 1916–1921 works of OPOJAZ as strictly scholarly, would be to ignore history."[65] The stock-taking that followed this period of *Sturm und Drang* was to lead to an intensive reexamination of the earlier position. The linguistic approach to verbal art and the key notion of poetic language were among the first to undergo this scrutiny.

Èjchenbaum himself launched this critique. He commended the recent confluence of poetics with linguistics as a healthy counterbalance to the traditional domination of poetics by psychology or sociology. "But," he warned,

a rapprochement with a neighboring discipline can be genuinely fruitful only if it does not lead to a new submission. In associating with linguistics, poetics ought to retain its independence. For linguistics, a poetic work is a "phenomenon of language" that furnishes interesting material for the study of phonetic, syntactic, or semantic issues. Linguistic observations about poetic language enrich the *general science of language* with new phenomena that occur only rarely in normal "practical speech." The literary theoretician, however fruitful he may find linguistic methods to be, should pose his questions in a completely different way. What emerges here is the distinction between the concepts of *language* and *style*, linguistic *phenomenon* and stylistic *device*. Linguistics belongs among the natural sciences, poetics among the humanities [*nauki o duche*]. Linguistics classifies poetic language as one of its varieties; it differentiates among them according to their goals merely to classify the phenomena of language as functions. Poetics begins with the separation of poetic language from other linguistic phenomena as an activity set toward a particular goal. And

65. "Teorija 'formal'nogo metoda,' " p. 132.

even though this goal cannot be defined with any precision, its symptoms are apparent. In this way, poetics is built on the foundation of a teleological principle and thus proceeds from the notion of the *device;* linguistics, like all natural sciences, deals with the category of causality and therefore proceeds from the notion of the *phenomenon as such.*[66]

Linguistically oriented Formalists tended to dismiss this statement of Èjchenbaum's as a relic of nineteenth-century scholarship. Viktor Vinogradov, for example, claimed that "both the inclusion of linguistics among the natural sciences and the disregard for the teleological principle in it are widespread but incorrect, narrow-minded ideas."[67]

Èjchenbaum was not the only Formalist in the early twenties to clash with the concept of poetic language and the linguistic approach to literature so central to OPOJAZ. In a proposal for a monograph on *Evgenij Onegin,* Jurij Tynjanov listed as one of his topics, "Why poetic language is not a poetic dialect and does not belong completely within descriptive linguistics."[68] Thus, Èjchenbaum's (and Tynjanov's) dissent from the other Formalists cannot be simply swept aside.

Any characterization of Èjchenbaum's position will depend on what we make of his concept of the device. At first glance, his contrasting of poetic teleology with linguistic causality may appear to be another version of Šklovskij's mechanistic model. However, Èjchenbaum speaks of stylistics and linguistics, and contrasts the stylistic device with the linguistic phenomenon. In this respect his polemics recalls Žirmunskij's critique of the mechanistic metaphor discussed in the preceding chapter. It was precisely through the notion of style that Žirmunskij reformulated the functional definition of the device. From his standpoint, style is a principle of unity determined by the overall artistic goal, which ascribes to each device a specific role within

66. *Melodika russkogo liričeskogo sticha* (Petersburg, 1922), p. 14.
67. "O zadačach stilistiki: Nabljudenija nad stilem žitija protop. Avvakuma," *Russkaja reč',* vol. 1, p. 206.
68. *Poètika, istorija literatury, kino,* p. 416.

the artistic whole. The device is thus not an a priori, independent monad of artistic form for the morphologists, but a functionally integrated element of the work. In the same way, though from a different theoretical perspective, Tynjanov argued against an atomistic approach to the device. In his systemic metaphor, the identity of each element is a function of the hierarchical relations within the work and the higher systems in which the element participates.

It is obvious that Èjchenbaum's rejection of the linguistic model was motivated by similar considerations. For the linguist, he believed, poetic and practical language are nothing but abstractions. In separating the two, the student of language might classify them, "among other ways" (Jakubinskij's words), according to their respective goals. To do so, however, is only a heuristic procedure, a matter of choice, as Jakubinskij himself demonstrated when in 1922 he rejected the goal as an inadequate criterion and proposed to classify utterances according to their actual forms.[69] Students of literature, however, do not have this choice, for they deal with concrete literary works, that is, intentionally created poetic wholes. From their perspective, the ontological difference between poetic and practical language (for example, the clustering of the same liquids) or between sound gestures and normal linguistic usage (for example, the occurrence of the speech sound p) is unimportant. It is not the presence or absence of these particular features that concerned Èjchenbaum as a literary scholar, but their functional place in the literary work. "Poetic language," he argued, "is characterized solely by a particular set toward certain elements of speech and a specific utilization of them."[70]

In more abstract terms, it might be said that the two factions in OPOJAZ used different "logics." Those advocating the linguistic model were quite close to the mechanists in casting their categories in the form of polar oppositions. Their critics shunned this

69. "O dialogičeskoj reči," pp. 115–16.
70. "Oratorskij stil' Lenina," *Literatura*, p. 250.

disjunctive stance, instead casting their categories in terms of a gradation, a relative difference. Thus, the linguist Jakubinskij, inspired by the Futurists' *zaum'*, split all linguistic behavior into two incompatible classes: poetic language oriented solely toward the phonic aspect of speech, and its opposite, practical language set toward the semantic aspect of speech. His critic, Èjchenbaum, though considering this a powerful working hypothesis, claimed that it was not supported by the facts. Commenting on practical language, he wrote, "It is quite doubtful that there actually exists a type of speech in which our attitude toward the word would be totally mechanical, in which the word would be exclusively a 'sign.' Forms such as oratory, for instance, regardless of their 'practical' character, are in many respects quite close to poetic language."[71] And Žirmunskij criticized the absolutism of the opposite category, poetic language, conceived as a purely phonic structure. "If the poet really wanted to affect us by mere sounds he would take up music." Poetry "does not affect the listener by sound *as such* but by sounding *words*, i.e., sounds tied to meaning."[72]

Though Žirmunskij and Èjchenbaum both conceived of style as the functional integration of elements in an artistic whole, they disagreed on the nature of this integration. Žirmunskij, faithful to his organic metaphor, favored a static notion of the whole in which elements were harmoniously related. Èjchenbaum, in contrast, prepared the way for the systemic metaphor by advocating a more dynamic view. According to him, the unity of a work was a fragile equilibrium of elements struggling for domination. I dwelt on this difference in the preceding chapter and repeat it only to avoid the false impression that Žirmunskij and Èjchenbaum were speaking the same language. In fact, Žirmunskij's criticism of those conflating literature and music was not addressed to the linguistically inclined OPOJAZ members at all but to Èjchenbaum, in a review of Èjchenbaum's book *The*

71. Ibid.
72. "Melodika sticha: Po povodu knigi B. M. Èjchenbauma, *Melodika sticha*, Pbg. 1922," *Voprosy teorii literatury*, p. 149.

Melodics of Russian Lyric Verse. In this work Èjchenbaum had formulated his dynamic notion of the poetic whole as a struggle between the organizing element (the dominant of the work) and the other subordinate elements constituting this whole. He illustrated his position with lyric poems in which the dominant intonation deformed all the other aspects of language, including semantics, to its needs.

The deformation of semantics that Èjchenbaum discussed, despite Žirmunskij's claims to the contrary, was quite different from that described by the early OPOJAZ members. We recall that they treated poetic language as sound that might but need not be accompanied by a cognitive meaning. Èjchenbaum was concerned not with the presence or absence of meaning in a particular verbal construction, but rather with its function there, a function determining its hierarchical position relative to the other elements of the construction. In other words, for him, meaning is always involved in a verbal construction, but sometimes it is subordinate to other elements and at other times it dominates them. Oratory, Èjchenbaum argued, may foreground the phonic aspect of language for the sake of persuasion, whereas artistic prose may be quite indifferent to sound if its goal requires this.

Joining Èjchenbaum against Jakubinskij's separation of poetic from practical language was Boris Tomaševskij, who wrote, "Instead of the clear, though perhaps terminologically unfortunate opposition of the old scholastic theory, 'poetry' and 'prose,' we, following a linguistic path, have advanced another opposition: 'practical' versus 'artistic' language. This opposition, however, does not cover all aspects of a verbal composition. It pertains solely to the sphere of language and, secondly, does not coincide with the bounds of 'poetry' and 'prose.' For the 'prosaic' perhaps as much as the 'poetic' should be contrasted to 'practical' language."[73]

73. "Konstrukcija tezisov," *Lef* 5, no. 1 (1924), 140.

Earlier in this chapter I described how Jakubinskij arrived at his frame of reference. He proceeded from Potebnja's original opposition between poetic and prosaic language, but replaced the second element with "practical language," which he considered more appropriate. His critics proceeded in the opposite fashion; they retained "prosaic language" and replaced the other element of the opposition with what they claimed to be the more accurate concept of "verse language." In the introduction to his pioneering 1924 monograph, *The Problem of Verse Language,* Tynjanov explained this step: "The notion of 'poetic language' put forth not so long ago is today in a crisis which is undoubtedly caused by the broad and diffuse character of this psychological-linguistic concept. The term 'poetry' that had long existed in our language and scholarship has now lost its concrete scope and content and gained an evaluative tinge. In this book I shall analyze the specific concept of *verse* (in opposition to the concept of *prose*) and the specific features of *verse language*."[74]

These conceptual shifts were not solely a matter of terminology. By substituting the notion of practical language for Potebnja's "prose," Jakubinskij was redefining the category of the poetic. The same was true of his critics. Their opposition between verse and prose is not equivalent to the earlier dichotomy of poetry and prose. The early OPOJAZ members ignored verse, considering verse rhythm just one of many artistic devices that de-familiarize the sound stratum of language, whereas their

74. *Problema stichotvornogo jazyka* (Leningrad, 1924), p. 5. In this passage Tynjanov insists on a subtle but untranslatable difference between two synonymic adjectives *stichotvornyj* and *stichovoj*, both rendered in English as "verse." His preference for *stichovoj* most likely can be attributed to the fact that Jakubinskij, who conceived of "verse language" as a mere subcategory of "poetic language," used *stichotvornyj* (see note 26 above). For this reason, it is quite surprising that *stichotvornyj*, rejected by Tynjanov, should have appeared in the very title of his book. Tynjanov's correspondence reveals, however, that this title was chosen by his publisher who was apprehensive about the original title *Problema stichovoj semantiki* (see Tynjanov's letter to Lev Lunc of January 14, 1924, reprinted in *Novyj žurnal,* no. 83 [1966], 142).

critics argued that verse and prose occur in both literature and *byt*.[75] What these two forms represent is not the opposition of art to nonart, but two different principles of verbal construction, or what Tynjanov called functions. Tomaševskij wrote in his comprehensive *Russian Versification* that "the difference between prose and verse rests in the fact that in verse the phonic imperative [*zvukovoe zadanie*] dominates the semantic one and in prose the semantic dominates the phonic one. Everything boils down to the relative role of these two origins."[76] Similarly, Tynjanov argued that "it would be premature to conclude that verse form differs from prose form merely because in verse the external sign of the word plays the exclusive role whereas in prose such a role is performed by its meaning." He concluded, "Prose and poetry, it seems, do not differ from each other in their immanent phonation and in the consequent set toward sound in poetry and semantics in prose, but rather in the way these two elements interact: how the semantic aspect of prose deforms its phonic aspect (the mental set toward the semantic) and how verse deforms the meaning of the word."[77]

In short, the linguistic model and its fundamental concept, poetic language, underwent a criticism within OPOJAZ in the early twenties that entailed a significant shift in the scholarly endeavors of the group. Of course, this shift was not a total abandonment of the previous Formalist tradition. Those who rejected the "vague" and "inadequate" concept of poetic language followed the path established by their predecessors in one

75. In the conclusion to his "Art as Device," Šklovskij promised to devote a special book to the problems of rhythm. This plan never materialized, however, perhaps because Šklovskij considered poetic rhythm nothing but a deformation of prosaic rhythm, a deformation that must remain unpredictable and hence unsystematizable in order to carry out its de-familiarizing function ("Iskustvo, kak priëm," p. 114).

76. *Russkoe stichosloženie: Metrika* (Petersburg, 1923), p. 8.

77. "O kompozicii *Evgenija Onegina*," *Poètika, istorija literatury, kino*, pp. 53 and 54.

important respect. They too focused their attention on verbal constructions in which sound played the dominant role. However, they no longer carried out their research under the banner of the theory of poetic language but under that of metrics and verse semantics.

Verse

I would define, in brief, the Poetry of words as *The Rhythmical Creation of Beauty*. Its sole arbiter is Taste. With the Intellect or with the Conscience, it has only collateral relations. Unless incidentally, it has no concern whatever either with Duty or with Truth.

—EDGAR ALLAN POE, "The Poetic Principle"

Perhaps the most influential among the early Formalist studies of verse was Osip Brik's 1920 lecture at OPOJAZ entitled "Rhythm and Syntax."[1] In it he coined the term "rhythmical impulse," which became the "focal point of the Formalist and Structuralist conception of verse."[2] To appreciate Brik's contribution fully it is necessary to sketch out its historical context.

The principles of Russian versification the Formalists inherited were those of the great poet-theoreticians of the Symbolist generation, A. Belyj and V. Brjusov. Though innovative in their approach to the study of verse (Belyj, for instance, was the first

---

1. Although quoted in the early twenties by many Formalists, "Ritm i sintaksis: Materialy k izučeniju stichotvornoj reči" was not published until 1927, when it appeared in four installments in the journal *Novyj Lef*.

2. M. Červenka, "Rytmický impuls: Poznámky a komentáře," *Z večerní školy versologie: Čtyři studie 1975–83* (Prague, 1983), pp. 52–53.

in Russia to apply statistics to metrics), their theories did not satisfy the young Formalists. In their eyes, the three major failings of Symbolist metrics were as follows: first, an atomistic approach to verse; next, the separation of meter from rhythm; and finally, prosodic egocentrism. The Symbolists considered the foot the minimal unit of verse. Unable to detect any overall gestalt in the verse under study, they arbitrarily analyzed even the most regular verse into heterogeneous feet. This blindness to the holistic nature of verse stemmed from their divorce of meter from rhythm. They insisted that meter was an ideal scheme existing prior to verse, whereas rhythm was the actual pattern of deviations from this scheme. Because the Symbolists attributed aesthetic value precisely to such deviations, in their own analyses they purposely sought to segment verse into as many different kinds of feet as possible.

To avoid the problems of Symbolist metrics, Brik's study did away with the concept of meter entirely. Instead it treated rhythm as the motoric or kinetic precondition of verse. "As a scholarly term, rhythm means a particular formation of the motor processes . . . motion shaped in a particular way."[3] Rhythmic shaping is a function of quantity (the increase or decrease in motion) and duration (the continuity or discreteness of motion). The projection of rhythm onto verbal material—the kinetic organization of an utterance in terms of stresses and intervals—constitutes what Brik terms the "rhythmical impulse." This impulse organizes the verse *as a whole,* a fact that had eluded the Symbolist theoreticians. Only if we know the rhythmical movement of the entire poem can we correctly identify its smaller units. Brik takes as an illustration a line from Puškin, which in isolation seems dactylic but within the poem as a whole turns out to be trochaic. He concludes, "one should not speak of strong and light syllables [downbeats and upbeats] but of stressed and unstressed ones. Theoretically, any syllable can be stressed or unstressed; everything depends on the rhythmical impulse."[4]

3. "Ritm i sintaksis," *Novyj Lef,* 1927, no. 3, 16.
4. Ibid., 17.

Brik's statement clearly reflects the iconoclastic attitude of his Hylaean friends toward traditional accentual-syllabic versification. As they wrote in 1913, "we stopped seeking meters in the schoolbooks; every motion generates a new, free rhythm for the poet."[5] To achieve such total rhythmical freedom, Futurist poets manipulated language in a particular way, as they themselves admitted. They "disregarded grammatical rules" and "shattered syntax." It soon became evident to Brik, however, that the majority of Russian verse is written in more traditional language than *zaum'*, language whose words are units of meaning combined semantically as well as prosodically.

To account for the semantic constraint upon the rhythmical impulse in ordinary Russian verse, Brik returned to the concept of syntax disdained by the Futurists. "Syntax," he wrote, "is the system of combining words in ordinary language. As long as verse language does not abandon the essential laws of prosaic syntax these laws are obligatory for it."[6] Thus, the relationship of sound and meaning in verse is necessarily complex; it is always a compromise between rhythmical and syntactic considerations. A verse line, in Brik's opinion, is the minimal implementation of this rhythmical-syntactic compromise. It is a unit separated from the rest of the utterance to which it belongs on the basis of its prosodic features, but at the same time containing syntactic connections among its elements. "A rhythmical-syntactic word combination differs from a purely syntactic one in that it incorporates words into a fixed rhythmical unit (a line); it differs from a purely rhythmical combination in that it links words not only phonetically but semantically."[7] Rhythmical and syntactic requirements may coincide in verse, as when a line is a complete sentence, or they may clash, for example, in caesuras or enjambments. In either case, words in verse are always subject to two sets of combinatory rules.

5. D. Burljuk, et al., *Sadok sudej* II (St Petersburg, 1913), reprinted in V. Markov, ed., *Manifesty i programmy russkich futuristov* (Munich, 1967), p. 52.

6. "Ritm i sintaksis," *Novyj Lef*, 1927, no. 5, 32.

7. Ibid.

The value of Brik's essay for Formalist metrics lay in its firm grasp of the structuring principle of verse. This grasp, however, was achieved only at the cost of considerable oversimplification, and all subsequent Formalist studies of the topic complicated Brik's clear-cut picture. Its first limitation was its equation of the vehicle of rhythm with word stress alone. Obviously, in addition to the stress within an isolated word there are a variety of stresses belonging to higher syntactic units. Once this premise is accepted, syntax can no longer be seen in simple opposition to rhythm as meaning versus sound. Syntax actually consists of both phonic and semantic strata. Furthermore, the phonology of syntax cannot be limited to the intensity of the voice (syntactic stress). The voice also has pitch, whose modulation creates syntactic intonation. It was this aspect of verse that Èjchenbaum examined in his study of the melodics of Russian lyric poetry.

Èjchenbaum divided the lyric into three categories according to the role played in each by intonation. In the *declamatory* (rhetorical) lyric, intonation supports the logical structure of the text; in the *conversational* lyric it serves to link the verse to everyday language. In both these types of lyric, intonation is subordinate to other verse elements. In the third lyric type, intonation performs a more significant function. This is the *singable (napevnyj)* lyric, which purposely imitates musical melody. In such poetry "we observe not a simple alternation of speech intonations but a developed *system of intonation* that determines the composition of the poem more than its verbal themes."[8] Only such intonational schemes—symmetries, repetitions, or cadences—can in Èjchenbaum's view be called melodics proper. Here intonation ceases to be a mere epiphenomenon and becomes the organizing principle of verse—its dominant.

The semantic aspect of syntax is subordinated to intonation in this type of lyric. For example, Vasilij Žukovskij, a Russian poet of the first half of the nineteenth century, exploited the syntactic patterns of emotive language for melodic ends. Some of his

8. *Melodika russkogo liričeskogo sticha* (Petersburg, 1922), p. 9.

poems are merely a series of interrogative sentences combined with exclamations. Afanasij Fet (1820–1892), in contrast, built his melodics on intonational emphasis. To attain it he inverted word order, repeated lexical items in significant positions (anaphora, epiphora) and employed syntactic parallelism. With such cases in mind, Èjchenbaum concluded that the "analysis of the melodic style in which the role of intonation is obvious suggests the need for a study of the role it plays in verse in general."[9]

The strength and the disadvantage of Èjchenbaum's study lie in its specialization. His scheme convincingly illustrated the idea that verse is a hierarchical structure and called attention to one hitherto neglected element of this structure. But given its author's mistrust of linguistics, the concept of syntax with which it operated was vague, to say the least. Furthermore, by focusing on intonation, it inevitably slighted other important factors. A study of melodics cannot substitute for a general theory of verse. The formulation of such a theory was left to the other Formalists.

In 1919, at a lecture before the Moscow Linguistic Circle, Boris Tomaševskij defined the role of rhythm in verse as the "distribution of expirational energy within the limits of one wave—the verse."[10] This definition is broad enough to subsume both Brik's rhythmical impulse and Èjchenbaum's melodics. In addition to "lexical-accentual" (*slovesno-udarnyj*) and "intonational-syntactic" (*intonacionno-frazovoj*) rhythm, Tomaševskij spoke of "harmonic" rhythm.[11] Borrowed from the French linguist Maurice Grammont (1866–1946), "harmony" designates the relation between speech sound distribution and the rhythmical organization of the line. In verse, according to Tomaševskij, "harmony fulfills a twofold task: first, dissimilation—the segmentation of speech into rhythmical periods; second, assimilation—the evocation of the idea that the segments thus marked are analogous."[12]

9. Ibid., p. 195.
10. "Pjatistopnyj jamb Puškina," *O stiche: Stat'i* (Leningrad, 1929), p. 182.
11. "Problema stichotvornogo ritma," *ibid.*, p. 25.
12. Ibid., p. 22.

Rhyme is a good example of a harmonic correlation. On the one hand, it demarcates one rhythmical unit (a line) from the text, and on the other, it renders the two lines analogous through the repetition of sounds. But rhyme is not the only such phenomenon in verse. As Brik argued, verse is always marked by the orchestration of speech sounds. Using Puškin's and Lermontov's poems as examples, he showed how thoroughly poetry is permeated with sound repetition.

Tomaševskij's attitude toward sound repetition differed considerably from Brik's. Tomaševskij was not interested in repetition as a manifestation of the "fundamental euphonic laws" of poetic language, but as a functional element of rhythmically organized speech. In the Russian trochaic tetrameter, he argued, even feet carry stress more often than odd ones and the line tends to break into two colons each composed of one strong and one weak foot. This rhythmical partition of the line is underscored by the distribution of vowels in Puškin's verse (where each downbeat is stressed):

> On imel odno viden'e
> o—e   o—e
> (He had a single vision)[13]

This, of course, is just one instance of the correlation of speech sound repetition and verse rhythm, and Tomaševskij provides many others to support his thesis that "verse 'harmony' belongs fully within the theory of rhythm."[14]

Not only was Tomaševskij's theory of verse rhythm more inclusive than that of the other OPOJAZ members, but it was constructed from the standpoint of the perceiving subject.[15] In discussing harmonic rhythm, for example, he stressed its capacity for evoking the idea of analogy in the subject. In this respect he departed considerably from both Brik and Èjchenbaum. Brik

13. Ibid., p. 23.
14. Ibid., p. 24.
15. For a detailed discussion of this topic see M. Červenka, "Rytmický impuls," pp. 73–84.

arrived at his concept of the rhythmical impulse from the perspective of the creating subject. The kinetic organization of the verse (the regular distribution of word stresses in it) engenders motor processes that are present during its generation. The perceiver merely re-presents this original motion in his or her reading. It might seem that *Ohrenphilologie* had reversed this hierarchy in stressing the aural perception of verse, so that the perceiving subject was its point of departure as well, but this shift was purely a heuristic device. Sievers's experiments with recitation in fact served as the basis for reconstructing what he took to be the correct authorial reading. And Èjchenbaum deliberately bracketed off the act of perception, seeking only the "objective" preconditions of verse melodics that he identified with syntax: "Independent of individual nuances in reading, syntactic structure is a totally objective fact and syntactic intonation, within the bounds of our requirements, is obligatory."[16]

This reduction of verse to its "objective" preconditions was clearly unacceptable to Tomaševskij. "We do not recognize verse through immediate perception," he argued in the opening paragraph of *Russian Versification.* "'Verse-quality' [*priznak stichotvornosti*] is generated not solely from the objective attributes of poetic language, but from the conditions of its artistic perception as well, from the hearer's judgment about it based on his taste."[17] Thus, the starting point of metrics should not be rhythm as such but its constitution in the perceiver's consciousness.

At the most abstract level, rhythm is experienced when a "phenomenon becomes arranged in 'periods' that are perceived as 'isochronous,' whereas in objective time they may be unequal."[18] This is a generalization of Tomaševskij's observations on the twofold task of "harmonic rhythm" discussed earlier. The constitution of rhythm in the perceiver's consciousness has both dissimilative and assimilative aspects. It dissolves the utterance

16. *Melodika russkogo liričeskogo sticha*, p. 16.
17. *Russkoe stichosloženie: Metrika* (Petersburg, 1923), p. 7.
18. "Ritm prozy," *O stiche*, p. 258.

into distinct rhythmical periods and at the same time, by rendering these periods rhythmically equivalent, reconstitutes the utterance. In terms of the inner experience of time, this act can be described as a continuous interplay of expectations and fulfillments. The reading of a "long series of repeated, analogous lines creates a sort of rhythmical inertia in the perceiver, a scheme of 'prosodic expectations.'"[19] Expectation alone is insufficient for the arousal of rhythm in consciousness: "Regularity distinguishes rhythmical speech from unorganized, unregulated speech only if the formed complex of phonic phenomena . . . recurs and is perceived as similar, thus enforcing in perception the sensation of this 'regularity.'" The fulfillment of expectations, the "'recognition' at every moment of a recurring regularity," must accompany the original expectation for the emergence of rhythm in the perceiver's consciousness.[20]

Conceptualized so generally, however, the notion of rhythm clearly exceeds the sphere of metrics. The experience of rhythm as just described occurs not only in poetry but in the other temporal arts, as well as in extra-artistic areas. Second, "rhythm" in Tomaševskij's usage refers to the "objective" stratum of rhythmical experience, the real phonic sequence that the perceiver faces. In its actual physical heterogeneity, this stratum inevitably defies systematic description. According to Tomaševskij, "rhythm can only be concrete, can be based only on the elements of phonation that we hear or actually take into account in both rhythmical and nonrhythmical speech."[21] In this respect, rhythm is a singular phenomenon: every utterance, every line, can have its own rhythm based on the repetition of any phonic element. In relation to verse, Tomaševskij prefers not to use the term "rhythm" but to speak instead of the "rhythmical impulse."

As I pointed out earlier, the concept of the rhythmical impulse was introduced into Formalist terminology by Osip Brik. With Tomaševskij, however, it acquired quite a different meaning.

19. "Pjatistopnyj jamb Puškina," p. 142.
20. "Ritm prozy," p. 260.
21. "Problema stichotvornogo ritma," p. 13.

Whereas Brik's rhythmical impulse pertained to the motor process generating verse, Tomaševskij's pertained to the process of interaction between verse and its perceiver. In this new meaning, the rhythmical impulse is an abstraction from the actual rhythm perceived by the subject. The isochronism of verse periods implies a selection among phonic features, the designation of those to be considered equal. Tomaševskij calls these "rhythm-creating elements." Thus, verse, in "dissolving itself into periods that are subjectively evaluated as equivalent, maintains the law common to all periods and orders its rhythm-creating elements analogously."[22] This reduction of all phonic data to those that are rhythm-creating, and hence regularly repeated throughout a poem, limits considerably the number of rhythmical possibilities and provides the perceiver with a grid or skeletal structure within which the interplay of expectations and fulfillments takes place. For under these conditions "rhythm is perceived against the background of an average rhythmical scheme, the most frequent, most expected one. We shall call this rhythmical expectation created in our perception by the aggregate effect of a series of recited lines, this 'general idea' about the rhythmical character of a poem, the *rhythmical impulse*."[23]

It must be stressed, however, that Tomaševskij distinguished rhythm in general from the rhythmical impulse proper to verse not only on intrinsic criteria. The heterogeneous phonic elements whose repetition constitutes rhythm lack a social and historical dimension. As rhythm occurs outside language, virtually any phonic feature can serve as its vehicle, but verse language is a linguistic phenomenon and its repertoire of rhythm-creating elements is necessarily restricted by the social nature of language. "Language," in Tomaševskij's view, "is what links the speaker to the hearer. The speaker not only utters words but also listens to them, and the hearer is not absolutely passive in his listening. Language is apprehended because the hearer knows it. The

22. "Ritm prozy," p. 260.
23. *Russkoe stichosloženie*, p. 65.

sounds reaching his ears are signals for him to recognize the speech as an utterance that he could have made himself. The most passive listening is always accompanied by an activity—inner speech. Thus, reception and production inextricably comprise any linguistic fact. Only those features copresent in pronunciation and perception can be essential to language. Only this link—the consonance of the utterer and the hearer—is real language."[24] In terms of the theory of verse, not every linguistic idiosyncrasy of interlocutors (such as a poet's stammer), but only those that are obligatory for both utterer and hearer, can become rhythm-creating elements in verse. This premise was elaborated in detail by Jakobson in a book on Czech metrics written about the same time as Tomaševskij's remarks (see below pp. 238–40). It became the cornerstone of his phonological metrics, which Tomaševskij himself embraced in the mid-1920s.

The social nature of literature and the history of verse impose another constraint on the selection of rhythm-creating elements. In encountering a poem, for example, hearers or readers are usually not a tabula rasa, innocent minds exposed to verse for the first time. Almost always they carry with them the memory of their previous dealings with poems, a backlog of literary education, tradition, and so forth. The fact that they are willing to see the various lines of a poem as comparable, even if quite dissimilar, indicates that the constitution of the rhythmical impulse has at its basis some canonized set of rhythmical conventions. This for Tomaševskij is "meter." Metrical norms function similarly to linguistic ones in the perception of verse rhythm. They "make the comparison [of verse units] easier by highlighting those features whose apprehension yields material for appraising the equivalence of speech periods. The goal of these norms is to provide a *prearranged system for organizing the system of phonations*, that necessary conventionality which links the poet with his audience and helps his rhythmical intentions to be perceived."[25]

---

24. "Problema stichotvornogo ritma," p. 30.
25. Ibid., p. 11.

In using the concept of meter, however, Tomaševskij did not revert to the Symbolist dichotomy of meter and rhythm. For him, the two were not absolutely distinct: "It is clear that the study of a norm cannot be separated from the study of actual possibilities, the concrete forms of the phenomenon that are subject to this norm."[26] The actual implementation of a metrical norm is not a series of deviations from an untenable ideal but a set of tendencies complying to one degree or another with this norm. Thus, Tomaševskij's 1919 study of Puškin's iambic pentameter measures statistically the tendency of syllables to be stressed. As might be expected, odd syllables are stressed only exceptionally; even ones are much more frequently stressed, but even these are not stressed equally. Only the last syllable (or the penultimate one in feminine endings) carries an obligatory stress, because "this syllable is the boundary of the rhythmical series (the line) and subsequent syllables . . . do not continue this series but lie outside of it."[27] On all the other even syllables, stress is distributed according to poetic style. Puškin's iamb differs in this respect from the iambs of other nineteenth-century poets, and even the proportion of stressed syllables varies in different stages of his career.

Tomaševskij's conception of meter also differs from the Symbolists' in its relativism. Different languages inevitably employ different prosodic elements as vehicles of the "same meter." And even within a single poetic tradition the metrical system changes in time. The change is triggered by shifts in the hierarchy of what Tomaševskij calls primary and secondary features of verse. A primary feature is a regular distribution of one phonic element canonized by a given metrical convention. "Thus, in classical [Russian] metrics, the canonized element of sound ordered according to the metrical norms is accent."[28] Because verse language is a complex structure of correlated elements, the canonized ordering of one phonic feature entails the regular distribution of others. This patterning, though often vague or

26. "Stich i ritm: Metodologičeskie zamečanija," *O stiche: Stat'i*, pp. 53–54.
27. "Pjatistopnyj jamb Puškina," p. 141.
28. "Problema stichotvornogo ritma," p. 8.

subliminal, creates the secondary features of verse, that is, its actual rhythm. Such a clear-cut distinction between primary and secondary features exists only at the moment when a particular metrical system is generally accepted as the only one possible. When its authority begins to be questioned, the secondary features come to the fore. Poets realize that "it is possible to write verse governed only by secondary features, that *an utterance can sound like verse even without meter.*"[29] Ultimately such a situation leads to the abandonment of the previous metrical norm and the establishment of one of the secondary features as a rhythm-creating element.

Given the paramount role of meter in generating the rhythmical impulse, it is not remarkable that Tomaševskij considered it the "specific differentia of verse vis-à-vis prose."[30] But insofar as he defined verse as the implementation of a specific metrical norm, he was unable to account for its overall unity. It was impossible for him to say what iambic and trochaic verse have in common, or, given the geographical and historical relativity of meters, what the connection is between, say, iambic verse in different languages or different historical periods. Therefore, Tomaševskij introduced the concept of verse language, which unites metrically disparate verse on the basis of other shared properties. For instance, "in contemporary European practice the custom was established of writing verse in even lines differentiated by capital letters, and to print prose in continuous lines without breaks. Despite the heterogeneity of *graphia* and living speech, this fact is significant, because there are specific linguistic associations with writing. The segmentation of the utterance into 'lines,' periods whose phonic potential is comparable or even identical in very simple cases, is evidently the distinctive feature of verse language."[31]

This fact, however, does not imply that prose written as verse will always and everywhere be perceived as such, or vice versa.

29. Ibid., p. 9.
30. Ibid., p. 10.
31. Ibid., p. 11.

The customary graphic arrangement merely signals to the European reader one formal difference between verse and prose, but does not establish either of them. Only the projection of an utterance against the current metrical norm can do that. For Tomaševskij meter is a relative category; therefore, "there is no hard boundary between prose and verse."[32]

Tomaševskij's claim was almost immediately challenged by Jurij Tynjanov, who devoted an entire monograph entitled *The Problem of Verse Language* to discovering a factor capable of differentiating verse from prose. However, Tynjanov's argument with Tomaševskij did not involve a radically different view of verse language. As I shall show, the two were quite close on many essential issues, but the logic of Tynjanov's systemic metaphor and his insights into the semantic dimension of verse led him to different conclusions.

As I argued in the preceding chapter, the key concept of Tynjanov's poetics was the literary system. Understood as a hierarchical set of variables, it consisted of a series of correlated subsystems (for example, genres), which in turn consisted of individual work-systems. Tynjanov related the interdependent variables through the concept of "function." Thus, every work exhibits a particular function—a correlation of the dominant constructive factor with the subordinate material. This function, dubbed by Tynjanov the "principle of construction," goes beyond the level of the single work. It unites individual works into literary subsystems—interdependent variables in the overall literary system. This system is not simply a logical construct; it has a historical correlate—the series of actual literary forms evolving in time.[33] These forms are not just accidents of history that cannot be systematically studied; they are embodiments of specific functions and their continuity or change is

32. *Russkoe stichosloženie*, p. 9.

33. For Tynjanov's discussion of the relation between form and function, see especially "O literaturnoj èvoljucii," *Archaisty i novatory* (Leningrad, 1929), pp. 38–41.

indicative of relations among the variables within the literary system.

From this perspective, the Formalist Tynjanov held that verse language should not be treated as a form alone, but also as a function. The fact that poetry, unlike prose, has long been written in even lines betrays a fundamental functional difference between them. For Tynjanov, verse and prose were the two most general literary subsystems constituted through the inversion of their respective principles of construction. "In verse the pivotal constructive factor is *rhythm* and the material (in a broad sense) is the *semantic grouping;* in prose the constructive factor is the *semantic grouping* (the plot) and the material is the rhythmical (in the broad sense) elements of the word."[34] The opposition between prose and poetry is thus not absolute but a function of the literary system as a whole. As the system evolves, the "time may come when it will be inessential whether a work is written in verse or prose, but as long as the distinction between prose and poetry remains palpable, their two contrastive principles of construction coexist within the literary system.[35]

Because by definition the principle of construction is always a correlation of two elements—in the case of verse, rhythm and meaning—one cannot adequately describe verse by describing only its dominant component, rhythm. On this point Tynjanov departs significantly from Tomaševskij, who confined his poetic study to metrics, a "discipline . . . studying the principles that underlie the ordering of actual rhythm."[36] Tynjanov believed the theory of verse language must also include verse semantics, which is a "discipline concerned with the meanings of words and verbal groups, and their evolution and shift in poetry."[37] The deformation of meaning in verse distinguishes it from prose as signifi-

---

34. "Literaturnyj fakt," ibid., p. 15.
35. "O literaturnoj èvoljucii," p. 39.
36. *Russkoe stichosloženie*, p. 11.
37. "Predislovie k knige *Problema stichovoj semantiki*," *Poètika, istorija literatury, kino* (Moscow, 1977), p. 253.

cantly as the dominance of rhythm. According to Tynjanov, "prose and poetry are enclosed semantic categories; prosaic meaning is always distinct from poetic meaning, and consequently poetic syntax and even its vocabulary are also essentially different from those of prose."[38] By systematically examining the meaning of the lexical units that make up verse, Tynjanov went beyond the other OPOJAZ members who (beginning with Brik) claimed they were including semantics within their schemes. In fact, these Formalists reduced semantics to syntax, the rules for combining words into more complex meaningful wholes, and neglected the actual lexical content of the words involved.

Tynjanov's treatment of rhythm, however, did not differ much from that of the other Formalists. In conceiving of it primarily as a "motor-energic" phenomenon, he was quite close to Brik. Instead of speaking of verse isochronism (whether objective or subjective), he treated rhythmical segmentation as a quantity of labor or energy expended.[39] As we have seen, the idea of verbal art as energy-extensive language was the basis for Šklovskij's conception of artistic de-familiarization, but in his purposive explanation of art the significance of rhythm lay in its effect upon the perceiver. Rhythmical irregularities were supposed to frustrate the reader's expectations, thus requiring more effort on his or her part. In Tynjanov's systemic metaphor, on the other hand, rhythm participates in the constructive function—a hierarchical correlation with other elements of the work. Here the labor involved in the rhythmical organization of verse seems to be the energy source for the ongoing struggle for domination of its elements.

Tynjanov's conception of rhythm was perfectly in keeping with his overall antisubstantialist position. As energy, rhythm cannot be identified with any of the phonic elements constituting verse. Rather, it is a system—a dynamic interplay of many factors: " 'Rhythm' [is] the entire dynamics of the poem compris-

38. "O kompozicii *Evgenija Onegina*," ibid., p. 55.
39. *Problema stichotvornogo jazyka* (Leningrad, 1924), p. 129–33.

ing the interactions among meter (accentual scheme), linguistic relations (syntax), and sound relations (repetitions)."[40] Among these, Tynjanov claimed, meter plays the dominant role. Although this apparently echoes Tomaševskij's belief in the paramount significance of meter for verse, a closer scrutiny reveals a difference. In Tynjanov's view, what dominates rhythm is not meter as a system of regularly alternating prosodic features, but rather the "principle of meter," in other words, the "dynamic grouping of verbal material according to a prosodic feature. Most elementary and basic to this is the singling out of some metrical group as a *unit*. This act also prepares dynamically for the isolation of a subsequent, similar group. If this metrical preparation is realized we get a metrical system."[41] Even if this preparation is not realized in the subsequent group, even if the metrical system is absent (as in free verse), we are still dealing with verse language. "'Unrealized preparation' is also a dynamizing instance. Meter is preserved in the form of a metrical impulse. Every 'nonrealization' involves a metrical regrouping: either as a coordination of the two units (carried out progressively) or as a subordination (carried out regressively). . . . Here the meter as a system is replaced by meter as a dynamic principle, namely, the set toward meter, the equivalent of meter."[42]

As the term "metrical impulse" indicates, Tynjanov's "meter" covered what Tomaševskij perceived to be two separate categories. In the sense of "metrical system," it coincided roughly with Tomaševskij's notion of meter, but as the "equivalent of meter," it overlapped with Tomaševskij's "rhythmical impulse." For Tomaševskij the rhythmical impulse alone could not constitute verse; for Tynjanov the principle of meter would.[43] This vari-

40. "Ob osnovach kino," *Poètika, istorija literatury, kino*, p. 341.
41. *Problema stichotvornogo jazyka*, p. 30.
42. Ibid.
43. Apparently in the mid-twenties, perhaps under Tynjanov's influence, Tomaševskij modified his position somewhat. Thus in 1925 he was willing to concede that "Majakovskij's verse is constrained merely by its rhythmical impulse" ("Stich i ritm," p. 59).

ance reflects the difference in Tomaševskij's and Tynjanov's orientations. Tomaševskij proceeded from concrete verse forms, concentrating on their heterogeneity, whereas Tynjanov proceeded from the general category of the literary system. Striving to discover the identity of verse as a function within this overall system, Tynjanov concentrated on what poems have in common.

Naturally then, Tynjanov rejected features that were characteristic of verse at one point but later disappeared. Meter, in the sense of a prosodic system, was such a case. "In a certain literary system the function of verse was fulfilled by the formal element of meter. But prose diversified and evolved, and so did verse. The diversification of one type of [sound-meaning] correlation involves, or better, is linked to the diversification of another type of correlation. The rise of metrical prose (with Andrej Belyj) was connected to the transference of the verse function from meter to other features of verse that were often secondary or concomitant, such as the rhythm-demarcating verse units, particular syntactic forms, or vocabulary. The function of prose or verse remains, but the formal elements fulfilling it are different."[44]

Thus, in a seeming paradox, Tynjanov reversed the hierarchy between central and peripheral features as markers of verse. Because central features are always the prime victims of historical change, the identity of a verse system lies in its peripheral features, in those elements that despite changes in the center continue to distinguish it from prose. "The principle of construction is revealed not in the maximum conditions comprising it, but in the minimal ones. For it is obvious that these minimal conditions are the ones intrinsic to the given construction and in them we should seek the key to the specific character of the construction."[45] Free verse, then, belongs to the verse system despite the fact that it does not correspond to any metrical system. By segmenting a continuous utterance into rhythmical periods it transforms the verbal material according to the same principle as metrically regular verse.

44. "O literaturnoj èvoljucii," p. 59.
45. *Problema stichotvornogo jazyka*, p. 17.

There is, however, one important difference between free verse and more traditional verse forms. In metrically regular verse, recurrent rhythmical units tend to be smaller than those of free verse. They are the syllable, foot, and hemistich, whereas in verse organized solely by the metrical principle, the basic unit is the entire line. In the absence of any prosodic system, the only marker of such a unit is its graphic form. In free verse "graphics plays a special role, for it stands not only for the rhythm but for the metrical unit as well. Here graphics is the signal of a line, of rhythm, and by the same token of metrical dynamics—the indispensable condition of rhythm."[46] For this reason, Tynjanov, unlike Tomaševskij, ascribed major importance to the graphic form of verse. Graphic form provides the minimal conditions for the rise of rhythm as the dominant factor of verse construction.

Tynjanov believed that not only rhythm, the constructive factor of verse, was reducible to its graphic form, but the subordinate material—that is, the semantic groups within it, was as well. In Puškin's poetry, for example, a series of dots sometimes replaces a line or a group of lines, as in the original version of the thirteenth stanza of "To the Sea":

> The world has emptied . . . .
> . . . .
> . . . .
> . . . .

Here, three and one-half lines of dots serve as the graphic equivalent of the same expanse of words. This substitution is purely graphic; no oral rendition is possible. The voice has at its disposal only a pause—a silence indicating the absence of words. The graphic equivalent signals the presence of this absence, and in doing so carries the metrical energy of the verse. "Obviously, the successive segmentation and reunification of metrical elements . . . does not occur [here]. The meter is given only as a

46. Ibid., p. 31.

sign, a *potential* that is hard to detect. To us, however, the fragment and the dots are equal to the entire stanza and we perceive the lines of the following stanza . . . precisely as the following stanza. That is, *a stanza has elapsed* between the fragment commencing the stanza discussed and the next stanza, and the fragment carries the metrical energy of the whole stanza."[47] As long as the semantically empty dots serve the constructive principle and fulfill the function of actual words, they are a minimal equivalent of the material in the verse construction.

Earlier I suggested that Tynjanov conceived of verse rhythm as a system composed not only of the dominant meter but of other rhythmical factors. The most important of these are sound repetition and rhyme, which Tomaševskij included under the rubric of harmonic rhythm, as we have seen. For Tomaševskij, sound repetition and rhyme operate on the principle of expectation and fulfillment, thus performing the twofold task of rhythmical dissimilation and assimilation. Tynjanov considered them only secondary rhythmical factors because the proportion of progressive and regressive forces they command differs from that of meter. In meter, the progressive force is most important. It in itself is capable of generating rhythm, as in free verse, where the regressive realization of the initial expectation is forever frustrated. The perception of sound repetition is just the opposite. It lacks all progressive force or, as Tynjanov cautiously added in a footnote, it "is extremely weak."[48] We usually do not expect a sound to be repeated. In rhyme, on the other hand, both forces—regressive and progressive—operate. Nevertheless, Tynjanov argues that here regression is the primary factor.

This claim may require some clarification. One could object that in a regularly rhymed and strophically organized poem the progressive force is paramount: the reader has every expectation of the recurrence of a rhyming ending. For Tynjanov, however, this situation merely shows rhyme under maximal condi-

47. Ibid., p. 24.
48. Ibid., p. 128.

tions. In texts with looser rhyme and strophic schemes, the reader's expectation that some subsequent lines will conclude with a group of sounds similar to those he or she is presently perceiving drops considerably. Tynjanov illustrates this claim with a poem of Tjutčev's in which a rhyme separated by five verse lines passes by virtually unnoticed.[49] What accounts for the weak effect of this rhyme is the lack of expectation on the reader's part, for he or she realizes it only regressively, and then only if he or she has retained the first rhyming ending over an interval of five lines. Rhyme, moreover, is secondary to meter because it depends on prior metrical segmentation: the rhyming sounds occupy the same positions within lines that have already been metrically delimited.

All utterances organized according to the constructive principle of verse just outlined exhibit, according to Tynjanov, four essential features.[50] The first he calls *the unity of the verse sequence* [*rjad*], which is created by metrically isolating a particular segment from the continuous speech chain. Through this segmentation the second property of verse language arises, namely, *the density of the verse sequence*. The isolation of a metrical segment from its linguistic context brings its constitutive elements closer together: new connections among them, nonexistent before this segmentation, are established. This explains "why the quantitative content of a verse sequence must be limited. A unit that is quantitatively excessive either loses its boundaries or itself becomes segmented into other units. In both cases, however, it ceases to be a unit."[51] The unity and density of the verse sequence generate the third feature of verse construction—*the dynamization of the verbal material*. The segmentation of an utterance into recurring rhythmical units makes the semantic units similar to each other not only because of their meanings but also because of their phonic and grammatical features, position in the line, and so forth. In the progressive-regressive buildup of

49. Ibid., p. 34.
50. Ibid., p. 47.
51. Ibid., p. 39.

the line, words and their groupings cease to be mere carriers of infinitely repeatable meanings and turn into heterogeneous entities whose multiple facets are constantly foregrounded in the ongoing process of rhythmical permutation.

The most difficult to grasp of Tynjanov's four features of verse construction is *the successivity of its verbal material.* In the first place, he opposes it to the simultaneity of the verbal material of prose. Language is a temporal medium, so the verbal material of any speech construction must be successive. In Tynjanov's usage, however, the words "successivity" and "simultaneity" refer not to the medium itself but to the mode of its perception. In prose, the dominant set toward semantics prevents us from perceiving the utterance as a process. The successivity of its elements is there merely to help us grasp the meaning of the utterance in its totality. This perception of wholeness occurs only after the utterance is finished and we retain all of its elements in our consciousness as a simultaneous whole. In verse, with its dynamized verbal material, the goal sought is not a simultaneous meaning but the sequence itself, the rhythmical unfolding of the verbal material. Such speech is perceived as a process—a continuous correlation of different facets of language whose heterogeneity resists any final semantic summation.

But amazingly, at the same time Tynjanov claims that in prose "time is perceptible," whereas in verse "time is not perceptible at all."[52] Here we are confronted by apparent oxymorons: the "temporal simultaneity" of prose and the "atemporal successivity" of verse. This contradictory notion arises from the fact that Tynjanov was really talking about two different temporal strata: the temporality involved in the perception of the artistic medium and the temporality of the extralinguistic semantic groupings that occur in it. This extralinguistic temporal stratum is especially important in prose, where such groupings are the dominant constructive factor. Through a series of gradual se-

52. Ibid., p. 119.

mantic buildups, the reader constitutes characters and events whose causal–temporal relations (the story) present one temporal flux. In addition to the indirect experience of temporal flow presented in the story (*fabula*), the reader experiences directly the flux of the plot (*sjužet*). That the reader is simultaneously aware of both of them is apparent in Gogol's short story "The Nose," in which the "decelerated . . . narrative about the barber Ivan Jakovlevič eating bread and onions produces a comical effect because too much of the (literary) time is devoted to it."[53] In verse language dominated by rhythm, semantics (in the broad sense) is merely a subordinate material. The constitutive elements of verse construction are organized primarily through their rhythmical permutations, and the experience of time in the story–plot interaction is largely missing. Moreover, as these permutations are an ongoing process, there are no breaks in its perception dividing the temporal continuum into "now" and "then" points. Every moment is simultaneously a function of its future (progressive preparation) and its past (the regressive realization of a previous preparation). Tynjanov's claim about the imperceptibility of time in poetry refers therefore to the fact that the unfolding of an entire verse construction takes place in a single perceptual "now" suspended from the temporal flow.

The discussion of temporal perception in prose and verse occurs in the second half of Tynjanov's monograph, which is concerned with the effects of verse construction on lexical meaning. The fact that he originally planned to call his book *The Problem of Verse Semantics* indicates how crucial he considered this part to be. The nearly six decades that have passed since its publication have rendered Tynjanov's many revolutionary insights about verse semantics commonplaces in modern literary scholarship, but within the context of Russian Formalism their value is unquestionable. And though Tynjanov's metrics often depended upon discoveries made by other members of the

53. Ibid.

movement, his study of verse semantics is without any doubt an original contribution to Formalist poetics.[54]

Tynjanov's analysis of verse meaning was firmly rooted in his systemic metaphor, according to which every phenomenon is relational. For semantics this meant that "it is not necessary to proceed *from the word* as the single indivisible element of verbal art, to regard it as the 'bricks with which an edifice is built.' *This element is analyzable into much finer 'verbal elements.'*"[55] Hence, as with rhythm, verbal meaning is a system of hierarchically correlated factors—semantic features.

The first distinction Tynjanov drew was that between the "basic feature" and the "secondary features" of semantics. A basic feature is a general lexical category common to all the usages of a word and hence guaranteeing its semantic identity. This identity is purely semantic, for though homophones share the same outer form, they do not share their basic semantic feature. Drawing a parallel with phonology, Tynjanov saw the "concept of the basic feature in semantics as analogous to that of the phoneme."[56]

The secondary features of meaning can be divided into the "vacillating" and the "steady." The former are a function of the immediate linguistic context in which the word appears. Every speech construction semantically colors the words which compose it by furnishing them with (slightly) different connotations. Steady secondary features are a function of a broader social context: the milieu from which the word comes (slangs, dialects, and so forth). Tynjanov calls it the "lexical coloring of the word" and claims that it is *discernible only outside the activity and situation which it characterizes.* Finally, in synthetic languages like Russian, words are usually composed of two parts: the "ref-

---

54. This, of course, does not mean that Tynjanov's semantic theory is without any intellectual predecessors. As the footnotes to his book indicate, he adopted some of his most important notions from French and German students of language: M. Bréal, C. Bally, J. Vendryes, H. Paul, A. Rosenstein, and W. Wundt, to name a few.

55. *Problema stichotvornogo jazyka*, p. 35.

56. Ibid., p. 52; p. 134.

erential" (*veščestvennyj*) part that carries the semantic charge of the word, and the "formal" part—the vehicle of its grammatical meaning.[57] The domination of rhythm in verse tends to realign the hierarchy of semantic features in its words according to their verse function. The unity and density of the verse sequence is perhaps the most obvious cause of such a semantic shift. In a verse construction the rhythmical and semantic divisions need not coincide, and syntactically related words may be separated by metrical boundaries. Enjambment is a case in point. A word separated from its context and incorporated into a metrical sequence gains strong new connotations because of the density of the sequence.

An interaction of rhythm and semantics also occurs within segments smaller than the line, for example, feet and syllables. If a line is composed of words whose boundaries coincide with foot boundaries, every word turns into a rhythmical unit (a foot) and its syntactic relation to other words weakens. Such word-feet tend to be perceived as if in isolation, so that their basic semantic features are intensified.[58] Caesura, an obligatory word boundary after a particular syllable, is another rhythmical division capable of interfering with semantics if, for example, the concomitant intonational pause divides words that are syntactically closely related. Thus, in Lermontov's line

> No ne s toboj / ja serdcem govorju
> (But not to you / with my heart I speak)

such a pause (accompanied by a seeming parallelism of the two hemistychs) even leads to a misreading (a "secondary semasiologization" in Tynjanov's terms), attested to by the fact that two years after the poet's death this line was printed as:

> No ne s toboj, / —ja s serdcem govorju

57. Ibid., pp. 56–57; p. 58; p. 56.
58. Ibid., p. 71.

(But not to you, / to my heart I speak)[59]

The lexical coloring of words (a steady secondary feature) enjoys a special position in the semantics of Russian verse. It results from the strong influence of liturgical Church Slavonic on literary Russian. Lomonosov's linguistic reform of the eighteenth century and his theory of three styles identified the high style with the use of Church Slavonic vocabulary. Although in modern Russian this factor has decreased considerably, there are still many cases in which a poet can play on the synonymity or homonymity of Russian and Church Slavonic words. Lexical coloring can even become a dominant semantic feature when the Church Slavonic word is no longer understandable to the reader but still carries the lofty, liturgical connotations belonging to that tongue. Vocabulary drawn from other foreign languages, proper names characterizing foreign cultures, or even Russian words connected to a particular region, trade, or milieu fulfill a similar function. All of them foreground secondary features in the words with which they comprise a verse sequence.

In addition to the semantic features that I have discussed so far, the word consists of referential and formal parts. Their relation, or more precisely, the change in this relation caused by rhythm, is equally important for verse semantics. Here secondary rhythmical factors—sound repetition and rhyme—play a central role. Needless to say, for Tynjanov these devices are complex phenomena, and in studying them he takes into account the proximity of repeated sounds and rhymes, their relationship to meter, the quantity and quality of the sounds utilized, the part of the word in which they occur, and the general character of the word.[60]

Sound repetitions affect lexical meaning in many ways, for instance, through the mimetic and expressive sound patterns that the early Formalists found especially intriguing. Tynjanov,

59. Ibid., p. 63.
60. Ibid., pp. 102 and 109.

A Synecdoche

however, was less interested in this direct link between the phonic and semantic aspects of individual words than in their relationship in words interlocked in a verse sequence. For example, his commentary on the line

Unylaja pora, očej očarovan'e
(Doleful time, the charm of eyes)

provides a good explanation of this phenomenon. "'Očej očarovan'e' is a group united both metrically and phonically, and we perceive the sounds očej, oča- as comparable. This perception involves two successive moments: the recognition in the word očarovan'e [charm] of an element from the previous word and the uniting of the two words into a group. In this, the referential part of the word očarovan'e becomes colored through its strong linkage to the referential part of očej [eyes]. It is as if the first stage in the redistribution of the referential and formal parts . . . had taken place, in this case, as though we derived očarovan'e from the root oči."[61]

Obviously, sound repetitions need not be limited to contiguous words. They may permeate an entire verse construction; by rendering words phonically similar they dynamize their verbal material, and through a regressive movement make this material successive. Summing up the role of sound repetition in verse semantics, Tynjanov wrote that its "evocation of the vacillating features of meaning (through the redistribution of the referential and formal parts of the word) and transformation of the utterance into an amalgamated, correlated whole, cause me to view them as a particular kind of rhythmical metaphor."[62]

The role of rhyme in verse semantics is to some degree similar to that of sound repetition. There are, however, certain differences between the two, the stronger progressive force of rhyme being the most important. Because of the anticipation raised by the first rhyming member, rhyme is capable of de-

61. Ibid., p. 107.
62. Ibid., p. 108.

197

forming not only the meaning of the rhymed words but also the "direction of the utterance itself." Put differently, the very play on the fulfillment or frustration of expectations in an actual rhyme can of itself motivate the unfolding of a lyrical "plot" outside of any story. The poem seems to come about only as an exercise in rhyming. Moreover, because of their fixed positions, rhyming words tend to retain their relative independence: they do not interpenetrate or amalgamate as do words in a sound repetition. "The moment of *juxtaposition, comparison,*" wrote Tynjanov, "is so important that I view rhyme as a particular kind of *rhythmical simile* with a partial change in the rhyming member's basic feature or the foregrounding of its vacillating features. Its significance as a powerful semantic lever is beyond any doubt."[63]

Tynjanov's *The Problem of Verse Language* was the most significant criticism of the early OPOJAZ notion of poetic language and the linguistic model that underlies it. Yet, despite such formidable opposition, the linguistic model and its key notion of poetic language did not vanish from Formalist discourse. Quite the contrary: this synecdoche not only survived the movement that spawned it, but after receiving a powerful boost from Prague Structuralism during the thirties and forties, continued into the present day. The reemergence of this theoretical model after its OPOJAZ critique was the work of the second wing of the Formalist movement whose institutionalized center was the Moscow Linguistic Circle. In particular, the genius of the vice-chairman of this group, Roman Jakobson, invested the linguistic model with a depth and sophistication that it had lacked in the early days of OPOJAZ. We now arrive at the complex topic of Jakobsonian poetics.

63. Ibid., p. 109; p. 117.

Expression

> Je dis: une fleur! et, hors de l'oubli où ma voix
> relègue aucun contour, en tant que quelque chose
> d'autre que les calices sus, musicalement se lève,
> idée même et suave, l'absente de tous bouquets.
>
> —STÉPHANE MALLARMÉ, "Crise de vers"

Within the limits of this study of Russian Formalism, Roman Jakobson's theoretical model poses a special problem. In July of 1920 he left Russia for Czechoslovakia, and with the exception of a handful of articles all his major works were published outside his native land. His stay abroad, which only subsequently turned into permanent exile, did not in the beginning preclude scholarly or personal contact with the Formalists he had left behind. His works were read in Russia and his ideas had an impact on several members of the movement. But the scholarly and political situation in Bohemia was quite different from that of Russia, and as time passed the difference grew. By the late twenties all the other Formalists discussed so far had yielded to

Epigraph: When I say: "a flower!" then from that forgetfulness to which my voice consigns all floral form, something different from the usual calyces arises, something all music, essence, and softness: the flower which is absent from all bouquets (Quoted from *Mallarmé: Selected Prose Poems, Essays, and Letters*, ed. and tr. B. Cook [Baltimore, 1956]).

199

official pressure and abandoned either their scholarly careers or their earlier theoretical views, whereas Jakobson's intellectual history does not contain any such caesura. This is not to say that his ideas stood still. In fact, as his research progressed, his approach to linguistics and poetics evolved into a wholly new scholarly paradigm that in 1929 he christened "Structuralism."[1] This development, unlike that of his former comrades, was not the result of an abrupt leap that negated an earlier position; rather, it was a series of gradual changes—an expansion of intellectual horizons and a shift in theoretical emphasis.

It is this very continuity in Jakobson's thought that makes my account of it rather difficult. Because of its organic development, it is impossible to pinpoint with any precision the moment at which Jakobson's Formalist period ended and his Structuralist phase began. And while it is obvious that his linguistic model was an integral part of the Russian movement, it is equally indisputable that a refined version of it informed Structuralist poetics as well. For these reasons, if I am to remain within the strict limits of my topic of Russian Formalism, I cannot treat Jakobson's approach to verbal art adequately; yet any serious attempt at a full analysis will lead me far astray.

To escape this dilemma, my treatment of the Jakobsonian model will be somewhat more arbitrary than that of the others I have discussed. As a way of stressing the Formalist quality of Jakobson's notion of poetic language I shall focus on his booklet on Chlebnikov "written in May, 1919, in Moscow as an introduction to Chlebnikov's *Collected Works* in preparation" and published some two years later in Prague.[2] The Chlebnikov book contains *in nuce* most of Jakobson's ideas about verbal art, but as it is not a full-fledged theory of literature but only a preliminary sketch (*nabrosok*), I shall extract from it the basic principles that came to underlie Jakobson's "literary science." At the same time, because many of the notions vaguely hinted at in the Chlebnikov

1. "Romantické všeslovanství—nová slavistika," *Čin* 1 (1929), 11.
2. *N. S. Trubetzkoy's Letters and Notes*, ed. R. Jakobson (The Hague, 1975), p. 17.

pamphlet are much more fully presented in Jakobson's works of the twenties and early thirties, I shall turn to them whenever they clarify the earlier principles of his linguistic model, though I shall make every effort to respect the diachronic development of his thought.

As Elmar Holenstein has argued persuasively, among the intellectual movements that shaped Jakobson's theoretical outlook, Husserlian phenomenology occupied an especially prominent position. Jakobson's acquaintance with this subject dated back to his student days at Moscow University in the mid-teens, as shown in the epistemological assumptions behind his earliest project in the new literary science. His conception of literary studies closely parallels the procedures of eidetic phenomenology, which in Holenstein's account "is concerned with the grasp of the essential features common to objects of the same category."[3] Accordingly, Jakobson believed that the literary scholar should bracket off the phenomenal heterogeneity of poetic works and focus on the underlying essence that endows them with their categorical identity. As he succinctly put it, "the object of literary science is not literature but literariness, i.e., what makes a given work a literary work."[4]

Jakobson's conception of this *eidos* yielded the first principle of his new poetics. It is the "set [*ustanovka*] toward expression," he wrote, "that I designate as the only factor essential for poetry."[5] Holenstein calls this principle "phenomenological" in that it defines poetry in terms of a perceiver's mental set, thus following the basic premise of phenomenology that no object can be studied "in itself" but only as it is apperceived by an experiencing or observing subject.[6] As we have seen, however, both Tomaševskij and Tynjanov advocated that the study of verse

3. E. Holenstein, *Roman Jakobson's Approach to Language: Phenomenological Structuralism* (Bloomington, Ind., 1976), p. 4.
4. *Novejšaja russkaja poèzija: Nabrosok pervyj* (Prague, 1921), p. 11.
5. Ibid., p. 41.
6. Holenstein "Einführung: Linguistische Poetik," in R. Jakobson, *Hölderlin. Klee. Brecht: Zur Wortkunst dreier Gedichte* (Frankfurt a/M., 1976), p. 9.

must begin with the particular mental set with which a perceiving subject approaches rhythmically organized speech. Thus, if I were to follow Holenstein's suggestion fully I would have to extend the label "phenomenological" to designate their metrical studies as well. However, for me, what is phenomenological in Jakobson's formulation is not the mental set alone but its qualification as the "set toward *expression*." That Jakobson himself considered this qualification crucial is obvious from his suggestion that his method of literary study be called "expressionist."[7] It would seem vital, then, to approach the phenomenological nature of Jakobson's poetics through the concept of the expression.

The expression (*Ausdruck*), a notion that Husserl advanced with great rigor in "Investigation I" of his *Logical Investigations*, served as the cornerstone of his search for a universalist semiotic theory. For Husserl, only a repeatable sign, a sign that retains its essential self-sameness under all circumstances, can serve as a vehicle of logical thought capable of embodying truth. The psychologistic and physicalistic doctrines of representation prevalent in his day failed to account for the ideal nature of the logical sign. By reducing it to a mere representamen of the mental states it indicates or the objectivities it denotes they opened the sign's identity to the vicissitudes of the phenomenal world. Radically stated, if every significative act posits the sign in a new and unrepeatable spatiotemporal nexus, each of these acts inevitably turns the sign into a unique, nonidentical event.

To avoid the relativism inherent in all naturalistic semiotics, Husserl divided signs into two incompatible categories: (1) the expression, identified as "each instance or part of speech" and "each sign . . . essentially of the same sort" that are capable of remaining self-same regardless of the actual context; and (2) the indication (*Anzeichen*), which is any sign lacking such identity and hence merely representing a fluctuating state of affairs.[8]

7. *Novejšaja russkaja poèzija*, p. 10.
8. *Logical Investigations*, vol. 1, tr. J. N. Findlay (New York, 1970), p. 275.

This scheme, however, was merely taxonomic and did not in any way explain why words (and this is what expressions primarily are) can remain unaffected by the context of the speech event. Thus, Husserl was forced to analyze the internal structure of the expression to discover a factor resistant to contextual change. "In the case of a name [for example], we distinguish between what it 'shows forth' (i.e., a mental state) and what it means. And again between what it means (the sense or 'content' of its naming presentation) and what it names (the object of that presentation)."[9] Both the "showing forth" and the "naming" are contingent upon empirical reality and thus cannot retain their sameness in repetition. Only the "content of an expression's naming presentation," the "meaning" (Bedeutung) of the linguistic sign, is independent of the phenomenal context. It is therefore this lexical meaning inherent in the word prior to its representing other entities that endows the expression with its identity and distinguishes it from the indication.

This distinction has a direct bearing on Jakobson's probe into the essence of verbal art. To the three functions of the name—showing forth, naming, and meaning—correspond Jakobson's three goal-oriented verbal activities, or more precisely, functional dialects—the emotive, the practical, and the poetic. He argued against the claims of F. T. Marinetti, the leader of the Italian Futurists, that their experiments in poetry were in fact perfect vehicles for the modern sensibility. Jakobson agreed that "in both emotive and poetic language, linguistic representations (both phonetic and semantic) attract attention to themselves; the bond between sound and meaning in them is closer, more intimate." However, "these facts exhaust what emotive and poetic language have in common."[10] For Jakobson, emotive language was a clear-cut case of the communicative use of language. By intimating a speaker's mental state, an emotive utterance refers

9. Ibid., p. 276.
10. Novejšaja russkaja poèzija, p. 10.

to a phenomenal entity very much as practical language speaks of an objective state of affairs. But "the poetic word is to a certain degree objectless"; it "lacks what Husserl terms *dinglicher Bezug*."[11] Poetic language stands apart from the other two functional dialects because the "communicative function inherent in practical and emotive language is minimal in it." Thus, "poetry, which is nothing but an utterance *set toward the expression*, is governed by its own immanent laws."[12]

The suspension of representation in verbal art profoundly affects the way the poetic utterance operates. Whereas in its communicative function the word is a mere transparent vehicle for the signification of other, nonlinguistic entities, in poetry the word itself, its internal structure, occupies center stage. Grigorij Vinokur—another influential member of the Moscow Linguistic Circle—drew attention to this fact. "A poetic creation," he claimed, "is work with a word that is no longer a mere sign but a *thing* endowed with its own structure, whose elements are reevaluated and regrouped in every new poetic utterance. . . . if the communicative function makes social intercourse possible through the word, the poetic function informs the perceiver about the very structure of the word, shows him the elements that compose its structure, enriches his mind with knowledge of a new object—the word. The poetic function tells us through the word what the word is, whereas through the other functions of the word we learn about objects ontologically different from the word: other functions tell us through the word about something else."[13]

Jakobson's conversion of the Husserlian expression from a logical to an aesthetic category was unorthodox, to say the least, and generated certain problems that had to be solved as his

11. Ibid., p. 47.
12. Ibid., p. 10.
13. "Poètika, lingvistika, sociologija: Metodologičeskaja spravka," *Lef*, no. 3 (1923), 109–110.

expressionist model developed.[14] Within its immediate historical context the rationale for his move was quite clear. By rendering the expression the key notion in his poetics, Jakobson staked out the territory of this discipline beyond the two opposing camps of contemporary Russian literary study. The expressionist model rejected the transrational theory of poetic language propounded by early OPOJAZ, but avoided slipping into the pre-Formalist notion of the literary work as an undistorted mirror of either the poet's soul or the social reality it depicted. With the expressionist model Jakobson could deny that the artwork was a mere psychological or sociological document without implying that it was therefore devoid of meaning. If poetry, as another critic of the transrational model, Jurij Tynjanov, wrote, "does not operate . . . with the *word* but with the *expression*," meaning is still always a component of its structure.[15]

Earlier I suggested that the theoretical gulf between the Petersburg and Moscow Formalists on the issue of poetic language corresponds in some degree to the two notions of *zaum'* among the Futurists. For Kručěnych, who inspired the founding members of OPOJAZ, transrational language was an attempt at liberating linguistic sound from the yoke of rationality; for Chlebnikov, the subject of Jakobson's first book, it was a return to an original language of pure rationality. "It is possible to say," Chlebnikov argued, "that everyday language is the shadow of

14. Although Jakobson's definition of verbal art proved to be quite workable for distinguishing poetic language from its emotive and practical counterparts, because of its origin in logic it tended to obliterate the difference between poetic language and another functional dialect which Jakobson later termed "metalanguage." Viktor Šklovskij, for example, when analyzing authorial metadiscourse in *Don Quixote*, viewed it as a manifestation of the "set toward 'expression' which is so typical in art" ("Kak sdelan *Don-Kichot*," *O teorii prozy* [Moscow, 1925], p. 85). Thus Jakobson and some other Prague Structuralists were eventually forced to come up with a secondary criterion to distinguish the metalinguistic from the poetic set toward expression; see, for example, J. Mukařovský, "O jazyce básnickém," *Slovo a slovesnost* 6 (1940), 114–15; or R. Jakobson, "Linguistics and Poetics," *Style in Language*, ed. T. A. Sebeok (Cambridge, Mass., 1960), p. 358.

15. "Illjustracii," *Archaisty i novatory* (Leningrad, 1929), p. 509.

the great laws of the pure word fallen on an uneven surface."[16] And the proper domicile of this pure word, as he observed elsewhere, is the human mind: "besides the language of words there is a mute language of concepts composed of mental units (a tissue of concepts governing the language of words)."[17] Or, in an anthropomorphic metaphor, "the word is a face with a hat tilted over it. The rational [*myslimoe*] in it precedes the verbal, the aural."[18] From Chlebnikov's standpoint, therefore, verbal art as the art of the word is forever caught in the conceptual web generated by rationality, is always permeated with cognitive meanings.

Such a view of verbal art, however, has in recent years become somewhat unpopular. It exhibits what the French philosopher, Jacques Derrida, calls a "logocentric" bias, for it conceives of the linguistic sign as an instrument of reason. This bias, Derrida argues, has its roots in the "Western metaphysics of presence," which forged the image of the sign as an instance of logos, the signification of Truth. Whatever Chlebnikov's reasons might have been for elevating rational meaning in the verbal parcel, Jakobson's seem somewhat less metaphysical than Derrida would suggest. They stem from another conviction of his—unexpected perhaps, given his phenomenological orientation—that literature is a social institution, a consensus among the members of a particular collectivity. Jakobson believed that poetic works are intersubjective signs involving some form of rationality which he conceptualized as the (imperfect) sharing of cognitive meanings. The OPOJAZ theorists who emphasized the transrational components of poetic language (the emotive and so forth) had in Jakobson's opinion lost sight of the social nature of verbal art. His 1922 comparison of the Moscow and Petersburg branches of the Formalist movement makes this point unequivocally: "Whereas the former [the Moscow branch] argues that the historical development of artistic forms has a so-

16. "Naša osnova," *Sobranie sočinenij*, vol. 5 (Leningrad, 1933), p. 230.
17. "Neizdannaja stat'ja," ibid., p. 187.
18. "Razgovor Olega i Kazimira," ibid., p. 191.

ciological basis, the latter [the Petersburg branch] insists upon the full autonomy of these forms."[19] Thus, accepting Derrida's notion of the "instituted trace"[20] as a substitute for the concept of the sign (damaged beyond repair by its millennia-long marriage to the Western metaphysics of presence), one might say that Jakobson's "logocentrism" stems at least in part from his taking too seriously the fact that the trace is *instituted*. For what else does the act of instituting a trace achieve but some form of presence, that is, a consensus among those whose vested power or interest enables them to promulgate one trace as opposed to another and those who recognize the others' efforts as an accomplished fact? Anyone like Jakobson, who had experienced revolution and civil war, would be well aware of the brutal force by which such a consensus is brought about.[21] Physically enforced presence hardly qualifies as metaphysical.

Rejecting the social determinism of pre-Formalist literary theory, but maintaining nevertheless that literature is essentially social, Jakobson formulated a rather unusual view of "literary sociology." Here the second, "linguistic," principle of the expressionistic model becomes relevant. This principle projects the social dimension of literature into its linguistic material. If verbal art, in contrast to communicative discourse, directs our attention to the internal structure of language, poetic forms are above all linguistic forms. Thus, in Jakobson's words, "poetry is language in its aesthetic function."[22] Because language is for him the social institution par excellence—a set of rules obligatory for the members of a particular speech community—verbal art cannot

19. P. Bogatyrëv and R. Jakobson, "Slavjanskaja filologija v Rossii za g.g. 1914–1921," *Slavia* 1 (1922), 458.
20. J. Derrida, *Of Grammatology*, tr. G. C. Spivak (Baltimore, 1974), p. 46.
21. See, for example, the joke that Jakobson quotes in his review of André Mazon's *Lexique de la guerre et de la révolution en Russie* about a peasant asking the direction to Ljubljanka (a quarter in Moscow where a penitentiary is located). The answer he got was: "Start to sing the Czarist anthem and you will get there quite quickly" ("Vliv revoluce na ruský jazyk," *Nové Atheneum*, no. 3, 2 [1920], 111).
22. *Novejšaja russkaja poèzija*, p. 11.

be asocial. "The theory of poetic language," Jakobson declared, "can be developed only if poetry is treated as a social fact, if a poetic dialectology of its own kind is established."[23]

To appreciate Jakobson's linguistic model fully it is necessary to introduce his overall concept of language. The great Swiss linguist, Ferdinand de Saussure, exerted the most decisive influence on the young Jakobson. As Jakobson recollected in 1956, he gained his first insights into Saussurean linguistics through Saussure's student Sergej Karcevskij, "who in 1917–1919, during his short-lived return to Russia, fired the young generation of Moscow linguists with the *Cours de linguistique générale*."[24]

Jakobson would have found Saussure's theory of language especially stimulating because the main problem it tackled—the identity of the linguistic sign—was also the central theme of Husserl's "Investigation I." The solution the Swiss linguist had to offer was, however, quite different. We have seen that Husserl found the meaning of the expression to be the vehicle of its sameness. But this step only raised the further question, "what is the nature of that meaning?" To answer it Husserl was forced, first, to come up with a situation in which the word would function as a pure meaning free of any indicative relations, and then to account for the self-sameness of meaning in repetition, its identity in every actual situation belonging under this heading. He fixed on the mental soliloquy to meet the first condition. In an interior monologue the subject knows what he means; his words do not serve him as indicators of his thought. Instead, in the directly experienced unity of the significatory act, the meaning of the expression merges with the subject's meaning-intention. This, however, does not imply that for Husserl meaning was a totally subjective entity: if it were, meaning would dissipate into a multiplicity of meaning-intending acts and so would lack any essential sameness. In addition to its intuitive presence in one's consciousness, meaning had to exist intersubjectively for

23. Ibid., p. 5.
24. Jakobson, "Serge Karcevski: August 28, 1884–November 7, 1955," *Cahiers Ferdinand de Saussure*, vol. 14, 1956, p. 10.

Husserl as a universal object (like numbers or geometrical figures) prior to and independent of its actualization. All subjective meaning-intentions would thus be merely tokens of a type, their identity being the ideal self-sameness of the members of a class.

What connects the Swiss linguist to the German philosopher is Saussure's mentalist stance. The starting point of Saussure's "semiology" was not the word in its physical existence but its representation in the subject's consciousness. The two constitutive elements of the linguistic sign (the signifier and the signified) are not the actual sound and referent whose materiality renders them unique, but instead infinitely repeatable mental representations—the "sound image" and the "concept." Like Husserl, Saussure is not a subjectivist, for such a stance would subvert the issue of semiotic identity from the very start. But unlike Husserl, who relegated the intersubjective sameness of the sign to the ideal realm of universal objects, Saussure sought it in the social nature of language.

The basic postulate of Saussurean linguistics is that every phenomenon of language has a strictly dualistic existence. On the one hand, it is a component of an actual utterance by an individual speaker (*parole*), and on the other it is an element within the potential and socially shared system of language (*langue*). Concrete utterances are nothing but particularized instances of the preexistent system, its implementations in physical, heterogeneous matter. In its purely material being every utterance inevitably differs, if ever so slightly, from any other one; therefore the sameness of a linguistic sign cannot be a fact of *parole*.

The situation, however, is radically different with *langue*. It is a homogeneous system of purely linguistic relations devoid of any physical substance, sheer form articulating sound images and concepts into linguistic units. The value of every such unit is precisely circumscribed by its incorporation into this differential grid. Moreover, though entirely conventional, at any given moment *langue* is fixed and obligatory for all users of a language. Thus, the sameness of the linguistic sign, which cannot be discerned in its manifold material manifestations, is a function of the linguistic system. The sign retains its identity through repetitions only because each of its occurrences is an embodiment of the self-same unit of *langue*. Needless to say, for Saussure the science of language should concern itself solely with this internal system of language. Eschewing the traditional preoccupation of linguists with cultural or natural phenomena contingent upon language, he declared: *"the true and unique object of linguistics is language studied in and for itself."*[25]

Though he accepted Saussure's postulate of the social nature of *language,* Jakobson was quite uneasy about the abstract character Saussure ascribed to it. From his point of view, the trace—to return once more to Derrida's terminology—is never instituted at random but rather for some particular purpose. In other words, language, he believed, is preeminently a means–end structure allowing the user to achieve particular goals.

Earlier I mentioned a similar notion of language advocated by the Petersburger Jakubinskij. The two Formalists differed in an important respect, however. For Jakubinskij, the classification of utterances according to *telos* was only a heuristic device, possible but definitely not the exclusive possibility. For Jakobson, in contrast, language existed in no other mode than as a means to a particular end, so that the teleological view was the only one possible. Furthermore, in accord with the strict binary structure of his transrational model, Jakubinskij recognized only two functional dialects—practical language, in which sounds are mere means, and poetic language, in which they are ends. This bifurcation of language was unacceptable to Jakobson because it juxtaposed sound and meaning as two incompatible phenomena. His own classification (inspired by Husserl) proceeded from the actual speech situation, allotting an appurtenant function to each of the indispensable components of the situation—the speaker, the referent, and the sign. For Jakobson, sound and meaning coexist in every functional dialect; only their relationship is a variable.

25. *Course in General Linguistics,* tr. and ed. W. Baskin (New York, 1959), p. 232.

Maintaining his means–end model for better or for worse, Jakobson challenged Saussure's credo that linguistics was concerned solely with language "in and for itself." "Language," Jakobson argued, "according to the correct definition of contemporary French linguists, is a system of conventional values, very much like a pack of cards. But because of this, it would be wrong to analyze it without taking into account the multiplicity of possible tasks without which the system does not exist. Just as we have no rules for a universal card game valid equally for rummy, poker, and card-house building, linguistic rules can be determined only for a system defined by its goal."[26] What is under attack here is not *langue* per se, but Saussure's notion of it as a homogeneous system uniformly governing each and every utterance. Instead, Jakobson conceives of language as a set of functional dialects each with its own system of rules structured in the way best suited to its specific goals.

Of course, the division of *langue* into functional dialects presents some problems of its own, the unity of the national language being perhaps the most important. It would seem reasonable to argue, for instance, that a Russian poem has more in common with utterances belonging to other Russian functional dialects than with a poem, let us say, in English. To account for this unity in variety, Vinokur proposed a modification of Saussure's rigid dualism of *langue* and *parole*. Between the social system of a language and its individual utterances, he posited sets of "stylistic" norms, each governing one particular type of goal-oriented verbal behavior. These norms, pertaining only to specific usages of a language, are less general than the norms of *langue*, but at the same time they are shared by at least some speakers of a language. Like *langue*, they are social.

Viewed through this conceptual prism, every utterance, poetic or otherwise, is simultaneously governed by two normative systems: a general *langue* and a particular style. "The word taken as

---

26. "Konec básnického umprumáctví a živnostnictví," *Pásmo: Revue internationale moderne*, nos. 13/14 (1925), 1.

a thing [i.e., the poetic word], insofar as it is a word, remains liable to *all the laws* that determine the life of a word in general, that rivet every kind of superstructure belonging to the sphere of the utterance to the firm, normative basis of language proper."[27] At the same time, a poetic word, Vinokur argued, is not just an utterance but a *poetic* utterance that belongs in the specific class of utterances united by the pursuit of the same goal. "Taken in itself, of course, each empirically concrete utterance (poetic ones included) is asocial. But the point is that stylistics in general and poetics in particular study these concrete utterances as elements of a *specific system* that is superimposed upon the system of language proper. An utterance is an individual, creative, volitional act. But several of these acts are no longer merely a sum total of individual acts but a *system* endowed with a purpose, a significance, that is generally valid within perhaps narrow, yet surely social, limits. This system of poetic utterances is, in fact, the genuine object of poetics."[28]

Although Jakobson did not at first discuss the unity of functional dialects as fully as Vinokur, his occasional statements on the subject reveal a more critical attitude toward Saussure. He rejected the notion of a homogeneous *langue* equally implemented in every utterance, instead conceiving of a national language as a "system of systems," a hierarchically organized structure of functional dialects each with its own *langue*. Within such a structure, each dialect is only relatively autonomous. Practical language is the most basic or, according to Jakobson's later terminology, the unmarked dialect. Every member of the speech community is inevitably competent in it, for through it one communicates one's everyday business. As the most universal functional dialect, practical language creates the background against which the utterances of all other dialects are perceived. As Jakobson argued in the Prague Linguistic Circle's 1929 "Thèses," "From a synchronic standpoint, poetic language has the form of

27. "Poètika, lingvistika, sociologija," 109.
28. Ibid., 111.

a poetic utterance (*parole*) and hence of an individual creative act evaluated both against the backdrop of the immediate poetic tradition (poetic *langue*) and against that of the contemporary practical [*sdělovací*] language."[29] A poetic utterance is perceived against the background of practical language because the two are functional dialects and not foreign languages. They share most of their linguistic elements and mechanisms, differing only in their methods of exploiting them. Arguing against Jakubinskij's definition of poetic language as a particular phonetic feature, Jakobson wrote, "The clustering of liquids is possible in both practical and poetic language, but in the former it is causal whereas in the latter . . . [it is] goal-oriented; i.e., they are two essentially different phenomena."[30] At this point, the concept of the "device" enters Jakobson's critical vocabulary. The clustering of liquids and other striking organizations of verbal material in poetry are not, as in other linguistic processes, mere accidents, but means to a specific end. They disrupt the communicative function of the verbal sign and in this way redirect attention from the subjective or objective realities signified to the internal structure of the sign itself. The *langue* of poetic language, the "immanent laws" governing this dialect, can thus be seen as a system of poetic devices. Hence Jakobson's oft-quoted slogan that "if the science of literature wishes to become scientific it must recognize the 'device' as its sole 'hero.'"[31]

This statement obviously suggests Šklovskij's mechanistic metaphor, in which the device, if not the sole hero, was definitely one of the main protagonists. The affinity between Šklovskij and Jakobson here is undeniable; however, there are several impor-

29. "Teze předložené Prvému sjezdu slovanských filologů v Praze 1929," in *U základů pražské jazykovědné školy*, ed. J. Vachek (Prague, 1970), p. 47. To maintain Jakobson's earlier nomenclature I have translated "*sdělovací*" as "practical" instead of the more correct "communicative." By the late twenties, however, Jakobson expanded his functional dialectology and "practical language" became a subcategory of the more general "communicative language."

30. *O češskom stiche preimuščestvenno v sopostavlenii s russkim* (Berlin, 1923), p. 17.

31. *Novejšaja russkaja poèzija*, p. 11.

tant differences between them as well. One of these, concerning the linguistic versus extralinguistic nature of the artistic device, was discussed in the preceding chapter. A second difference is that for Šklovskij, the device functioned to de-familiarize, and hence was crucial to the process of artistic perception. For Jakobson, however, the device was important to the process of artistic signification: a poetic utterance de-familiarizes language because of its peculiar semiotic status, because it does not refer in the manner of communicative utterances. Finally, the two Formalists approached the device with different epistemological economies. Šklovskij clearly multiplied the entities designated as devices, cataloguing as many different varieties as possible. Jakobson, in accord with his general phenomenological orientation, was decidedly reductivist. Rather than describing the manifold heterogeneity of poetic devices he strove to isolate a few elementary structuring principles implemented in all of them.

What are these basic principles that govern every poetic utterance? Because the "set toward expression" renders prominent the internal structure of the word, verbal art operates with the constitutive elements of this structure—phonic and prosodic factors, morphemes of all types, semantic features—which play only a subsidiary role in communicative language. From this point of view, poetic praxis is the restructuring of an utterance to bring to the foreground the constitutive elements of language. This goal is achieved through two correlated processes: the uncoupling of the speech chain into its basic linguistic elements, and their reassemblage into new patterns determined by some form of equivalence. As Jakobson wrote, "in poetry, the role of mechanical associations is minimized, for the dissociation of verbal elements is the exclusive goal. The dissociated fragments are [then] easily regrouped into new combinations."[32] This view was subsequently reiterated by Vinokur, for whom the "specificity of the poetic tendency" in language "ultimately boils down to the dissolution of a linguistic structure into its

32. Ibid., p. 41.

elements, which are then recombined. But here, in contrast to the language system proper, the relations among the parts are reshuffled and displaced and thus *the very significance, the valency, the linguistic value of these constitutive parts are laid bare and precisely calculated.*"[33]

This dual process of analysis and resynthesis operates, according to Jakobson, at all levels of poetic language. Analysis occurs in such devices as the rhythmical splitting of the word, poetic etymologizing, and "accentual dissimilation," that is, the reaccentuation of a word or the juxtaposition of accentual doublets. Resynthesis is implemented in such devices as "rhyme, assonance and alliteration (or repetition)" and "all forms of parallelism: partial parallelism—the simile; parallelism unfolding in time—the metamorphosis; [and] parallelism reduced to a point—the metaphor."[34]

The poetic restructuring of an utterance not only affects the individual strata of language, but establishes new relations among them. Most importantly it realigns the link between sound and meaning. Throughout this chapter I have noted the keen interest of the Formalists in the similarity of poetic sound to what it signifies. Jakobson was no exception. He also believed that in poetic language "the link between sound and meaning is closer, more intimate . . . insofar as the habitual associations based on contiguity retreat to the background."[35] Earlier we saw OPOJAZ's preoccupation with expressive and mimetic sound metaphors and Tynjanov's study of the semantic amalgamation of similar sounding words within a verse line. Jakobson described yet another similarity between the phonic and semantic aspects of poetic language, which might be characterized as the thematization of sound. It occurs when the phonic structure of several semantically disparate words is repeated in the key word of an utterance. A Russian proverb mentioned by Jakobson is a good illustration:

33. "Poètika, lingvistika, sociologija," 109.
34. *Novejšaja russkaja poèzija,* pp. 47–48.
35. Ibid., p. 10.

Sila solomu lomit
(Power breaks the straw)

Here "two members of a construction intersect in the third one."[36] The key word *soloma* (straw) contains both the consonants of the initial word *sila* (power) and the root of the final verb *lomit* (breaks). This sound equivalence creates a semantic rapprochement among the words composing the sequence.

The poetic restructuring of an utterance not only disrupts its communicative function, but affects poetic perception through a third principle of expressionist poetics, which might be called "Futurist" (in accord with Holenstein's terminology).[37] The nonreferential poetic word transforms our attitude to language; it makes what seemed intimately familiar into something strange and unknown. According to the "Futurist" principle, the distinctive feature of verbal art as a type of linguistic behavior is that it de-familiarizes language and renders its forms unusual.

Like Šklovskij, Jakobson insisted that poetic "form exists only insofar as we feel it, as we sense the resistance of the material, as we wonder whether we face prose or verse."[38] Hence de-familiarization is a historical process in which all three dimensions of time interpenetrate. As the "unknown is comprehensible and striking only against the background of the known,"[39] so de-familiarization necessarily involves the past: the old automatized forms that serve as a backdrop to the new perception. At the same time, the novelty of the present poetic forms is merely transitory. "There comes a time," wrote Jakobson, "when traditional poetic language ossifies, ceases to be palpable and becomes outlived like a ritual or a sacred text whose very lapses are considered holy. . . . the form masters the material, the material becomes fully dominated by its form, the form turns into a ster-

---

36. Ibid., p. 51. For a more detailed discussion of this proverb see Jakobson's essay, "Quest for the Essence of Language," *Diogenes* 51 (1965), 32–33.
37. Holenstein "Einführung," p. 18.
38. *Novejšaja russkaja poèzija*, p. 5.
39. Ibid., p. 30.

eotype and dies out."[40] New, unusual forms must at this point be created to rejuvenate poetic language. Yet this future de-familiarization is contrastively related to the forms now becoming automatized, and these present forms, as the cause of the subsequent development, contain the seeds of the future within them. Moreover, Jakobson held that de-familiarization takes place not among isolated poetic phenomena but among phenomena integrated into structures corresponding to literary schools, groups, movements, or even individuals. Thus, like *langue*, the system of poetic language is not homogeneous. Rather, it comprises various subsystems interlocked in an ongoing historical struggle. Jakobson describes this process in terms of geographical linguistics. "From this point of view, Puškin is the center of the poetic culture of a particular time with a particular zone of influence. The poetic dialects of one zone gravitating toward the cultural center of another can be subdivided, like the dialects of practical language, into: transitional dialects, dialects with a transitory tendency, and mixed dialects. The first have adopted a group of canons from the center toward which they gravitate; the second have adopted certain poetic tendencies from it; and the third, only individual heterogeneous elements—devices. Finally, one must take into account conservative archaic dialects, whose centers of gravity belong to the past."[41]

The de-familiarization of language is not fully exhausted by the interaction of old and new poetic forms. I noted previously that in the expressionist model, poetic language is closely related to another functional dialect—practical language. Within this dialect too a historical clash goes on between the conservative tendency of standard literary language to preserve traditional forms and the innovative tendency within living colloquial speech to generate new ones. Russian poets, according to Jakobson, have always exploited the creative potential of colloquial speech for the sake of de-familiarization. "From Simeon Polockij

40. Ibid.
41. Ibid., pp. 5–6.

on, through Lomonosov, Deržavin, Puškin, Nekrasov, and Majakovskij, Russian poetry has continuously adopted newer and newer elements of the living language."[42] Raw, uncultivated colloquialisms replace old poetisms-turned-clichés to render the medium of verbal art vivid once again.

The Futurist principle introduces another facet denied by Saussure into the language system: time. In Saussure's *Course*, *langue* is defined as atemporal, and linguistic change as asystemic. The motivation for this decision is obvious: concern over the identity of the sign. Once different stages of *langue* are included in one system, the precise value of linguistic units is compromised. By functioning simultaneously in different relational grids, their identity becomes ambiguous. Moreover, Saussure maintained that the impulse for change came not from within the homogeneous system of language, but only from without it, through the accidental destructive intervention of extra-linguistic factors. Therefore he split the science of language into its *synchronic* and *diachronic* branches and identified the study of *langue* solely with the former.

But can we actually purge a linguistic system of its history? The Jakobsonian de-familiarization of poetic language would argue against it. This process inevitably brings together past, present, and future states of the system. Moreover, the resulting mutations are not caused by accidents external to the system but by its immanent need for constant rejuvenation. True, in Jakobson's opinion, the impulse for change is greater in poetic language than in other functional dialects, but synchrony and diachrony interpenetrate in other linguistic systems as well. Hence, a *langue* devoid of temporality would be a fiction. In every synchronous linguistic system "there are styles of pronunciation, grammatical variants, phrases, which are interpreted by a collectivity of speaking subjects as belonging to and appropriate to a generation of older people, and others which are considered the prerogative of youth, the latest fashion." Besides these

42. Ibid., p. 30.

time-marked variants, Jakobson argues, diachrony mingles with synchrony because of the functional heterogeneity of the linguistic system. "The most characteristic form of the projection of diachrony into synchrony is the attribution of a different function to the two terms of a change; thus, two phonological stages are judged as attributes of two functional dialects, two 'styles.' The characteristic form of the projection of synchrony into diachrony, on the other hand, is the generalization of a style; two styles become two [developmental] stages."[43]

The difference between Saussure's and Jakobson's notions of the linguistic system might be represented as shown in the diagram.

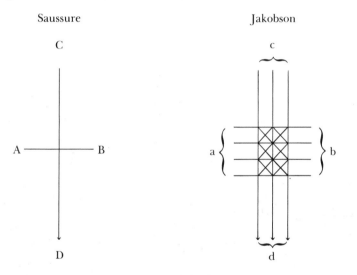

Saussure's diagram contains the following coordinates: "(1) the axis of *simultaneity* (AB), which stands for the relations of coexisting things, from which the intervention of time is excluded, and (2) *the axis of succession* (CD), on which only one thing can be considered at a time but upon which are located all the things on

43. *Remarques sur l'évolution phonologique du russe comparée à celle des autres langues slaves* (= *Travaux du circle linguistique de Prague* 2 [1929]), p. 15.

the first axis together with their changes."[44] The system of language, then, is the geometric point at which the two axes intersect.

For Jakobson, as my diagram suggests, the axis of simultaneity (ab) is impregnated with history, for in language at every moment a number of time-marked variants (archaisms, modernisms) always co-occur. By the same token, the axis of succession (cd) contains more than one element at a time. Language consists of several systems of functional dialects each involving a number of subsystems linked both synchronically and diachronically. Thus, rather than a *hic et nunc* point, the Jakobsonian linguistic system is a field comprising homogeneous and heterogeneous elements.

What my diagram omits, however, is the profoundly dialectic nature of Jakobson's linguistics, which makes any separation of the system from its history impossible a priori. According to this view, language is not a harmonious, symmetrical whole but an ongoing struggle between revolutionary tendencies aiming to alter the status quo and their conservative counterparts set on preserving it. At any moment the system is both balanced and imbalanced; it is simultaneously a state and a mutation. The ruptures in previous equilibriums coexist with the equilibriums that mended these ruptures, and all of them point to subsequent changes that will redress this situation in the future. This dialectic conception of language also contradicts Saussure's claim that the causes of linguistic change are necessarily extrasystemic and hence accidental. For Jakobson, linguistic development is triggered by internal contradictions within language, and as such is subject to the rules of the system. External factors, therefore, are neither accidental nor destructive to *langue*. They are able to penetrate and affect it only if they satisfy some of its internal demands, that is, only if they correspond to the developmental tendencies of the system itself.

To return to verbal art, de-familiarization there according to

44. *Course in General Linguistics*, p. 80.

Jakobson operates on three planes. "We perceive every fact of contemporary poetic language in necessary relation to three factors: the current poetic tradition, contemporary practical language, and the prior poetic tendency."[45] In the case of Chlebnikov—the poet with whom Jakobson's booklet was concerned—the poetic tendency of the immediate past was Russian Symbolism. Whereas Symbolist poetry strove to emulate music, Chlebnikov considered the word the only proper material of verbal art. His *zaum'*—speech transcending the utilitarian rationality of practical language—had no counterpart in Symbolist poetry. Equally new was his penchant for what the Formalists termed the "laying bare of devices," that is, the pure unfolding of verbal material in poetic constructions lacking any psychological, natural, or metaphysical motivation.[46] And in contrast to the predominantly lyrical mode of Symbolist poetry, Chlebnikov returned to the epic genre. In Jakobson's assessment, "Chlebnikov gave us a new *epos,* the first genuinely epic creations after many decades of drought."[47]

Central to Chlebnikov's rebellion against the Symbolists was his use of the Russian vernacular. "Most of Chlebnikov's work," Jakobson observed, "is written in language derived from colloquial speech."[48] This introduction of colloquialisms into poetry was a deliberate challenge to the Symbolist dogma that the profane language of the mob is incompatible with the sacred language of poets. According to Vjačeslav Ivanov, an outstanding poet-theoretician of this movement, "in all ages in which poetry has flourished as an art, poetic language has been contrasted to the colloquial, common language. Both singers and the people loved its differences and peculiarities—singers, as their prerogative, a liturgical or imperial robe; the crowd, as a national treasure and cult."[49]

45. *Novejšaja russkaja poèzija,* p. 4.
46. Ibid., p. 28.
47. "O pokolenii rastrativšem svoich poètov," *Smert' Vladimira Majakovskogo* (Berlin, 1931), p. 8.
48. *Novejšaja russkaja poèzija,* p. 30.
49. "Sporady," *Po zvezdam: Stat'i i aforizmy* (St. Petersburg, 1909), p. 355.

Naturally, Chlebnikov was not the only Russian poet reacting against the Symbolist canon in the second decade of this century. There were at least two antipodal tendencies within Russian post-Symbolist poetry: the archaizing of Akmeists such as N. S. Gumilëv and O. E. Mandel'štam, who sought inspiration in the poetic tradition of past ages, and the iconoclasm of Futurists such as Chlebnikov, who claimed that they were inventing the art of an epoch yet to come. And even within Futurism there was a distinct struggle between the old and the new, as manifested in the writings of its three leading figures, Majakovskij, Pasternak, and Chlebnikov. Jakobson described this conflict as follows: "In the evolution of Russian post-Symbolist poetry Majakovskij personifies the *Sturm und Drang*, Chlebnikov the most clear-cut, characteristic conquests, and Pasternak the link of this new art with Symbolism."[50]

This sketch of the Futurist movement is a good illustration of Jakobson's dialectic conception of the linguistic (poetic) system as a synchronous state containing conservative tendencies pointing toward the past and revolutionary tendencies pointing to the future. The de-familiarization of language in verbal art is not a simple unilateral progression in which every new work leaves all previous ones automatized. The interaction of old and new is instead an oscillation, a seesaw movement, as the contemporary literary reception of the three Russian Futurists verifies. "Despite the fact that Chlebnikov's poetic personality crystallized prior to Majakovskij's and, in turn, Majakovskij's before Pasternak's . . . the reader brought up on Symbolism was willing to accept Pasternak first, then he stumbled over Majakovskij, and only after conquering him was he ready to begin the strenuous siege of Chlebnikov's fortress."[51]

Chlebnikov's belated critical recognition, eloquently described by Jakobson, is a function of what might be called the dialogic nature of the literary process: the spatiotemporal gap between

50. "Kontury *Glejtu*," repr. in R. Jakobson, *Slovesné umění a umělecké slovo* (Prague, 1969), p. 387.
51. Ibid.

the author and reader. Here we reach a crucial contradiction, for to conceive of the poetic utterance as dialogic is utterly inconsistent with Husserl's or Saussure's semiotic concept underlying the expressionist model.

Husserl's contempt for the dialogic form of language was absolute. Once the word is addressed to someone and leaves the safe haven of a single consciousness, its identity is totally compromised, for "all expressions in communicative speech function as indications."[52] Saussurean linguistics is equally monological. It relegates any actual verbal intercourse to the sphere of *parole* and focuses solely on *langue*—the set of all linguistic elements at a given moment which are uniformly internalized by the speech community. And because Saussure deemed language prior to thought, the linguistic system is not merely a seamless semiotic web connecting all individual minds but their identical content as well. Thus, even though his *Course* begins with a discussion of the speech-circuit through a schematized dialogue between Mr. A. and Mr. B, ultimately these gentlemen are nothing but two identical instances of a hypostasized social consciousness, two interchangeable voices in a single monologue, two terminals whose semiotic input and output are one.

Saussure's postulate that the linguistics of *langue* is possible only if the distance between the interlocutors is obliterated had repercussions among the Russian Formalists. Those who paid attention to the dialogic form of language turned against the notion of system, whereas those concerned with system ignored the dialogic. Jakubinskij and Tynjanov are the two most obvious representatives of these opposite tendencies. In his 1923 essay "On Dialogic Speech," Jakubinskij rejected the teleological view that divided language into functional dialects according to their respective goals (though he himself had earlier propounded one variant of this view) because he considered it too abstract for the classification of concrete utterances. This classification, Jakubinskij insisted, must proceed from the linguistics of *parole*,

52. *Logical Investigations*, vol. 1, p. 277.

actual discourse. Accordingly, he drew the criteria for his classification from the two characteristics of every human interaction: the type of contact between the subjects (immediate/mediated) and the directionality of the information flow (alternating/continuous).

> To the immediate (face-to-face) form of human interaction correspond immediate forms of verbal interaction. These are characterized by the immediate visual and aural perception of the speaker. To mediated interaction corresponds, for example, the written form of an utterance. Correlated with the alternating forms of interactions involving a relatively quick exchange of actions and reactions between interacting individuals is the dialogic form of linguistic intercourse. And for the continuous form we have the monologic form of utterance.[53]

Jakubinskij believed that in contrast to the "artificial" monologue, dialogue is the "natural" form of language and that the "dialogic form is, in fact, almost always linked to the immediate form of interaction."[54] As a result he concentrated on the oral dialogue and described various linguistic, paralinguistic, and social features of such exchanges.

Fruitful as it might be for the study of dialogue in general, Jakubinskij's approach was incapable of dealing with what I have termed the dialogic quality of the literary process. From a purely formal standpoint, the literary work is nothing but a mediated continuous communication, the monologue of an absent author read by a passive audience. The curious delayed reaction to Chlebnikov's work (as described by Jakobson) suggests that the relationship between the author and reader is much more com-

53. "O dialogičeskoj reči," Russkaja reč': Sborniki statej, vol. 1, ed. L. V. Ščerba (Petersburg, 1923), pp. 116–17.
54. Ibid., p. 117. The concept of dialogue gained a rather prominent status in the subsequent development of Russian intellectual life as a rallying point for the scholars connected with Michail Bachtin. But with their negative attitude toward Formalism, the Bachtinians approached dialogue from a different perspective. They saw it primarily as a metalinguistic phenomenon—a chain of utterances commenting upon each other from different points of view. Thus, for the Bachtinians, dialogue was a predominantly ideological phenomenon.

plex. The literary audience is not merely a sounding board for the poet's words: its choice of reading matter, the timing of its choice, and so forth are, in fact, the audience's replies to the author's poetic message. Clearly, such replies are a function not only of the actual literary discourse but of the socially shared literary system as well, the poetic tradition that conditions the reader's interaction with the text.

Tynjanov opposed Jakubinskij in that he built his model specifically on the notion of the system. In doing so, he, like Saussure, collapsed the space between author and reader. Because he believed that a work's identity is determined by its evolutionary position within a literary system, this gap is irrelevant to its identity and is simply another name for the work's alienation, its inauthenticity. Paying attention to it merely subverts the systemic metaphor and leads to subjectivism and psychologism, to a "naive evaluation," which instead of viewing the "'value' of a given literary phenomenon . . . in its 'developmental significance and character,'" arbitrarily "transfers the value from one era-system to another."[55]

Despite the fact that Tynjanov conceives of the era-system as a diachronic lamination of several contrastive principles of construction, there seems to be no gap between the author and the reader within it. A "literary fact" is identical for everybody. "Whereas a hard *definition of literature* is more and more difficult to make," Tynjanov claimed, "every contemporary can point his finger at what is a *literary fact*."[56] But once again, the reaction of the Russian reading public to Chlebnikov's experiments contradicts this assertion. By refusing to read them, the majority of Chlebnikov's contemporaries indicated that for them his works belonged among the facts of *byt*, somewhere between infantile babble and the ravings of a madman; only a miniscule minority considered them literary works. Thus, even within a single era-system, one person's literary fact is not necessarily another's.

55. "O literaturnoj èvoljucii," *Archaisty i novatory,* pp. 31–32.
56. "Literaturnyj fakt," ibid., p. 9.

The de-familiarization of poetic language takes place among a multitude of individuals whose reactions will differ considerably. Jakobson's expressionist model stands between Jakubinskij's and Tynjanov's. It acknowledges the dialogic relationship between the artist and audience but accommodates it within a shared system of artistic conventions. Jakobson explored the difference between the subjects involved in the artistic process in his essay "On Realism in Art," published the same year as his Chlebnikov pamphlet. The notion of realism, because of its apparent simplicity, offered especially fertile ground for debunking the monologic view of art. According to the simplest definition, realism is an "artistic movement that strives for the closest possible representation of reality, for maximal probability." But within a dialogic context, "representation" and "probability" acquire a curious duality: "On the one hand we deal with an intention, a goal; that is, a work is realistic if the author conceived of it as probable (meaning A); on the other hand, a work is realistic if I, the judging subject, perceive it as probable (meaning B)."[57]

The difference between the author and the perceiver described by Jakobson need not, however, lead to the subjectivism that Tynjanov feared. The degree of realistic probability is not totally idiosyncratic; it is measured against the background of a given artistic tradition, the socially valid norms for representation in art. Thus, authorial realism can be subdivided into "A_1 = the tendency to deform a given artistic canon, interpreted as an approximation to reality" and "A_2 = the conservative tendency within the bounds of a given artistic tradition, interpreted as faithfulness to reality." The same holds for the perceiver. In the "meaning B_1 [he] is a revolutionary vis-à-vis the given artistic conventions, who comprehends their deformation as an approximation of reality." In "meaning B_2 [he] is a conservative who sees the deformation of the artistic conventions as a shortchanging of reality."[58]

57. "O realismu v umění," Červen 4 (1921), 301.
58. Ibid., 302.

Jakobson succeeded in accommodating the spatiotemporal gap between the participants in the artistic process within the concept of system because of his dialectic outlook. As I argued earlier, he conceived of the system not as a homogeneous *langue* but as an ongoing struggle among antithetical tendencies and heterogeneous elements. Moreover, the system was not internalized uniformly and totally by every subject. Rather, each individual appropriated only a particular segment of it. From this perspective, the author is neither identical to nor absolutely distinct from the reader. Despite the fact that the two are separate, insofar as they share a similar attitude to past artistic canons they are closer to each other than two contemporaneous authors who represent opposing artistic tendencies. At the same time, conservatives and revolutionaries are not unrelated either, although their connection is a negative one. They embody the thesis and antithesis of a single artistic state and as such they are inseparably bound to each other within the given system.

One important problem arises with this argument. The interplay of sameness and difference occurs within the limits of a system. But what are the limits of the system, or in other words, how far apart can an author and reader be before they cease to share anything (whether positive or negative)? This problem is aggravated by the particular modality of literary discourse—its written form. Once a work is fixed in a permanent substance, it can transcend the moment of its origin and become available to a distant reader, projected against a poetic system that is radically different from the one that generated it. When Jakobson and another Moscow Circle exile in Prague, Pëtr Bogatyrëv, compared high literature and folk poetry, they discovered that the primary difference between the two is their respective utilization of permanent and transient linguistic substances—writing and speech.

Their findings, published in "Folklore as a Special Form of Creativity," can be summarized as follows. A literary work is usually written, so its existence does not coincide with its acceptance by the reading public. It can be ignored by the author's contemporaries and become popular decades or even centuries later. This fact explains the considerable freedom of the writer in respect to the poetic canon of his or her time. The writer may not only emulate or reject it, but ignore it totally. "In the domain of political economy," Bogatyrëv and Jakobson wrote, "so-called production for the market provides a close parallel to the relationship of literature to the consumer." In folklore, on the other hand, this relationship "is closer to 'production on demand.'"[59] A folkloric work, framed in the transient oral medium, comes into existence only when accepted by the community. In fact, it is nothing but a potential set of norms, a living artistic tradition, which persists in the collective memory of a given group to be actualized in every individual performance. Any innovations introduced by these performances can survive only if they correspond to the immanent developmental tendencies of the normative structure, and fulfill a collective demand. Asocial aberrations are rejected and, unrecorded, they vanish without a trace. The performer's attitude toward his or her creation reflects this state of affairs. The performer exercises a "preventive censorship" and voluntarily conforms to the collective tradition.

Projected into Saussurean terminology, the difference between oral and written poetic works thus corresponds to the opposition of *langue* and *parole*. Bogatyrëv and Jakobson wrote:

> The role of the performer of folkloric works may not be identified with that of either the reader, the reciter, or the author of literary works. From the folklore performer's standpoint, the work is a fact of *langue*, i.e., an extrapersonal, given fact independent of the performer, even if the fact allows for deformation and the introduction of new poetic and quotidian material. To the author of a work of literature, the work appears as a fact of *parole*. It is not given a priori, but is subject to an individual realization. There is simply a set of artworks effective at a given moment. The new work of art is to be created and perceived against the background of their formal requisites (in that the new work of art appropriates some forms, transforms others, and rejects still others).[60]

59. "Die Folklore als eine besondere Form des Schaffens," *Donum natalicum Schrijnen* (Nijmegen, 1929), p. 906.
60. Ibid., p. 905.

This is a radical statement; indeed, it is seemingly at odds with Jakobson's notion of verbal art as a social institution. "As a fact of *parole*," the poetic work is above all a unique and individual product definitionally exceeding the linguistic system of a given collectivity. One could argue that I am reading too much into Bogatyrёv and Jakobson's essay. As its title suggests, it does not pretend to deal with the entire literary process but only with its production. Such a reduction is possible because the principal topic of the piece is folklore, in which creation and reception coincide. Had the two authors dealt with *literary* reception, the issue of poetic *langue* would have inevitably emerged.

This objection does not invalidate the point I made earlier, however. If, as Bogatyrёv and Jakobson argue, high literature is unlike folklore in the separation of its production and reception, then written literary texts must eventually outlive the system that spawned them, only to be "misread" by later audiences subscribing to totally different poetic canons. And considering the actual conditions of the literary process, one might wonder how things could be otherwise. This was, of course, in part the point Šklovskij made in his article on Puškin, discussed in the preceding chapter. Jakobson, like most of the other Formalists, rejected the radical relativism of Šklovskij's *Rezepzionsästhetik*. In his booklet on Chlebnikov, he assailed the aesthetic egocentrism of old-fashioned critics who "usually impose upon the past current modes of poetic production" for negating the social nature of verbal art.[61]

To check the relativism creeping into his expressionist model, Jakobson had to deal with two problems: the need to bridge the gap between author and reader, that is, to find a system obligatory for the two parties; and the need to neutralize the written substance of literature, whose permanence opens the identity of the literary work to the vicissitudes of history. These problems turned out to be two sides of the same coin, and a single solution proposed by Jakobson took care of both of them.

61. *Novejšaja russkaja poèzija*, p. 5.

The path that led Jakobson into this difficulty is worth considering. The starting point of his poetics, we recall, was the concept of the expression—a sign whose self-sameness was absolute. Jakobson departed from Husserl, however, in conceiving of this semiotic identity in terms of a Saussurean "social consciousness"; he then further relativized it by breaking up *langue* into historically changing functional dialects. Among these, poetic language, propelled by its need for incessant de-familiarization, exhibited the highest degree of change and thus, ironically, was the least reliable guarantor of long-term semiotic identity.

To mitigate the tension between phenomenological stability and Futurist instability in the aesthetic sign Jakobson's strategy was to turn to language itself, a move I call the "linguistic principle" of his poetics. For him, the literary work is always perceived against the background of contemporary practical language. Poetic language, to appropriate Vinokur's "Marxist" lingo, is a mere superstructure built upon this normative basis; the aesthetic efficacy of a literary work is founded upon it. Once the author and audience cease to share the system of practical language, the text can no longer function poetically. Jakobson made this point clear in the introduction to his edition of two Czech poetic compositions of the early fourteenth century: "Literary works are so connected with language, they are linguistic facts to such a degree that the distance between the linguistic structure giving rise to the medieval poem and modern linguistic usage is a serious hindrance to its living perception. It is easier to perceive the aesthetic value of an ancient painting or building than to live out the linguistic consciousness of a writer or a reader from that period. This explains why the resurrection of the medieval poetic work as an aesthetically experienced fact lags behind our surmounting of the merely archaeological approach to the medieval visual arts."[62]

This argument, of course, has its roots in Jakobson's "logo-

---

62. "Dvě staročeské skladby o smrti," *Spor duše s tělem. O nebezpečném čase smrti* (Prague, 1927), p. 9.

centric" notion of language, according to which every linguistic fact is a vehicle for intersubjective, cognitive meanings. A poetic utterance, as an expression, is a prime example of such a sign. The same holds for communicative utterances. They differ from expressions not in being without such meanings, but in subordinating them to the referential functions they carry out. This intrinsic bond between the two functional dialects limits the possible spatiotemporal displacement of the literary work that threatened its identity. Therefore, the writer and the reader cannot be totally isolated from each other as long as they share a language. They might subscribe to different literary canons, but the more conservative system of practical language is still common to them. Thus, the "misreading" of a work, its projection against a set of poetic norms totally alien to it, still implies that the work makes sense as an utterance. Such a misreading is qualitatively different from the simple incomprehension that occurs when a work is produced in a language unknown to the reader.

At this point, however, it might appear that Jakobson would like to have it both ways. He claims that "every word of poetic language is in essence phonically and semantically deformed vis-à-vis practical language" and thus he can speak of "language in its aesthetic function" as a specific dialect "governed by its own immanent laws."[63] Yet at the same time he maintains that in some respects poetic utterances are not totally unlike those fulfilling a communicative function.

Ultimately though, Jakobson comes down on the side of non-uniqueness. If verbal art is the "organized violence of poetic form upon language," such violence is necessarily circumscribed by certain limits, and these are the limits of language itself.[64] A poetic form cannot distort its material to such a degree that it loses its linguistic nature. There is a sacrosanct structure underlying all functional dialects and rendering articulated sounds

63. *Novejšaja russkaja poèzija*, p. 47.
64. *O češskom stiche*, p. 16.

(even the Futurist *zaum'*) linguistic facts. This structure is the phonological system of a given national language. It was thus phonology that Jakobson chose as the key to the self-sameness of the literary sign.

For Saussure, the study of phonology outlined in his *Course* was an important aspect of linguistic science. This discipline was charged with the task of examining the verbal signifier outside its historical development. It proceeded from the premise Jacques Derrida has termed "phonocentrism," namely, the view that the spoken word is the original, authentic form of language.[65] Phonocentrism counters the infinite spatiotemporal dislocation of the sign that relativizes its identity by eliminating the cause of this slippage—written language. In Saussurean linguistics, the absolute self-sameness of the verbal sign is guaranteed by its participation in the synchronic system of *langue* internalized uniformly by every member of the speech community. Because of its transience, intangibility, and absolute proximity to the speaking subject, voice is much better suited to embodying the signifier than writing is. Fixed in permanent and tangible matter, the inscription falls outside the purely mental *langue*, and hence is subject to the vagaries of external forces. The numerous discrepancies between pronunciation and spelling, in Saussure's opinion, reveal the inability of the graphic substance to represent faithfully the internal system of language. Whether flukes of history, geography, or false etymology, they lead to a single conclusion: "writing obscures language; it is not a guise for language but a disguise."[66]

It is, however, obvious that in its raw physical heterogeneity the *phonè* cannot participate in the system of language as Saussure conceives of it. Its amorphous multiplicity must be reduced to a limited inventory of elements which can be incorporated into the relational grid of *langue*. Here Saussure's phonocentrism merges with his logocentric view, according to which voice

65. See, for example, *Of Grammatology*, pp. 27–44.
66. *Course in General Linguistics*, p. 30.

is solely the vehicle of reason and has no value outside this relationship. "Sound," as he sees it, "is only the instrument of thought; by itself it has no existence."[67] The phoneme—the minimal unit of the signifier—is, therefore, defined through its relation to the signified—the rational meaning it expresses. "The important thing in the word is not sound alone but the phonic differences that make it possible to distinguish this word from all others, for differences carry signification."[68] Thus, the phoneme is nothing but a speech sound that is capable of differentiating morphemes. Saussure illustrates this point with the Russian speech sound *t*. It can be pronounced in a number of ways: aspirated, palatalized, and so forth. The aspirated variant, though acoustically quite distinct, does not differentiate meaning in Russian and, hence, is not an element of its phonological system. The palatalized *t*, on the other hand, as a verbal desinence, signals an infinitive form of the Russian verb, in contrast to the nonpalatalized *t* which in the same position indicates the third person singular form, and therefore is a phoneme.

This approach to phonology provided Jakobson with a solution to the two possible sources of relativism within his expressionist model. By proclaiming the voice to be the original substance of language, phonology eliminated one cause of the spatiotemporal dislocation of the literary work: its written form. As a mere secondary representation of sound, the written text must always relate to the primary substance—voice—whose basic structure is provided by the phonological system of a given language.

Phonology also takes care of the second cause of semiotic slippage—the distance between the participants in the literary process. Of the multitude of norms making up language, the phonological system is the most obligatory, the one the interlocutors *must* share if any intercourse at all is to take place. This postulate stems from the Saussurean conception of language as a semiotic

67. Ibid., p. 8.
68. Ibid., p. 118.

233

system whose significatory mechanism is by definition double-tiered. Full-fledged signs or signifiers that carry meaning require the existence of smaller sound elements which do not signify in themselves but serve to differentiate the signifiers of unlike meanings. These meaning-differentiating elements, or phonemes, thus constitute the most elementary linguistic system, which is indispensable to the semiotic functioning of language. In other words, according to this view there can be no language without a phonemic system. Therefore, poetic violence cannot deform this system in any significant way, or verbal art would lose its linguistic nature and become a "variety of less than perfect vocal music."[69]

The phonological conception of the linguistic signifier enabled Jakobson to treat poetic sound in a way radically different from the transrational model of OPOJAZ. Even if the phonic stratum of poetic language is deformed on purpose, its relation to cognitive meaning is not eliminated, for verbal art "operates not with sounds but with phonemes, i.e., acoustic representations capable of being associated with semantic representations."[70] Even utterances that "deliberately strive to avoid any relationship with a given practical language" (such as the *zaum'* of the Russian Futurists) cannot escape the constraints of phonology, "for insofar as [a given practical language] exists and a phonetic tradition is present, transrational language is as distinct from prelingual onomatopoeias as a nude contemporary European is from a naked troglodyte."[71]

Jakobson's claim extended not only to poetic production but to reception as well. Once a subject internalizes the phonological

69. *Novejšaja russkaja poèzija*, p. 48. A special problem that deserves more attention than I can devote to it here is the historical changeability of phonemic systems. In contrast to Saussure, Jakobson maintained that these systems evolve. At the same time, he regarded this change as purely phenomenal, not affecting their "deep structures"—the universal and absolute inventory of hierarchically correlated distinctive features that in one way or another is implemented in every actual phonological system.

70. *Novejšaja russkaja poèzija*, p. 48.
71. Ibid., p. 67.

system, he or she perceives every linguistic sound in terms of it. Here the expressionist model diverges from the purely acoustic approach to poetry characteristic of *Ohrenphilologie* and its Formalist followers. Arguing against one of its basic postulates propounded by Saran—that the "theoretician of verse . . . ought to adopt toward verse the attitude of a foreigner who listens to it without knowing the language"—Jakobson wrote: "Not a single person perceives the sound form of poetry in his native tongue, its rhythm in particular, as Saran's foreigner does. Indeed, even this foreigner is fictitious; even his perception would not be purely acoustic. He would merely approach the foreign utterance from the standpoint of his own phonological system, with his own phonological habits. He would, so to speak, transphonologize this utterance."[72]

Jakobson did not stop at criticizing older conceptions of poetic sound; he advanced his own theories about the phonic organization of poetry. The most ambitious was the project of a "phonological prosody" launched in a comparative study of Czech and Russian verse in 1923. Earlier we encountered the polarization of the OPOJAZ membership on the issue of poetic language as opposed to verse language. Those on the side of poetic language considered rhythm just one among many devices characterizing poetic language, and hence largely ignored it, whereas the others rejected the notion of poetic language as too vague, and focused on the specific problems of verse rhythm. The expressionist model, however, managed to bring these two perspectives together by integrating versification into the overall study of poetic language.

Jakobson's discussion of verse was indirectly a polemic against Brik's identification of verse with the single device of rhythm. According to Jakobson, the mere presence of rhythm in an utterance does not render it poetic, for rhythm may equally occur in practical language. It is the role rhythm performs in these functional dialects that differs. "The dynamic rhythm of prac-

72. *O češskom stiche*, p. 21.

tical language is a process that automatizes exhalation during an utterance. In contrast, poetic rhythm is one of the ways to de-automatize the utterance. It is the prerequisite of the [mental] set toward the time of the utterance, what the German psychologists call the experiencing of time (*Zeiterlebnis*). The division of an utterance into subjectively equal segments, the rhythmical inertia that makes us expect the repetition of a specific signal at a specific moment, the repetition of this signal that foregrounds that signalized sound vis-à-vis its neighbors, all of this is missing in practical language, where time is not experienced."[73]

This delimitation of practical and poetic rhythm proceeds from the same principles that Jakobson employed to distinguish poetic language from the other functional dialects. What is involved, first of all, is the phenomenological principle: verse triggers a particular set toward the utterance in the perceiving subject. Its temporal dimension, which in communicative discourse is irrelevant, becomes the center of attention in verse language. According to Jakobson, "poetic time is a typical *Erwartungszeit;* after a particular period expires we expect a particular signal. This time superimposed upon the utterance subjectively transforms it."[74] What is in question here is another manifestation of the Futurist principle. By foregrounding a feature which in practical language is merely a means toward a communicative end, verse de-familiarizes the verbal medium and renders prominent the internal structure of the verbal sign. Moreover, this transformation employs a particular variant of the two basic devices operating in every poetic utterance. The speech chain is dissolved into rhythm-creating elements only to be reassembled on the basis of their regular repetition.

At this point, it might appear that Jakobson's phonological prosody does not differ significantly from the other Formalists' positions on verse. Viktor Šklovskij, for example, arguing against Spencer's conception of rhythm as an energy-saving mechanism, had already pointed out the difference between

73. Ibid., pp. 17–18.
74. Ibid., p. 19.

prosaic and poetic rhythm—between the regular rhythm of a work song, which by automatizing movements tends to save labor, and the violation of this rhythm in art for the sake of defamiliarized, difficult perception.[75] One could also draw a parallel between Tynjanov's and Jakobson's discussions of the temporality of verse language. Tomaševskij's redefinition of the "rhythmical impulse" is also quite close to Jakobson's understanding of verse perception as the pendulum-like process of expectations and fulfillments aroused in a perceiver's consciousness by the regular recurrence of rhythm-creating elements.

As I observed earlier, the Formalists never reached an agreement as to what those rhythm-creating elements were. Tynjanov's graphic approach, according to which the ultimate source of poetic rhythm is the visual property of the verse line, was rejected by other Formalists as too simplistic to have any explanatory value. Tomaševskij wrote that in verse, "graphics is merely a sign, not unlike punctuation, that expresses other linguistic correlations but only sometimes is the sole objective evidence of these correlations (as when it happens that only punctuation makes a sentence understandable). For often the other factors are so powerful that graphics becomes redundant and merely accompanies an utterance that is understandable without it. Thus, Puškin's classic verses will remain such even if printed as prose."[76] It is the various prosodic features existing in language, Tomaševskij asserted, whose regular alternations create the rhythmical impulse. But even though he seemed intuitively aware of what these features were, he failed to specify them, and went on to embrace Jakobson's phonological prosody, which provided a coherent and simple hypothesis about the nature of the rhythm-creating elements in verse.[77]

75. "Iskusstvo, kak priëm," *Poètika: Sborniki po teorii poètičeskogo jazyka* (Petersburg, 1919), p. 114.
76. "Ju. Tynjanov, *Problema stichotvornogo jazyka,*" *Russkij sovremennik* 3 (1924), 267.
77. See especially his 1925 essay, "Stich i ritm," *O stiche: Stat'i* (Leningrad, 1929), pp. 39–42.

Jakobsonian metrics evolved from the linguistic principle of poetic language, according to which, as we have seen, verse is an utterance with a particular organization of its sound stratum. This organization, moreover, must be rooted in the phonological system of a particular language. Given the resistance of this system to poetic violation, the linguistic principle leads to two conclusions: first, verse deforms above all the extraphonemic elements of language, and second, it is the inviolable phonological elements that provide the organizational base for this violence. That is, phonological features are those hitherto elusive rhythm-creating elements.

Earlier I tried to show how the differences among the various Formalist theories of verse were conditioned by their points of departure. The same applies to Jakobson. The other members of the movement dealt primarily with Russian verse: Jakobson's orientation was comparative. As an exile in Prague, he was in fact Saran's foreigner forced to experience poetry in an alien language. Indeed, it was this experience that convinced him of the intimate link between verse and language. While the other Formalists considered prosodic features such as stress non-problematic, Jakobson, transplanted into a foreign linguistic milieu, directly witnessed their relativity. This relativity was especially evident because Czech and Russian are so similar. At first glance Puškin's line appears almost identical to its Czech translation:

Russian: Burja mgloju nebo kroet
Czech: Bouře mlhou nebe kryje[78]

And yet an actual reading reveals a tremendous prosodic difference between them. This difference, Jakobson argues, results from the dissimilarity of the Czech and Russian phonological systems. While both languages contain dynamic stress, only in Russian is it a phonological element; for example, múka (tor-

---

78. *O češskom stiche*, pp. 46–47. In English the line means "The storm covers the sky with haze"; it is from Puškin's poem "Zimnij večer" (Winter Evening).

ment) differes from *muká* (flour) only in the position of its stress. Czech stress, on the other hand, always falls on the initial syllable of the word and, therefore, is nonphonemic. But vocalic length differentiates words in Czech, for example, *byt* (apartment) and *by:t* (to be), something it cannot do in Russian, where vocalic length is obligatorily bound to stress.

Given Jakobson's premise that the rhythm-creating elements must be phonologically based, it might appear that the difference between Czech and Russian prosody lies in the fact that the former is quantitative (tied to vocalic length), whereas the latter is accentual (tied to word stress), but, with the exception of the early nineteenth century when a few attempts at quantitative metrics appeared, modern Czech verse, like Russian verse, has been based on the regular alternation of stressed and unstressed syllables. Accordingly, Jakobson introduced another phonological element into his theory—word boundary. Just as Russian quantity always coincides with stress, Czech stress (fixed on the initial syllable of the word) always coincides with word boundary. Therefore, Jakobson concluded, not stress but word boundary is the rhythm-creating element in Czech verse.[79]

The foregoing discussion yields the following typology of phonic phenomena that play a role in the constitution of verse: "(1) the phonological basis of rhythm, (2) concomitant extraphonemic elements, and (3) autonomous phonological elements, or more precisely, phonological elements that in a given poetic language are not a factor in the rhythmical inertia."[80] The profound difference between the Czech and Russian systems of versification becomes obvious if we superimpose this grid upon the prosodic features with which they operate: stress, quantity, and word boundary.

79. This is the most controversial point in Jakobson's theory. For the opposing view, which maintains that stress rather than word boundary constitutes the prosodic basis of Czech verse, see, for example, J. Mukařovský, "Roman Jakobson: *Základy českého verše,*" *Naše řeč* 10 (1926), 217–20; or M. Červenka, "Der versologische Band von Jakobsons *Selected Writings:* Bemerkungen eines Bohemisten," *Wiener slawistischer Almanach,* no. 7 (1981), 260–65.
80. *O češskom stiche,* p. 46.

RHYTHMIC SEGMENT	Phonological basis of rhythm	Concomitant extraphonemic element	Autonomous phonological element
CZECH	word boundary	dynamic stress	quantity
RUSSIAN	dynamic stress	quantity	word boundary[81]

Returning to Puškin's line and its Czech translation, it is obvious now why the two are so different despite their surface similarity. First of all, Jakobson argues, they differ in their distribution of quantity. In the Russian original, following the regular trochaic alternation of stresses, every odd syllable is long, whereas in the Czech version only the first and fourth syllables with the diphthong *ou* are quantitatively different from the rest. Second, because Russian stress is free, the fact that every word in Puškin's line is disyllabic is "perceived as an *episodic* coincidence of the normally autonomous word boundary with the rhythmical inertia." In Czech, on the other hand, with its fixed stress and with "word boundary the basic rhythm-creating factor . . . the quoted line in respect to its word boundaries is *canonical.*"[82]

This example illustrates the plausibility of Jakobson's hypothesis about the close link between the prosodic and phonological systems. It would be wrong to interpret this link in a totally deterministic fashion, to say that one particular phonological system inevitably gives rise to one particular system of versification. On the contrary, as the history of Czech verse has shown, the early nineteenth century witnessed a struggle between quantitative and accentual (or, more precisely, accentual-syllabic) prosodies, both based on different phonological elements coexisting in Czech. Thus, the actual victory of accentual-syllabic verse cannot be explained in terms of phonology. This was the conclusion Jakobson reached in the final paragraph of his study: "I think that a versification system can never be totally deduced

81. This is a truncated version of Jakobson's table from ibid.
82. Ibid., p. 47.

from a given language. If a versification system is the unknown X, and what is given to us are only the prosodic elements of the language, we can arrive merely at an indeterminate equation, i.e., the possibility of several values for the X. An explanation for the historical choice of this or that solution from among the several possible ones involves factors that are outside the phonetics of the given language, namely, the present poetic tradition, the relationship of the given poetic movement to this tradition, and cultural influences."[83]

This conclusion was not at variance with the universalistic thrust of the expressionist model. Despite its possible heteromorphism, the essence of verse is still provided by the phonological system of the language underlying it, the ultimate system connecting the participants of the literary process. But, as Stephen Rudy has observed, Jakobson's conclusion contains the seeds of the full subsequent development of Jakobsonian poetics: "It anticipates his later realization that literature is part of a 'system of systems' and its study necessitates a 'correlation between the literary series and other historical series.'"[84] The quotation within Rudy's passage is taken from the nine-point thesis written in 1928 by Tynjanov, the leading theoretician of the then-defunct OPOJAZ, and Jakobson, the vice-chairman of the newly established Prague Linguistic Circle. These theses are generally recognized as marking the end of the Formalist era and the beginning of a new stage of literary studies that emerged in Prague under the name of Structuralism.[85]

83. Ibid., p. 118.
84. S. Rudy, "Jakobson's Inquiry into Verse and the Emergence of Structural Poetics," in Sound, Sign and Meaning: Quinquagenary of the Prague Linguistic Circle, ed. L. Matejka (Ann Arbor, Mich., 1978).
85. Cf., for example, V. Erlich, Russian Formalism: History—Doctrine, 3d ed. (The Hague, 1969), p. 135; or L. Matejka and K. Pomorska, "Preface," in their anthology, Readings in Russian Poetics: Formalist and Structuralist Views (Ann Arbor, Mich., 1978), p. viii. Unfortunately, a description of the transformation of Jakobson's linguistic poetics into Structuralism lies beyond the scope of this book.

4

The Developmental
Significance of
Russian Formalism

[The scientist] accepts gratefully the epistemological
conceptual analysis; but the external conditions,
which are set for him by the facts of experience, do
not permit him to let himself be too much restricted
in the construction of his conceptual world by the
adherence to an epistemological system. He therefore must appear to the systematic epistemologist as
a type of unscrupulous opportunist.

—ALBERT EINSTEIN, "Reply to Criticism"

Readers who have patiently followed my discussion up to this
point might now find themselves uneasy about its metapoetic
method. I began by berating those who dealt with Formalism in
a piecemeal fashion, and demanded instead a holistic approach.
Yet have I not treated the Formalist movement as a cluster of
loosely connected theoretical models without any obvious common denominator? Furthermore, in chapter 1 I argued that the
epistemological assumptions behind the individual Formalist
models were too disparate to provide a unified basis for the

movement. I also insisted on the futility of a purely historical approach for distinguishing Formalism from the other schools that preceded or followed it. Given all these counterindications, it must surely appear strange to persist in seeking an overall unity for Russian Formalism. Yet persist I will. For the separation of Formalist epistemology from its history with which I began is ultimately the cause of the difficulties that we now encounter. Such a separation is quite inappropriate for this movement, whose theoretical heterogeneity is largely a function of its historical situation, and, vice versa, whose vague historical boundaries can be traced to its epistemological eclecticism. It is a mistake to seek the unity of the school in either of these spheres alone; it must be sought in their conjunction. In my opinion, there is an intellectual coherence to Russian Formalism, and that coherence lies in its evolutionary significance, the developmental role it played in the history of Slavic literary theory. This role, as I shall argue subsequently, consisted above all in destabilizing the traditional patterns of literary scholarship and in opening up new and provocative vistas.

Such an assumption, I believe, is appropriate for dealing with a movement as aware of its place in Russian literary study as Formalism. The young theoreticians conceived of their enterprise as a deliberate departure from previous critical practice. Theirs was to be a truly scientific approach to literature. According to Victor Erlich, "the driving force behind Formalist theorizing was the desire to bring to an end the methodological confusion prevailing in traditional literary studies and systematize literary scholarship as a distinct and integrated field of intellectual endeavor."[1] Given this goal, the "state of the art" of literary study could not but strike the Formalists as deeply unsatisfactory. "The status of literary history among the other sciences of culture," Tynjanov complained, "remains that of a colony."[2] This is so, Jakobson pointed

1. *Russian Formalism: History—Doctrine*, 3d ed. (The Hague, 1969), pp. 171–72.

2. "O literaturnoj èvoljucii," *Archaisty i novatory* (Leningrad, 1929), p. 30.

out, because "literary historians have found a use for anything that came to hand: *byt*, psychology, politics, philosophy. Instead of a literary science they created a conglomerate of homespun disciplines."[3] The criticism that literary history was a totally disunified field, however, was not unique to the Formalists. As early as 1870, Aleksandr Veselovskij had declared, "The history of literature reminds one of a geographical zone that international law has sanctified as a *res nullius,* where a historian of culture and an aesthetician, a savant and a student of social thought hunt [side by side]. Everyone takes out of it whatever he can, according to his talents and opinions. The goods or booty carry the same label but are far from having the same content. With no prior agreement as to norms, everyone constantly returns to the same question: what is literary history?"[4]

Veselovskij's answer was that literature should be defined in terms of the history of ideas. But this solution did not satisfy the Formalists either, for it simply confirmed their belief that literary study is unscientific because it, unlike any other discipline that claims the status of a science, has no distinct object of inquiry. For Tomaševskij, when traditional critics approached the literary work as a facet of its author's biography, a sociohistorical document, or a manifestation of some particular philosophical system, they were dissolving literary studies into a series of disconnected disciplines.[5] The lesson that the Formalists drew from their predecessors' forays into such heterogeneous cultural domains was purely negative. "Thanks to these inquiries," Grigorij Vinokur wrote, "we have gradually begun to learn at least what the object of poetics or literary history is *not.*"[6]

Nevertheless, out of this negative lesson came a positive pro-

3. *Novejšaja russkaja poèzija: Nabrosok pervyj* (Prague, 1921), p. ll.
4. "Iz vvedenija v istoričeskuju poètiku: Voprosy i otvety," *Istoričeskaja poètika* (Leningrad, 1940), p. 53.
5. "Nová ruská škola v bádání literárně-historickém," tr. J. Mukařovský, *Časopis pro moderní filologii* 15 (1929), 12–13.
6. "Poétika, lingvistika, sociologija: Metodologičeskaja spravka," *Lef*, no. 3 (1923), 104.

gram for a new literary science, a Copernican revolution in literary study. Before Formalism, literary studies revolved around other branches of knowledge, but the Formalists provided the discipline with its own center of gravity by insisting that it had a unique and particular object of inquiry. In Vinokur's words, the Formalist revolution boils down to a "simple idea, that literary science studies *literature itself*, and not anything else; that the student of an artwork has as his subject matter the *structure* of this work and not factors that are historically or psychologically concomitant to its creation."[7] Or as Èjchenbaum put it, "the prime concern of the 'Formalists' is . . . literature as the *object* of [literary] studies."[8]

This step necessarily involved a new conception of what literature was. Traditional critics had not treated literary texts in terms of psychology, sociohistory, or philosophy just to be perversely "unscientific," but because they saw these works as expressions of their authors' mental lives, documents of their time, or philosophical meditations. The Formalist view was quite different. For them literature was an autonomous reality governed by its own regularity and more or less independent of contiguous spheres of culture. From this perspective the vital issue for literary science was no longer the investigation of other realities that literary texts might reflect, but the description of what it was that made them a *literary* reality. "There should be only a single principle that establishes the content or the object of a science," Èjchenbaum declared. "Our principle is the study of literature as a specific series of phenomena. Next to it . . . there can be no other principle."[9]

This primary principle of Formalist literary science—the specificity of its subject matter—was utterly unacceptable to other Russian literary critics, regardless of their theoretical stripe. Their reactions can be summed up in the question: What are the

7. Ibid.
8. "Teorija 'formal'nogo metoda,'" *Literatura: Teorija, kritika, polemika* (Leningrad, 1927), p. 116.
9. "Vokrug voprosa o 'formalistach,'" *Pečat' i revoljucija*, no. 5 (1924), 4.

grounds for this principle? The Marxists offered a predictable answer. In the Formalists' attempt to de-ideologize literature they saw the classical move of bourgeois ideologists to neutralize literature as an effective weapon of class struggle. Others, for whom this analysis was too crude, traced the Formalists' view of literature to avant-garde artistic practice, and in particular to Futurist poetics, with its stress on the "self-valuable" word. Though theirs was a more perceptive objection than the Marxists' it still requires some modification, for as we have seen, the Formal school was as heterogeneous in its origins as in its theoretical models. Some of its members did begin as proponents and interpreters of Futurist art. Others came to Formalism from the mainstream of traditional literary study and still others entered its orbit after the close relationship with Futurism was over. True, not all the Formalists completely severed their ties to avant-garde art. But the young scholars aspired to be more than mere spokesmen of a poetic movement. They set out to establish a science of literature capable of dealing with verbal art in all its historical manifestations.

These and similar attempts to "deconstruct" Formalism by pointing out its ideological or aesthetic basis proceed from a fundamental misunderstanding of its aims. Though Èjchenbaum argued for the specificity of the subject matter of literary science, he did so not as an article of faith needed to advance either bourgeois or Futurist interests, but as a heuristic device needed to advance science. The postulate of the specificity of literary phenomena, the Formalists maintained, was not an apodictic statement or an expression of some ontological commitment, but merely a hypothesis, a cognitive lens for focusing the material at hand and unfolding a literary theory. It was not sacrosanct, and if proven unproductive it could be replaced by any other such device.

> We did not and do not have [Èjchenbaum wrote in 1925] any . . . ready-made system or doctrine. In our research we value theory only as a working hypothesis which helps us to discover facts and make sense of them: that is, to ascertain their regularity and render them a material of study. Therefore we do not care

for definitions, so dear to epigones, and do not construct general theories, so appealing to eclectics. We advance concrete principles and stick to them to the extent that they are justified by the material. If the material requires their further elaboration or alteration we elaborate or alter them. In this respect we are free enough of our own theories, as a science should be if there is a difference between theory and conviction. A science lives not by establishing certitudes but by overcoming errors.[10]

This "laying bare of heuristic devices," however, did not placate the detractors of Formalism. It perhaps refuted the claim that Formalist literary science depended on certain ideological or artistic assumptions, but that refutation only invited a different criticism. The notion that basic principles are mere hypotheses falsifiable by the facts is a sign of philosophical naiveté, the critics argued. Theories should not be advanced in such a random fashion if science is to make any sense. To proceed properly, students of art should first of all seek a secure epistemological basis for their theorizing, which can be provided only by the most general branch of knowledge—philosophy. The denial of this truth, the argument goes, betrays either naive realism or facile empiricism.

Ippolit Uduš'ev's philosophical debunking of Formalism exemplifies this attitude.

The Formal method exists, but the Formalists themselves lack any philosophy of this method. . . . Do not bother asking them about the philosophical foundations of their own method. In vain would you inquire why, while rebelling against the dualism of "form" and "content," they introduced another dualism, "form" and "material." And why is the latter better than the former? . . . Why do they break the integral work into the elements of form and motivation? Where did they get the criterion for this delimitation? On the basis of what world view do they eliminate the artist's world view from their studies? How can one explain anything, even the rejection of a world view, without some alternate world view? . . . Why must literary phenomena be severed from all other cultural domains, particularly the domain of cultural

10. "Teorija 'formal'nogo metoda,'" p. 117.

unity: philosophy in its broadest sense? Why do the Formalists (I know very well why!) deny any philosophical-aesthetic foundation of their theory? Do they really think (alas, they do!) that the theory of art can be founded outside of philosophical aesthetics?[11]

The charge of philosophical naiveté that Uduš'ev (whoever is hidden behind this nom de guerre) and like-minded critics leveled against the Formalists should not, however, be accepted without reservation. We have seen that the Formalists were not ignorant of modern philosophical developments, and if certain procedures or concepts from that discipline suited their needs they did not hesitate to put them to use. As the flippant Šklovskij remarked in a statement that shocked the Marxist establishment, "We are not Marxists, but if in our household this utensil proves necessary we shall not eat with our hands out of spite."[12]
Moreover, if we look at Èjchenbaum's pre-Formalist essays, we quickly realize that the concerns voiced by Uduš'ev were not at all alien to him. "Every literary historian," Èjchenbaum maintained in 1916,

> no matter what particular field he chooses to investigate, must rely on a whole series of aesthetic and even epistemological presuppositions that he accepts as self-evident and that are, therefore, totally heteronomous. No matter how well he is insulated in his particular field, no matter how remote he seems at first glance from aesthetics and epistemology, those hidden presuppositions will show up in his method. For in the humanities, more than in other branches of knowledge, there is no method in itself, separate from the principle that founds it. There is no particular distinct from a generality, there is no analysis without a synthetic intuition. If the history of literature has a future, it will come about only when the philosophical attitude of the scholar toward his discipline becomes an absolute necessity for him.[13]

This statement suggests that Èjchenbaum was definitely a bet-

11. "Vzgljad i nečto: Otryvok," *Sovremennaja literatura: Sbornik statej* (Leningrad, 1925), pp. 176–78.
12. "Delo, kotoroe ja plocho vedu," *Tret'ja fabrika* (Moscow, 1926), p. 88.
13. "Deržavin," *Skvoz' literaturu: Sbornik statej* (Leningrad, 1924), pp. 5–6.

ter historian than a prophet. It might also explain why of all the Formalists he was the most capable of providing a synthetic overview of the movement's intellectual program. Above all, it offers an alternative to Uduš'ev's view of Formalism. What characterized the Formalist mode of inquiry was not a naive neglect of philosophical assumptions but a well-calculated rejection of philosophy as the ultimate arbiter of scientific theory. For the young scholars (as Èjchenbaum noted in his diary in 1922), "a concrete science [is] not a direct and immediate extension of philosophy."[14] Rather than being aphilosophical, the Formalists' theoretical posture was consciously antiphilosophical.

Moreover, this posture was perfectly in keeping with the latest trends in the philosophy of science, which were well known to the Formalists. I have in mind in particular Husserl's *Ideen*, published in 1913 and popularized in Russia by his student Gustav Špet.[15] In this book the founder of phenomenology drew a strict line between sciences of a specifically *philosophical standpoint* and those of a *dogmatic standpoint*. The former "are concerned with the sceptical problems relating to the possibility of knowledge. Their object is finally to solve the problems in principle and with the appropriate generality, and then, when applying the solutions thus obtained, to study their bearing on the critical task of determining the eventual meaning and value for knowledge of the results of the dogmatic sciences."[16] The objectives of those practicing sciences of a dogmatic standpoint are radically different. "*The right attitude* to take in the *pre-philosophical* and, in a good sense, *dogmatic* sphere of inquiry, to which all the empirical sciences (but not these alone) belong, is in full consciousness *to discard all scepticism together with all 'natural philosophy' and 'theory of knowledge'* and find the data of knowledge there where they

14. Quoted in M. O. Čudakova's commentary to Ju. Tynjanov, *Poètika, istorija literatury, kino* (Moscow, 1977), p. 454.
15. See Špet's letter to Husserl of February 26, 1914, quoted in E. Holenstein, "Jakobson and Husserl: A Contribution to the Genealogy of Structuralism," *The Human Context* 7, no. 1 (1975), 62.
16. *Ideas: General Introduction to Pure Phenomenology*, tr. W. R. Boyce Gibson (New York, 1962), p. 87.

actually face you, whatever difficulties epistemological reflection may *subsequently* raise concerning the possibility of such data being there."[17] It is noteworthy that Husserl specifically rebuffs skeptics (of Uduš'ev's type) who block the progress of the dogmatic sciences by raising epistemological issues. This procedure he sees as not only unwarranted but premature, for the basic problems of knowledge have themselves not been satisfactorily solved. "*Having regard to the present situation,* and so long as a highly developed critique of knowledge that has attained to complete rigour and clearness is lacking, it is in any rate *right to fence off the field of dogmatic research from all 'critical' forms of inquiry.* In other words, it seems right to us at present to see to it that epistemological (which as a rule are sceptical) prejudices upon whose validity as right or wrong philosophical science has to decide, but which do not necessarily concern the dogmatic worker, shall not obstruct the course of his inquiries."[18]

Husserl's characterization of the mode of inquiry proper to the dogmatic sciences explains well the Formalists' steadfast refusal to engage in philosophical discussions about the epistemological ramifications of their theorizing. Given the variety of mutually incompatible systematizations of knowledge that competed for recognition in the Russian intellectual life of the time, it was obvious to them that such an undertaking could hardly yield satisfactory results. Moreover, becoming embroiled in the philosophical fray would only distract them from what they considered their main objective: the advancement of a new literary science. "Yes," Tomaševskij replied to those who accused OPOJAZ of methodological unreflexiveness, "the Formalists deal with methodology, but only as a concrete testing of the literary historical methods in their research, and not as a methodology masking basically empty talk about what is literature, how it relates to the general problematic of spirit, epis-

17. Ibid., p. 86.
18. Ibid., p. 87.

temology, and metaphysics."[19] In a similar vein, Èjchenbaum blasted his scholarly contemporaries for forgetting literature in the heat of lofty philosophical discussions: "Hence the new ardor of scientific positivism characteristic of the Formalists: the rejection of philosophical presuppositions, aesthetic interpretations, and so on. The break with philosophical aesthetics and ideological theories of art was dictated by this state of affairs. It was necessary to turn toward the facts, leave behind general schemes and problems, begin in the middle—at the point where the artistic fact faces us. Art had to be tackled directly and sciences to become concrete."[20]

We now have an answer, I believe, to the problem with which this chapter opened. The common denominator, the "absolute" presupposition of the Formalists' literary science, was that there should be no presuppositions in scientific inquiry. This seemingly simple and reasonable program, the demand for the elimination of all "metaphysical" commitments from science, under closer scrutiny becomes quite a complex issue. In the first place, the idea of presuppositionless knowledge by no means originated with Russian Formalism; in fact its wide circulation caused it to acquire a great variety of meanings. In the second place, because of the heterogeneity of the Formalist movement itself and its developmental fluidity, different members on different occasions utilized the idea of presuppositionless knowledge in quite dissimilar ways. Therefore, it might be useful to specify at the onset of our discussion the main functions of this notion in Formalist discourse.

First of all, "presuppositionless knowledge" signified a Socratically naive, "know-nothing" attitude toward the subject matter of literary studies, which the Formalists waved as a polemical flag before the literary-theoretical establishment. On a more sophisticated level, this idea implied not so much the abolition of all presuppositions as the Formalist quest for a secure basis for

19. "Formal'nyj metod: Vmesto nekrologa," *Sovremennaja literatura,* p. 148.
20. "Teorija 'formal'nogo metoda,'" p. 120.

251

the discipline of literary science. Such a basis would not itself qualify as a presupposition in the usual sense of this word. It would be self-evident or certain and hence, unlike its traditional counterparts, obligatory and impervious to any further epistemological critique (which as a rule invites an infinite regress). Finally, in what seems the most fruitful approach to this idea, "presuppositionless knowledge" expressed the Formalists' deep-seated skepticism about the adequacy of any systematic or unified account of presuppositions in science. Given this impossibility, the Formalists conceived of their own scientific enterprise as a process unfolding in spite of this impossibility and in the course of time consistently negating all of its own presuppositions.

The first meaning of "presuppositionless knowledge" as an epistemologically fresh start—is understandable within the historical context that gave rise to Formalism. Dissatisfied with contemporary literary studies whose approaches derived from metaphysical, speculative sources, the young scholars wished to start all over again, to wipe the slate clean. And this goal could best be achieved, they believed, by expunging not only previous presuppositions but *all* presuppositions. Yet obviously the positive science of literature, at least as the Formalists envisioned it, could not proceed from a mere negation. If, according to their primary principle, literary study has a specific subject matter, its task would have to be to pin down and describe this specificity, to explain what makes literature literature. In my very formulation of this notion, though, I cannot but notice the deliberate vagueness of the specificity principle. It hypothesizes the distinctness of literary phenomena from other cultural domains without stipulating in the least in what this distinctness consists. By programmatically excluding all prior presuppositions from their inquiry, the Formalists seemed to be caught in an obvious paradox. They insisted that literature has a distinctness of its own; yet any specification of this distinctness would entail a commitment on their part, a presupposition of their own.

At this point the idea of presuppositionless knowledge in its second meaning becomes vital for Formalist theory. The young scholars were willing to put their necks on the line and propose that what they saw was the distinctive feature of literature. They held that this ultimate ground of their literary science was qualitatively different from the traditional presuppositions of the discipline. It was self-evident or certain, in the sense that it was derived from the very subject matter of their inquiry and not from any speculative, nonscientific sources. In this quest for a secure ground of literary science, the Formalists associated themselves with some of the most productive currents in modern thought which pursued the same objective in other disciplines or for knowledge in general.

Nineteenth-century positivism was certainly one of those currents. The positivists declared themselves totally free of metaphysical presuppositions, deriving their knowledge of the world solely from observable facts as sensory experience furnishes them. This positivistic empiricism—the reduction of facts to sensory data—found its most sustained application in OPOJAZ in the early days. In a radical move the young scholars reduced the literary work solely to its phonic stratum and directed all their efforts to discovering the immanent laws of sound that characterize poetic discourse. This is not to say that the Formalists were unaware of the fact that literary texts are semantically charged, and hence involve values, ideas, and other qualities not open to direct sensory experience. Rather, they would argue that these qualities do not constitute the essence of literature. What makes texts literary is the particular organization of their palpable substance: sound. Whether speaking of the "clustering of liquids," "sound repetitions," or "sonorous chords," the early Formalists were arguing that the differential quality of verbal art lies in its phonic stratum. The reduction of literature to its sensory vehicle might appear quite strange taken outside its historical context. But at the same time that it was formulated, the Futurist experiments with *zaum'*—transrational language deprived of meaning—provided the young theoreticians with empirical evidence that the manipulation of the *phonè* alone is sufficient to generate poeticity.

Even when in the early twenties the Formalists rejected the belief that the specificity of literary phenomena resides only in its sensory stratum, they did not accordingly abandon their commitment to presuppositionless knowledge, the program for a literary science that would be solely a cognitive extension of the facts under study. They merely changed their minds about what the literary facts were.

In doing so, they were perfectly consistent with other turn-of-the-century scholars who searched for self-evident grounds of knowledge. Positivist science was then coming under heavy attack, but not all critics disagreed with its goal of eliminating metaphysical presuppositions and relying exclusively on the facts. What critics did question was positivist phenomenalism, the belief that only observable facts, those furnished by sensory perception, are the genuine object of scientific inquiry. They considered the positivist commitment to experience as the sole source of knowledge too limiting and offered more adequate procedures for a direct, unmediated grasp of reality.

Among the welter of postpositivist notions of science, the most influential for the Formalists were Husserl's phenomenology and Saussure's linguistics. Husserl was far from denigrating the scientific vigor of positivism. "Empiricistic Naturalism," he wrote in *Ideen*, "springs, as we must recognize, from the most praiseworthy motives. It is an intellectually practical radicalism, which in opposition to all 'idols,' to the powers of tradition and superstition, to crude and refined prejudices of every kind, seeks to establish the right of the self-governing Reason to be the only authority in matters that concern truth."[21] However, a fallacy was built into the positivist program, Husserl insisted, which stemmed from its conflation of facts with sensorily perceptible phenomena. "The fundamental defect of the empiricist's argument lies in this, that the basic requirement of a return to the

21. *Ideas*, p. 74.

'facts themselves' is identified or confused with the requirement that all knowledge shall be grounded in *experience.*"[22] No scientist, Husserl argued, proceeds in research through pure experience. Such an approach could provide no more than knowledge of a single fact in a unique spatiotemporal nexus, that is, an accident. Scientific laws, in order to qualify as such, must have broader implications, must apply to a category of phenomena. The notion of the category clearly exceeds the empirical realm and is not a product of direct experience. It is grounded in what Husserl terms the "essential insight" that discerns in a sensory multitude the categorical *eidos* common to all the objects of the same category, in fact, constituting it.

Husserl's name for the "science which aims exclusively at establishing the 'knowledge of essences' [*Wesenerkenntnisse*] and absolutely no 'facts'" was "pure phenomenology."[23] Such a science would proceed not from sensory experience but from *intuition*— the direct grasp of the essences underlying the phenomenal world which provide it with its categorical identity. And whereas positivism, in Husserl's opinion, by uncritically privileging experience as the ultimate guarantor of truth, had actually betrayed the idea of presuppositionless knowledge, phenomenology postulated it in its full purity. "We start out from that which antedates all standpoints: from the totality of the intuitively self-given which is prior to any theorizing reflexion, from all that one *can* immediately see and lay hold of, provided one does not allow oneself to be blinded by prejudice, and so led to ignore a whole class of genuine data. If by '*Positivism*' we are to mean the absolute unbiased grounding of all science on what is 'positive,' i.e., on what can be primordially apprehended, then," Husserl declared, "it is *we* who are the genuine positivists."[24] In this respect, the later work of Formalism can be seen as a "purified" positivism as well.

Whereas Husserl was providing a prescription for the science

22. Ibid., pp. 74–75.
23. Ibid., p. 40.
24. Ibid., p. 78.

of all sciences, Ferdinand de Saussure was pursuing a more limited goal. He wished to establish the ultimate foundations of a single discipline—a science of language. In this respect, his undertaking was much closer to that of the Formalists, who aspired to do the same for literature. The task that the Swiss linguist set out to accomplish might be characterized in Husserlian terms as the construction of a "regional ontology," the isolation of the *eidos* that makes linguistic facts linguistic. Traditional approaches to language were unsatisfactory, Saussure maintained, because they never asked the essential question, "what is language?" Instead, they stopped at the empirical level and rather than studying language, concentrated on its physical, psychological, and cultural manifestations. Inevitably, from this perspective "the object of linguistics appears as a confused mass of heterogeneous and unrelated things."[25] To rectify this situation, Saussure proposed the strict separation of what is linguistically phenomenal, individual, and accidental from what is essential, social, and rule-governed. He bisected language into actual speech (*parole*) and potential linguistic system (*langue*) and proclaimed the latter the sole object of linguistics.

Saussure argued that linguists should not start with the observation of empirical reality, for in their psychophysical actuality, individual utterances are totally disparate. Instead, linguists should proceed from an insight into the essence of language, from their intuitive grasp of *langue*, which provides all utterances with their linguistic identity but is never fully implemented in any of them. Second, in organizing this knowledge linguists need not draw on patterns and schemes extrinsic to language. Because linguistic facts are by their very essence systemic, they can be treated adequately only on the basis of the system (*langue*) that they engender. And because Saussurean linguists proceed from an intuitive grasp of *langue*, the object of their inquiry furnishes them with a framework for the systematization of their knowledge.

25. *Course in General Linguistics,* tr. and ed. W. Baskin (New York, 1959), p. 9.

Saussure's and Husserl's influence on the Formalists was profound, as we have already seen. Husserl's program found its most faithful follower in the vice-chairman of the Moscow Linguistic Circle, Roman Jakobson. By postulating that literariness rather than literature was the object of literary science, Jakobson was conceiving of poetics as an eidetic discipline. Furthermore, in defining the distinctive feature of literature, he utilized Husserl's concept of the expression, a sign whose identity lies in the nonempirical domain. It was exactly this concept that enabled him to transcend the empiricism of the early OPOJAZ members, for whom the specificity of poetic language lay in its sensory stratum. Though the impact of Husserl's thought on the other Formalists is less clear, in general, phenomenology was an important component of the antipositivist climate surrounding the later phases of Formalist theorizing. Yet its methods for grasping essences appeared to them too abstract and too implicated in what they regarded as purely philosophical issues to be directly applicable to their own enterprise. Accordingly, they sought their inspiration for treating the specificity of literary phenomena elsewhere—in Saussurean linguistics.

As I observed earlier, Saussure and the Formalists were pursuing the same objective: to wrest their respective fields from other disciplines that had traditionally dominated them. Saussure's *Course* provided the young Russians with a well-elaborated program for what they themselves wished to achieve in literary studies: a science generated intrinsically, on the basis of its own subject matter. Saussure's path-breaking discussion of the essence of language suggested where the specificity of literary phenomena might lie. Like language, literature is a social institution, and it is the literary system—the set of norms valid for a given collectivity—that ultimately determines whether a particular text is poetic or not. This conception of literature clearly informed Tynjanov's notion of literary history, Jakobson's poetic language, and to a great extent Tomaševskij's metrics.

The antipositivist rebellion in European intellectual life also provoked interest in scientific models that predated positivism.

In rejecting the scientific inquiry of the immediate past, scholars were drawn to achievements that the positivists had branded passé. This development helps to account for the revival of Goethe's morphology, which several Formalists transplanted into the realm of literary studies. The theory of organic forms advanced by the German poet-turned-naturalist was in some respects quite similar to the notion of science that was emerging some hundred years later. In the spirit of a Spinozan "*scientia intuitiva*," Goethe had striven to grasp the "formal essence" of living beings, the ideal *Ur-Typ* that underlies all actual organisms despite their perplexing empirical heterogeneity.[26] The dynamic notion of nature in Goethe's thought provided a particular attraction for the modern period. What Goethe hoped to discover were the generative rules governing the formation and transformation of all organic forms. This approach was close to the hearts of Formalists seeking the essential invariant of literary genres and dissatisfied with Šklovskij's overtly static conception of the literary work as a "sum of devices." Thus, positivism, the phenomenological purification of positivism, and the science preceding positivism all entered Formalist thought through their search for the ultimate grounds of literary science.

The foregoing discussion helps illustrate how the Formalists went about their science of literature. They started from a general hypothesis that the literary series has an identity of its own and that literary facts constitute a reality of a different order from other cultural phenomena. Guided by their belief that a scholarly theory must be above all a cognitive extension of its subject matter, they at first looked for the specificity of verbal art in its sensory stratum and later in a variety of nonempirical "deep structures" underlying the literary process and manifested in actual works.

Nevertheless, even a quick glance reveals the obvious inconsistency of Formalist procedures. These proponents of a "pure

26. "Brief auf F. H. Jacobi, 5. Mai 1786," *Goethes Werke* (Weimar, 1887–1912), sec. 4, vol. 7, p. 214.

science of literature" indiscriminately borrowed frames of reference from other disciplines: linguistics, philosophy, or biology. Every Formalist model, despite the claim that scientific knowledge must be presuppositionless, arose from preconceived ideas about literature and molded its data according to a preexistent matrix. Given this fact, should we not assume that the Formal school failed to accomplish its own program? The answer to this question, I believe, is no. Here we should return to the third meaning of presuppositionless knowledge in Formalist parlance. Profoundly mistrustful of any unified or systematic account of scientific presuppositions, the Formalists conceived of science as a contention among theories, a self-correcting process of elimination and attrition. According to Jurij Striedter's keen observation, "the history and theory of Russian Formalism are an uninterrupted dialogue between the Formalists and their opponents, but even more so among the Formalists themselves, who opposed and criticized one another. . . . They were all at one and the same time partners and adversaries in the fascinating dialogue which produced and represented the formal method."[27] What characterizes Formalism, thus, is its "eristic" mode of theorizing: its refusal to reduce the heterogeneity of art to a single explanatory scheme. "Enough of monism!" Èjchenbaum had declared in 1922. "We are pluralists. Life is diverse and cannot be reduced to a single principle."[28] By proceeding from very dissimilar premises, the young scholars turned their presuppositions against themselves, undercutting, subverting, and refuting each other.

Thus, in its historical dynamics, Russian Formalism is not the sum total of its theories—a static set of models derived from a variety of sources—but a *polemos*, a struggle among contradictory and incompatible views none of which could become the absolute ground of a new literary science. Tomaševskij's remark that

27. "Zur formalistischen Theorie der Prosa und der literarischen Evolution," quoted from English tr. by M. Nicolson, "The Russian Formalist Theory of Prose," *PTL* 2 (1977), 435.
28. "5=100," *Knižnyj ugol*, no. 8 (1922), 40.

"the Formalists rejected more than anything else the excessive tendency toward inertia" encapsulates the movement's attitude not only toward previous critical schools but also toward its own theories.[29] "In the moment," Èjchenbaum wrote, "that we ourselves are compelled to admit that we have a universal theory, ready for all the contingencies of past and future and therefore not in need or capable of evolving, we would have to admit that the Formal method had ceased to exist, that the spirit of scientific inquiry had departed from it."[30]

Such a view of scientific inquiry as an incessant struggle among provisional frames of reference was conditioned, I believe, by certain pragmatic considerations, the first of which is the collective nature of Formalist theorizing. "The evolution of the Formal method," Èjchenbaum insisted, "appears as a consistent development of theoretical principles, independent of the role any one of us individually played in it."[31] This self-abnegation is quite understandable if we do not forget that the Formalists as a group pursued a higher goal: the transformation of literary studies into a science. Measured by this goal, it seemed more reasonable to stress the impermanence, the transience of one's own theory than to maintain it at any cost and thereby endanger the group's loyalty and the commonality of their enterprise. Strategically speaking, the centrifugal tendencies so strong within Formalism had to be balanced by an implicit agreement to disagree if this movement were to succeed.

The eristic mode of theorizing was useful in still another way.

29. "Nová ruská škola v bádání literárně-historickém," 12.
30. "Teorija 'formal'nogo metoda,'" p. 148. Readers familiar with recent developments in the philosophy of science might recognize that the Formalist view of the "spirit of scientific inquiry" anticipates to some degree Paul Feyerabend's "anarchistic theory of knowledge" (*Against Method* [London, 1975]). It is noteworthy that the Formalists in their polemics with Marxism occasionally invoked the "anarchy of life," a notion that is always incomprehensible to the adherents of the rigid and doctrinaire Marxist *Weltanschauung*. Explicitly comparing the struggle between the traditional philologists and the Formalists to that between the Marxists and anarchists, Èjchenbaum exclaimed, "Life is not built according to Marx—all the better" ("5=100," 41).
31. "Teorija 'formal'nogo metoda,'" p. 147.

The Developmental Significance of Russian Formalism

As I argued earlier, by rejecting the presuppositions of the older critical schools as "metaphysical" the Formalists could distance themselves from the past and launch their new literary science from point zero. To compete with elaborate principles and methods that had been in circulation for decades, however, the rising scholars had to advance convincing substitutes in the shortest time possible, and here their notion of presuppositionless knowledge proved extremely effective. Bound merely by a general hypothesis about the specificity of the literary series and an agreement to disagree, the young scholars were able to generate, seemingly overnight, an amazing variety of theories concerning the most disparate fields of literary study: versification, narratology, genre theory, and literary history. True, some of their more flamboyant hypotheses fell by the wayside, but many others took firm root, becoming the common property of modern literary scholarship.

Despite this success, the Formalists' victory was to some degree Pyrrhic. They changed the entire course of Russian literary study; yet no sooner had they done their work and suffered dispersion than their closest heirs, the Bachtin circle and Prague Structuralists, were already declaring them passé. The Bachtinians set themselves up as uncompromising critics of Formalism. They viewed its members as their enemies, with the important qualification that one should "appreciate a good enemy much more than a bad ally."[32] The Prague theoreticians, perhaps because of the Formalist contingent among them, were much better disposed toward their Russian predecessors. Nevertheless, the two groups mounted quite similar campaigns against their Formalist precursors.

The main target of the Bachtinians' critique was the Formalist vision of literature as an autonomous reality independent of other cultural domains. By challenging this view, the Bachtinians were not, however, returning to the old approaches dis-

---

32. P. N. Medvedev, *Formal'nyj metod v literaturovedenii: Kritičeskoe vvedenie v sociologičeskuju poètiku* (Leningrad, 1928), p. 232.

credited by the Formalists. Their new perspective is apparent in the very first sentence of Medvedev's book-length critique of Formalism: "Literary study," he wrote, "is one branch of the extensive science of ideologies that encompasses . . . . all the spheres of man's ideological creativity."[33] This opening sentence indicates the direction of the entire study: the presentation of literature as an ideological phenomenon closely related to other such phenomena (politics, religion, and so forth), yet possessing an identity of its own. For the Bachtinians, a limited rather than total autonomy characterized literature as a specific series. Of course, this position was not utterly alien to Formalism. The Formalist principle of the specificity of the literary series was vague enough to allow some members of the school to study the relationship between literature and social life. What set the Bachtinians apart was their semiotic frame of reference. Every ideological phenomenon, according to Valentin Vološinov, is a sign, a reality that stands for some other reality. "Within the sphere of signs, i.e., within the ideological sphere," however, "there exist profound differences. After all, this category includes the artistic image as well as the religious symbol, the scientific formula as well as the juridical norm. Every sphere of ideological creativity has its own orientation toward reality and refracts it in its own way. Every domain performs its own function in the totality of social life."[34]

The Bachtinians' definition of literature in semiotic terms may seem to paraphrase Jakobson, who also conceived of verbal art as a specific type of sign—the expression. In fact the two are quite different. As an expression, the literary work is an oxymoron: a semiotic nonsign. It is endowed with meaning, yet it does not represent any other reality. For the Bachtinians, however, literature differs from other ideological domains not in failing to signify but in its mode of signifying. Literary signs, Medvedev claimed, are metasigns—representations of represen-

33. Ibid., p. 11.
34. *Marksizm i filosofija jazyka: Osnovnye problemy sociologičeskogo metoda v nauke o jazyke*, 2d ed. (Leningrad, 1930), pp. 14–15.

tations. "Literature reflects in its content an ideological horizon: alien, nonartistic (ethical, cognitive), ideological formations. But in reflecting these alien signs literature creates new forms—literary works—new signs of ideological intercourse. And these signs—literary works—become in turn an actual component of the social reality surrounding man. By refracting what lies outside them, literary works are, at the same time, self-valuable and distinct phenomena of the ideological milieu. Their presence cannot be reduced to the simple, technical, auxiliary role of refracting other ideologems. They have their own ideological role and refract socioeconomic reality in their own way."[35]

This metasemiotic definition led the Bachtinians to a thorough revision of Formalist theories of language, the medium of literature. From a linguistic point of view, a verbal sign that reflects or refracts another verbal sign is exactly like an utterance commenting on or replying to another utterance. It forms a *dialogue*. This concept is the controlling metaphor of Bachtinian literary-theoretical discourse. Moreover, the dialogic conception of language was a direct challenge to Saussure's linguistics and Husserl's logic. The Formalists, as I showed earlier, did relativize the asocial and ahistorical categories of their intellectual predecessors, but they were primarily concerned with the centripetal forces operating in language that make it systemic. The Bachtinians' priorities were precisely the opposite. As a dialogue, language is not a system (*ergon*) but a process (*energeia*), an ongoing struggle between different points of view, different ideologies. Hence, what intrigued them was not the homogeneity of discourse but its heterogeneity, the centrifugal forces that resist integration.

Like the Bachtin group, the Prague Structuralists also rejected the radical Formalist view of literature as an autonomous reality. "It would be wrong," wrote the Circle's leading aesthetician, Jan Mukařovský, in 1934, "to place poetry in a vacuum under the pretext of its special function. We should not forget that the

35. *Formal'nyj metod v literaturovedenii*, p. 29.

developmental series of individual structures changing in time (e.g., the political, economic, ideological, literary) do not run parallel to each other without any contact. On the contrary, they are elements of a structure of a higher order and this structure of structures has its hierarchy and its dominant element (the prevailing series)."[36]

The attentive reader might hear in Mukařovský's "structure of structures" an echo of Tynjanov and Jakobson's conception of culture as a "system of systems," a notion advanced by the two in 1928 as a corrective to the purely immanent approach to literary history that had characterized earlier Formalism. But Tynjanov and Jakobson had failed to explain the mechanism that makes the interaction among different cultural systems possible. Within six years of their time, however, Mukařovský developed such an explanation. Like the Bachtinians, he accounted for the relative autonomy of the literary structure by means of the general theory of signs. "Without a semiotic orientation," he declared at the 1934 Congress of Philosophy in Prague, "the theoretician of art will always be inclined to regard the work either as a purely formal construction or as a direct reflection of its author's psychic or even physiological dispositions, of the distinct reality expressed by it, or of the ideological, economic, social, or cultural situation of a given milieu. . . . Only the semiotic point of view will permit the theoretician to recognize the autonomous existence and essential dynamism of the artistic structure and to understand its development as a movement which is immanent yet in constant dialectic relation to the development of other spheres of culture."[37]

Because they considered "all of reality, from sensory perception to the most abstract mental construction" a "vast and complex realm of signs," the Structuralists had to introduce some

36. "Polákova *Vznešenost přírody:* Pokus o rozbor a vývojové zařadění básnické struktury," *Kapitoly z české poetiky,* 2d ed., vol. 2 (Prague, 1948), p. 166.

37. "L'art comme fait sémiologique," *Actes du huitième congrès international de philosophie à Prague 2–7 septembre 1934,* ed. E. Rádl and Z. Smetáček (Prague, 1936), p. 1070.

criterion to differentiate individual semiotic structures from each other.[38] Here the notion of *function* entered Structuralist thought. Rooted in a purposive view of human behavior, it designated "the active relation between an object and the goal for which this object is used."[39] The Structuralists stressed the social dimension of functionality, the necessary consensus among the members of a collectivity about the purpose the object serves and its utility for such a purpose. From the functional perspective, every individual semiotic structure—art, religion, science—appeared as a set of social norms regulating the attainment of values in these cultural spheres.

The Structuralist concept of the aesthetic function was especially important to their revision of Formalism. It might be said that this function was the dialectic negation of all other functions. Whereas in "practical" functions, the *telos* lies outside the object used, in the aesthetic function the *telos* is this object. That is to say, in extra-artistic activities functional objects are instruments whose value stems from their suitability for particular purposes. Works of art, on the other hand, as the objects of the aesthetic function, do not serve any practical goal directly and thus constitute ultimate values in and of themselves.

The dichotomy between the aesthetic and practical functions may appear simply to restate in different terms the Formalist notion of de-familiarization, according to which the displacement of an object from its customary context—*byt*—makes it a "self-valuable" work of art. It is necessary to point out, however, that Structuralists conceived of an object's functionality in terms of hierarchy rather than in terms of the Formalists' mutual exclusivity: the dominance of one function did not preclude the presence of others. Further, because of their semiotic outlook, they did not see the aesthetic set toward the object as a total break from the social context. On the contrary, a dominant aesthetic function prevents the practical functions contained in the

38. B. Havránek et al., "Úvodem," *Slovo a slovesnost* 1 (1935), 5.
39. Mukařovsky, "Problém estetické hodnoty," *Cestami poetiky a estetiky* (Prague, 1971), p. 17.

work from realizing their corresponding values; therefore these values are transferred from the empirical to the semantic plane. Extra-aesthetic values become meanings that contribute to the total semantic structure of the work. Thus, "from the most abstract point of view," Mukařovský claimed, "the work of art is nothing but a particular set of extra-aesthetic values. The material components of the artistic artifact and the way they are exploited as formal devices are mere conductors of energy represented by extra-aesthetic values. If at this point we ask ourselves where aesthetic value lies, we find that it has dissolved into individual extra-aesthetic values and is nothing but a general term for the dynamic totality of their interrelations."[40]

We have seen that both the Bachtinians and the Prague Structuralists redefined the primary principle of Formalist literary science from a semiotic perspective. They did not stop there; they also questioned the "ultimate" presupposition of this science, namely, that its theories must be generated solely from the data studied. Medvedev's critique of Formalism takes up this point several times. "In the humanities, to approach the concrete material and to do so correctly is rather hard. Pathetic appeals to the 'facts themselves' and the 'concrete material' do not say or prove much. Even the most extreme specimens of the biographical method are founded on facts and concrete material. Eclectics of all kinds are especially 'factual' and 'concrete.'" But since a correct grasp of the material at hand influences the entire theory that follows from it, "the onset of research, the first methodological orientation, the mere sketching out of the object of inquiry, are crucially important. They are of decisive value. One cannot establish this initial methodological orientation ad hoc, guided solely by his own subjective 'intuition' of the object."[41]

This, of course, was precisely what Medvedev thought the Formalists had been doing. Sprung from an "unholy union" of

---

40. *Estetická funkce, norma a hodnota jako sociální fakty* (Prague, 1936), p. 69.
41. *Formal'nyj metod v literaturovedenii*, p. 108.

positivism and Futurism, Formalism lacked any solid philosophical foundations and molded its object of inquiry according to the aesthetic sensibility of modernist art. Obviously, many of Medvedev's charges were polemical exaggerations, but the overall thrust of his argument was straightforward: literary study, in order to treat its material adequately, must proceed from a well-defined, correct philosophical point of view. This, he happily announced, is Marxism. The "ultimate presupposition" of Medvedev's sociological poetics is that the literary fact is first of all an ideological fact and literary study a branch of the general science of ideology. "The foundations of this science concerning the general definition of ideological superstructures, their functions in the unity of social life, their relationship with the economic basis and partially also their interaction, were laid deeply and firmly by Marxism."[42] Although one may ask how well the Bachtinians' metasemiotics squared with the official Soviet Marxism-Leninism and its flat-footed theory of reflection (and hence whether they should be called Marxists at all), the choice of a tag is not important. The point is that the Bachtinians saw philosophy as the necessary ground of literary study and the Formalists did not.

On this issue the members of the Prague school were perhaps more reserved than the Bachtinians; yet they certainly did not deny the relevance of philosophy to theory. The Formalists had considered themselves specifiers, pioneers in the new science of literature, but the Structuralists emphasized the interdisciplinary nature of their research and the similarity of their principles and methods to those in other fields of knowledge. "*Structuralism*," as the coiner of the term, Roman Jakobson, stated in 1929, "is the leading idea of present-day science in its most various manifestations."[43] Its emergence heralds the eclipse of one era in European intellectual history and the beginning of a new one. "European Romantic scholarship," Jakobson argued,

42. Ibid., p. 11.
43. "Romantické všeslovanství—nová slavistika," *Čin* 1 (1929), 11.

"was an attempt at a general, *global* conception of the universe. The antithesis of Romantic scholarship was the sacrifice of unity for the opportunity to collect the richest factual material, to gain the most varied *partial truths.* Our time seeks a *synthesis:* it does not wish to eliminate general meaning from its purview, a law-governed structure of events, but at the same time it takes into account the great reservoir of facts gathered during the previous epoch."[44] This view of Structuralism was echoed by other members of the Prague Circle. According to Mukařovský, the modern history of European scholarship was marked by an oscillation between Romantic deductivism, which subordinated scientific data to an overall philosophical system, and positivistic inductivism, which reduced philosophy to a mere extension of the empirical sciences. The novelty of Structuralism, Mukařovský believed, lay in its efforts to bridge this dichotomy. "Structuralist research . . . consciously and intentionally operates between two extremes: on the one hand, philosophical presuppositions, on the other, data. These two have a similar relation to science. Data are neither a passive object of study nor a completely determinant one, as the positivists believed, but the two are mutually determining." For Mukařovský, "Structuralism is a scientific attitude that proceeds from the knowledge of this unceasing interrelation of science and philosophy. I say 'attitude,'" he continues, "to avoid terms such as 'theory' or 'method.' 'Theory' suggests a fixed body of knowledge, 'method' an equally homogenized and unchangeable set of working rules. Structuralism is neither. It is an *epistemological stance* [my italics] from which particular working rules and knowledge follow to be sure, but which exists independently of them and is therefore capable of development in both these aspects."[45]

Against these two philosophically oriented schools, the nature

44. "Společná řeč kultury: Poznámky k otázkám vzájemných styků sovětské a západní vědy," *Země sovětů* 4 (1935), 110.
45. "Strukturalismus v estetice a ve vědě o literatuře," *Kapitoly z české poetiky,* 2d ed., vol. 1, pp. 13–15.

of Russian Formalism is apparent. It served as what can only be termed an "interparadigmatic stage" in the evolution of Slavic literary scholarship. Thomas Kuhn, who introduced this notion, argues that normal scientific practice is characterized by the presence of a "paradigm," a "strong network of commitments—conceptual, theoretical, instrumental and methodological" shared by researchers in a given field.[46] The paradigm provides the scientific community with everything it needs for its work: the problems to be solved, the tools for doing so, as well as the standards for judging the results. At a certain moment, however, the hitherto accepted paradigm comes under suspicion because of its persistent failure to yield the results it predicts. Kuhn noted, "Confronted with anomaly or crisis, scientists take a different attitude toward the existing paradigms and the nature of their research changes accordingly. The proliferation of competing articulations, the willingness to try anything, the expression of explicit discontent, the recourse to philosophy and to debate over fundamentals, all these are symptoms of a transition from normal to extraordinary research."[47]

Such interparadigmatic hallmarks are the prime characteristics of Russian Formalism. Though it might be argued that the situation in the humanities is somewhat different from that in the exact sciences, inasmuch as the total domination of a single paradigm never occurs there, Kuhn's remarks fit the picture of the Formalist movement quite well. Motivated by the desire to provide a "more rigid definition of the field," the Formalist scholars raised fundamental questions about the principles and methods of literary study. In order to destabilize the older paradigm, they strove to open the theoretical space as wide as possible rather than to limit it by some a priori agreement. Hence the extreme heterogeneity of their enterprise, the proliferation of widely divergent and often incompatible models. What ties the individual Formalists together is the goal they

46. *The Structure of Scientific Revolutions*, 2d ed. (Chicago, 1970), p. 42.
47. Ibid., pp. 90–91.

pursued: to change the scholarly practice of their discipline. The unity of Formalism is thus of a special kind. It is a unity of action, a dynamic configuration of multiplex forces converging in a particular historical context. As such, Russian Formalism does not represent a single paradigm of literary study but a cluster of diverse theories. Despite this fact, or perhaps because of it, some seventy years after its inception Formalism still exerts considerable influence on literary study. Its debunking of earlier paradigms and its wealth of insights into the nature of the literary process provided a fertile ground for the new syntheses, new disciplinary matrices, that began to appear at the very moment of Formalism's demise in the late twenties. One of these emerged in Prague under the label of Structuralism, and for the next forty years achieved an ever-growing worldwide influence. The other was Bachtinian metasemiotics, forcibly suppressed for many decades, but since the seventies enjoying an international reputation as a viable alternative to Structuralism. Russian Formalism was without a doubt a transitional and transitory period in the history of literary study. But insofar as the literary-theoretical paradigms it inaugurated are still with us, it stands not as a mere historical curiosity but a vital presence in the critical discourse of our day.

Index

Index

Index

Index

Index

Library of Congress Cataloging in Publication Data

Steiner, P. (Peter), 1946–
    Russian formalism.

    Based on the author's thesis.
    Includes index.
    1. Formalism (Literary analysis)—Soviet Union. I. Title.
PN98.F6S73 1984   801'.95   84–7708
ISBN 0–8014–1710–4 (alk. paper)